WHAT OTHERS ARE SAYING
REFLECTIONS ON RISK IV

"As in the previous three collections of Reflections on Risk, Annie's students have delved into the ever-increasing variety of threats to our collective safety, providing in-depth analysis and thoughtful recommendations for potential solutions. This newest volume in the series provides a new set of stimulating and thought-provoking insights into critical issues in our society, whether at a global scale or a personal level. The range of material covers examples from the realms of global policy, technology, social equity, corporate safety, and personal well-being—topics that touch all of us, no matter what our role or political persuasion. Annie's continuing efforts to expose the work of her students to the public is a stellar example of leveraging the educational process to provide broader awareness of these issues; and in the process produce future leaders and employees who will have a heightened awareness of their own role in shaping our collective future."

Michael Crandall
Principal Research Scientist
University of Washington Information School

"An engaging compilation of fresh thinking on a range of key themes impacting risk governance. If you are looking for fresh perspectives on topics ranging from cyber-security to critical infrastructure protection, financial networks, and surveillance, pick up this volume. Great job by Annie Searle and her students!"

Kevin C. Desouza
Author, *Intrapreneurship: Managing Ideas Within Your Organization*

"It is said that the past is prologue to our future. However, our future sometimes defies the lessons of the past. Fortunately, there is Annie Searle who bridges both with her experience and the perspectives of her students."

Ron Worman
Managing Partner
The Sage Group

REFLECTIONS ON RISK
VOLUME IV

ASA INSTITUTE FOR RISK AND INNOVATION

ANNIE SEARLE & ASSOCIATES LLC

EDITED BY EMILY OXENFORD

TAUTEGORY PRESS
SEATTLE, WASHINGTON

Printed in the United States of America

First edition: November 2017

Tautegory Press, Seattle, Washington USA

Printing History

All research notes here were previously published as "ASA Research Notes" in ASA Newsletters ©Annie Searle & Associates LLC and at its website www.anniesearle.com, from September 2015 through July 2017.

USA Library of Congress Control Number: 2015960608

ISBN # 978-0-9839347-8-3

Cover design by Jesse Brown

Contents

Forward

Since Volume III of this series was published late in 2015, global risks and threats have increased exponentially, as have issues that surface around information ethics, policy and law, identity management, culture risk, privacy and security. In my operational risk seminar this spring, students ranked and then restacked and ranked the top operational risks present in 2017. No one was especially pleased with the results, and the top three risks – cyber-threats, global uncertainty, and terrorism – seemed nearly interchangeable, depending upon the month. A fourth close contender was regulatory uncertainty. You will find research notes in this volume that speak to all four of these risk areas.

At the same time, technology has evolved so rapidly in areas like Big Data, the Internet of Things (IoT) and Artificial Intelligence (AI) that it is difficult to find a range of basic materials to read or reference. I hope that one consequence of this fourth volume of research notes is that readers are offered not only the author's perspective, but a good set of references as well.

This volume is the first in which you will find research notes written by undergraduates. There are eight of them, a direct result of an undergraduate course in enterprise risk management that I teach in the University of Washington's Informatics program.

We are looking to broaden our scope to include research notes from risk practitioners, including former students but also colleagues in specialized fields mentioned above who may not previously have thought about publishing their expertise.

Finally, my thanks to Emily Oxenford, editor of this and two other volumes of **Reflections on Risk**. Emily is also the editor of *ASA News & Notes*, which appears monthly, and which is the first platform on which these research notes can be read.

Annie Searle

November 2017

The Contributors

Colin Andrade is a consultant at PwC focusing on data & analytics technologies where he helps large organizations use their data more effectively. He holds a Bachelor of Arts in History from The College of the Holy Cross and a Master of Science in Information Management with a specialization in information consulting from the University of Washington. Prior to returning to school to obtain his master's degree, Colin spent four years working for a German Investment Bank in their Sales & Trading division where he learned the true value of data and information.

Jorge Borunda received his Bachelor of Science degree from Heritage University with a major in computer science and a Master of Science in Information Management degree from the University of Washington. Being a "dreamer", Jorge is passionate about bridging the gap among minority communities and technology, doing research as a Mellon Fellow scholar at Heritage University and the University of Chicago. His past work experience ranges from the agricultural sector to sales and management. Jorge is currently employed as an enterprise architecture analyst for a top global retailer.

Ross Braine -- "Iisaaksiichaa (Good Lad)" -- is a citizen of the Apsaalooke (Crow) Nation and descendant of the Tsitsistas (Northern Cheyenne) of the Big Sky state of Montana. He is also a member of the Biglodge Clan and Nighthawk Warrior Society. He currently serves as both the tribal liaison and director of wəɬəbʔaltxʷ - Intellectual House at the University of Washington." He received his Bachelor of Science degree in Forestry Management in 2009, and his Master of Science in Information Management in 2015.

Michael Callier is an attorney and information scientist with over 15 years of experience helping clients to achieve their goals. His time working for Nike, Inc. and providing legal counsel and directing operations for a consulting firm in China led to his expertise in process improvement, project management, and technology. Michael currently brings his cross-functional background together to design innovative solutions, improve business processes and to lead cross-functional teams for Davis Wright Tremaine's legal solutions design team, De Novo. Michael received his Master of Science in Information Management from the University of Washington; Chinese language training at Suzhou University in Suzhou, China; his Juris Doctorate from the University of Oregon School of Law; and his bachelor's degree from the University of Oregon.

Evan Cottingham received his Bachelor of Science in Informatics degree with a focus in information assurance and cybersecurity from the University of Washington in 2017. His professional experience includes completing a summer internship with Costco Wholesale's information security team, where he conducted digital forensics investigations and authored procedural casework documents. Currently Evan works as an information security analyst at First Information Technology Services, helping CSPs meet their compliance goals.

Courtney Harris is a user experience designer for Alaska Airlines, where she uses human centered design thinking to create internal tools that are used across the enterprise by airline employees. She holds a Master of Science in Information Management, with a focus on UX Research, and a Bachelor of Science in Mathematics, both from the University of Washington. She is a core member and treasurer of the Alaska Airlines Women in Tech group.

Andy S. Herman is an information security consultant for West Monroe Partners. He holds a Master of Science in Information Management degree from the University of Washington and various industry certificates in information security; as well as a Bachelor of Science degree with departmental honors in microbiology from the University of Washington. His previous work experience is in conducting and assisting various information security audits for large technology companies. He was the co-founder of the ISACA Student Group at the University of Washington and is currently serving as the education coordinator of the ISACA Puget Sound Chapter.

Divya Kothari recently graduated from University of Washington with a Master of Science in Information Management. She also holds a

Bachelor of Science in Business Administration and Juris Doctorate from India. She is interested in cybersecurity, operational risk and robotics. Divya is currently employed as a cyber risk advisory consultant at Deloitte. Her past work experience includes working as a security analyst at Coalfire in the fields of payments and federal government work.

Kenny Lee is a seasoned cybersecurity professional for the past 12 years, working at small start-ups and Fortune 100 companies. Currently, Kenny is a Senior Security Manager at Microsoft, responsible for minimizing risk as related to mergers & acquisitions and third-party suppliers. Kenny has authored articles on cybersecurity and risk management, and co-reviewed the latest COSO framework for the Microsoft Advisory Council. Kenny earned a Bachelor's degree in management information systems from Washington State University, a Master of Science degree in Information Management from the University of Washington. He holds three industry certifications: CISSP, CISM, and CEH.

Adam Lewis recently received a Master of Science in Information Management degree from the University of Washington, where he focused on information architecture and human-centered design. He received his undergraduate degree in finance from the University of Puget Sound. He lived and travelled outside the U.S. from 2001 to 2011, including two years of living, working, and studying in China. Adam is currently a user experience designer at Microsoft, researching and designing applications for Microsoft's cloud infrastructure management and planning.

Kristine Tomasovic Nelson, CFA, received her Master of Science in Information Management from the University of Washington and her Bachelor of Science in accounting from Villanova University. She is currently a senior research analyst in the investment division at Russell Investments, a firm she joined in March of 2016. Prior to her current position, Kris was a senior vice president of research at Palisade Capital where she identified and directed equity investments in the consumer sector for three strategies including U.S. small, mid- and mid-cap growth. Previous to assuming consumer sector coverage at Palisade,

Kris was responsible for managing investments in the technology sector. Over the course of her career, she has covered multiple sectors and sub-sectors including media, telecommunications, autos, housing, and industrials.

Joe Pollack recently graduated from the University of Washington with a Bachelor of Science in Informatics. He is a technology consultant based in San Francisco, California. He is interested in databases, web technologies, as well as risk management and finance. He enjoys combining his passion for business and technology to create effective and meaningful solutions.

Kevin Rawls received a Bachelor of Science in Informatics from the University of Washington in 2016. Kevin is currently employed as a Software Engineer at a company in Renton (WA) that manufactures on-board weighing systems for commercial vehicles. His experience includes developing and maintaining all web-based software for the company as well as managing the security for all data involved with the software and websites.

Ermenejildo "Meadow" Rodriguez, Jr. is currently employed as an information security policy analyst/coordinator at Costco Wholesale's corporate office, where he earlier interned by supporting security risk and vendor risk management teams. Meadow earned a Master of Science in Information Management from the University of Washington, specializing in information management and consulting; a Bachelor of Science in computer science from Heritage University; and a Bachelor of Arts in social sciences from Washington State University. Meadow has interests in application development, compliance, and local and world events; and aspirations in corporate management and entrepreneurship.

Jyotsna Saxena graduated from the University of Washington with a Master of Science degree in Information Management in 2016, where she specialized in information security and UX research. With her undergraduate degree in computer engineering from the University of Mumbai, her background blends seamlessly with her passion for making technology products and services user-friendly and accessible.

She is currently working for Deloitte as a cyber risk consultant, and focuses on enabling better risk management and decision-making through design thinking.

Jeffrey B. Seward, Jr. received his Bachelor of Science in Business with Management as well as a Bachelor of Arts in Modern Languages and Literature in German Language from Montana State University in 2010. He has worked in environmental restoration as a GIS specialist and worked in criminal defense and civil litigation as a legal assistant and IT specialist. Jeffrey is interested in business analysis and business intelligence. He received his Master of Science in Information Management with a specialization in Business Intelligence from the University of Washington in 2017.

Cory Schyu has a Master of Business Administration degree from UCLA and later received a Master of Science in Information Management degree from the University of Washington with a focus in Data Science and Analytics. She started her career in financial audit at a Big Four accounting firm, then spent a few years in private equity. Currently, she is a market research consultant specializing in consumer retail.

Keith Snodgrass is the managing director and outreach coordinator for the South Asia Center at the Henry M. Jackson School of International Studies at the University of Washington. He has been engaged in teaching about South Asia for over 20 years, and has written numerous articles and reviews. He recently completed his Master of Science in Information Management at the University of Washington. His interests include information security, data collection and analysis, and the limits of electronic communications in conveying accurate information.

Ayush Soni is a graduate of the University of Washington. He received his dual degrees in Law, Societies, and Justice (BA) and Informatics (BS) in June 2016. Ayush's experience in industry ranges from doing paralegal & administrative work at a tax law firm to developing software for UW. His focus is in cybersecurity & information assurance. After graduation, Ayush completed an internship at the Starbucks Coffee

Company where he worked as an information security engineer. Ayush is now a security consulting analyst specializing in identity and access Management at Accenture. As a technologist with a legal background, he is equipped to provide positive changes in demanding and competitive enterprises.

Brian Stanley holds a Master of Science in Information Management degree, with a business intelligence specialization, from the University of Washington. His professional experience spans three decades in wireless telecommunications beginning, initially, as a mainframe computer technician and, most recently, as a software development manager. He currently serves as a software development consultant in the business intelligence and data analytics space.

Mark Tchao received his Bachelor of Science degree from the University of Washington, majoring in Informatics with a concentration in information assurance and cybersecurity. Mark has several years of experience as an educational technology consultant at the University of Washington, and is now currently employed as a cybersecurity consultant for PwC. His professional experiences include work within vendor risk management, PCI-DSS compliance, security auditing, and framework implementation.

Sukhman Tiwana is pursuing a Bachelor of Science in Informatics with a focus in information assurance, cybersecurity, and data science from the University of Washington. She has also two minors in Diversity and Gender, and Women & Sexuality Studies. She enjoys developing data visualizations, analyzing data and business risks, and enhancing data management. She has worked for UW Capital Planning & Development, El Rescate Non-Profit, CBRE, and iD Tech in their respected IT departments. Her work ranges from business analyst to teaching programming. She is known for developing visualizations that allow the client to make business decisions.

Matthew Welden received his Bachelor of Science in Business Administration from Westminster College of Salt Lake City. Matthew is currently a global research manager at Amazon in Seattle, Washington. He also holds senior certifications in the field of human resources. His past work experience includes managing the Seattle Space Needle, running a Beard Award-winning bakery, and consulting with global organizations on people management strategies. He received a Master of Science in Information Management from the University of Washington in 2016.

Jared Williams is a student finishing a Bachelor of Science in Informatics and is strongly interested in cybersecurity. Jared is currently employed at Tempered Networks, where he is expanding his knowledge of network security in general while furthering his technical skills in an innovative environment. He plans to continue working in the field of cybersecurity after graduation.

Dominik A. Zmuda received his Bachelor of Science degree from the University of Washington, majoring in Informatics. His special interests include software development, mobile application design, web development, and database administration. Having flown over a million miles and visited more than fifty countries, Dominik is currently highly involved in the travel industry - working with airlines and their partners on development of new technologies which aide travelers worldwide.

Emily Oxenford was ASA's research associate for the academic year of 2010-2011, during her final year in the Master of Science of Information Management at the University of Washington. She is a contributing author to the first volume of Reflections on Risk published in 2012, and edited the second and third volumes published in 2014 and 2015. Emily currently works as a senior analyst for Moss Adams LLP, a Seattle-based accounting, tax, consulting, and advisory services firm, performing a wide variety of operational and strategic research and consulting services.

Chapter I
Cybersecurity

The Harmonious Blend of Policy and Technology

The Need for an IoT Compliance Framework

Andy Herman

Publication Month: April 2017

Abstract: This paper discusses the rising concerns associated with the Internet of Things, and the lack of a comprehensive cybersecurity compliance framework. The rising number of internet-connected devices has created increasing number of cybersecurity risks, as network of devices are hijacked for malicious purposes.

The first "networked device" was demonstrated in 1990 at the Interop Networking Conference where MIT researcher John Romkey and Simon Hackett presented an "Internet Toaster," where the researchers could control the settings of the toaster through a connection made through the internet.[1] It took another decade for these networked devices to become a popular trend and Kevin Ashton coined the term "Internet of Things."[2] Since then, the number of connected devices has rapidly increased. Strategy Analytics forecasts that the 1.4 devices per person average at the end of 2014 will nearly quadruple to 4.3 devices per person in the next few years, predicting over 33 billion connected devices by 2020.[3] There are many benefits to the connected devices - simplicity of installation and use; convenience and automation of daily tasks; potential for increased productivity and efficiency; and even new avenues for innovation. Though there are many advantages, the rapid increase of connected devices is paralleled by an increase in inherent risks for cybersecurity attacks. As technology continues to develop and improve the way tasks are handled, the development and enforcement of policies will help guide these new technological advances to have a greater positive impact.

The new products purchased today come with less and less documentation. If users are confused on how to set something up, they can typically refer to online searches to find answers. The simplicity of products has reached a point where the term "set-up" is synonymous to "plug in the power and turn it on." A common experience is now to pull things out of boxes and intuitively see exactly how to plug devices in and connect to a PC or mobile phone without referring to the user manual. These natural reactions to technological devices contribute to high risk of breach. Bruce Schneier, author and thought-leader in information security, recently commented about this complacent consumer attitude and lack of concern for security in connected devices by saying that "[t]he owners of those devices don't care. Their devices were cheap to buy, they still work, and they don't even know [the victims of DDoS attacks]. The sellers of those devices don't care: They're now selling newer and better models, and the original buyers only cared about price and features."[4] Though the interest in new technological devices is high, the understanding of what connected devices are is still lacking to many consumers. Per Accenture, 87 percent of the consumer had not heard of the term 'Internet of Things,' prior to the study.[5] With this consumer uncertainty of how devices create an "Internet of Things," hackers can exploit vulnerabilities using fewer resources.

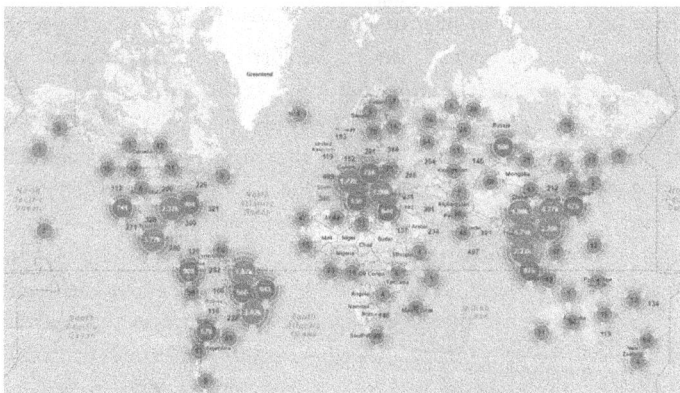

Figure 1 Geographic representation of where Mirai-infected devices are. (Bekerman et al, 2016)

One of the ways that compromised connected devices have been used maliciously has been the recent increase in distributed denial of service (DDoS) attacks. DDoS attacks do not take personal identifiable information from consumers but they can be nuisances to victims. Connected devices have been used to conduct DDoS attacks by using an army of infected devices and computers known as "botnets" that can be remotely controlled by the attacker to send traffic to a single target. By sending traffic to a single target by a large number of bots, you can overload the system and crash the system. To create a botnet, attackers spread the malware through clickable links on websites, emails, and social media. When people click on links that contain the malware, their computers become compromised and can be part of the botnet without detection. The MIRAI malware, which was responsible for creating disruptions to Dyn, is the latest example of the use of connected devices to DDoS an Internet service provider server.[6] The MIRAI malware has roughly 100,000 connected devices in its' botnet army and is expanding as infected devices conduct wide-ranging scans of IP addresses, with the intent of "locat[ing] under-secured IoT devices that can be remotely accessed using brute-force attacks".[7] With more awareness of the malware, hackers have become more creative in its ways to distribute the malware. Recently, MIRAI malware was found to use a new Windows Trojan with the name "Trojan.Mirai.1" which targets Window's PCs. Prior to this new attack vector, the MIRAI malware was mainly attacking Linux OS to scan the user's network for "compromisable Linux-based connected devices".[8] These recent discoveries demonstrate the rapid spread of malware and the constant adjustments that attackers are implementing to avoid detection and increase infection.

The main reason why connected devices have helped hackers exploit this effective method of attack is that the devices themselves are shipped out from their manufacturers with default security settings. Default passwords are set on devices to reduce the complications of creating random passwords for each device being produced. Manufacturers and developers provide the option to consumers to change the default settings to something more secure to prevent the hassle of implementing random passwords on the thousands of products that they are manufacturing. A common example of this would be wireless routers: consumers have become more aware of setting passwords on their wireless routers to prevent others from using it without your permission. To help contribute to the increased awareness of the risk of not changing passwords and developing an awareness of cybersecurity, it is important that regulations be put in place to oversee products before they reach the consumer. This would ensure that consumers not follow old habits, forced to become more vigilant in their cybersecurity awareness.

Recently, there has been a huge push for security policy firms to research and publish guidelines to help companies become more aware of the security issues associated with IoT devices and guidelines to help mitigate some of these problems. The National Institute of Standards and Technology (NIST) published NIST 800-160: Systems Security Engineering, to provide guidance to software engineers to build secure systems.[9] Other groups like the Open Web Application Security Project (OWASP) group has created a working group "designed to help manufacturers, developers, and consumers better understand the security issues associated with the Internet of Things, and to enable users in any context to make better security decisions when building, deploying, or assessing IoT Technologies."[10] The increase in attention and research into connected devices is critical especially because of the impact that connected devices have on our lives. In fact, connected devices are slowly becoming a larger part of our daily routine that it should be considered one of the critical infrastructures in the U.S. Treating these devices as a critical infrastructure would help create a defensive mindset. Imagine attackers compromising healthcare connected devices and remotely shutting off all devices. Furthermore, think about what would happen if compromised connected devices can be traced back to a power plant and the attackers decide to DDoS servers in power plants. Manufacturers of connected devices must be regulated to provide security to this critical component of our infrastructure. There are many potential solutions that policies can help enforce, though these rules and regulations must blend with technology to create the most effective defense. First, connected device manufacturers should require users to reset default device passwords the first time a consumer turns on a device. This standard must be incorporated into software development requirements. In addition, there should be an international effort by groups that are conducting research into best practices to create a framework that manufacturers would want to become certified in to show that the products that they are selling are secure - like PCI compliance for the payment card industry.

How to change the password on a DVR from the following series : 3000, 4000, 1000, 3200, 4200, 3450, 3425, 1250, 1425, 1450, 7072, 7082, 7085

Last Updated: Jun 23, 2015 10:37AM AEST

It is not possible to change the user and password information through the software MyDVR or Swannview Link. It has to be done on the DVR itself.

In order to do so, you need to connect a monitor to the DVR, using either the VGA or the HDMI port of the DVR. Then you open the main menu, you go in System, click on the User Tab, select the Username for which you wish to modify the password, click on modify and you can then change the password. The default password for the admin account is 12345 . It is by default just not enabled.

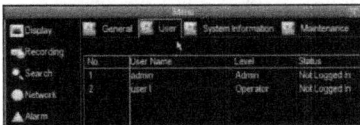

Figure 2: Swann DVR Support Webpage showing the default password. (support.swann.com)

Enforce Password Reset when Consumers Start their Device

Many connected devices such as refrigerators and thermostats often do not have a user-friendly interface. Some devices require connecting devices right out of the box to an application on a mobile phone. Others will allow users to simply select an "express set-up" to help with ease of use. Providing consumers fewer hassles is always one of the targets that manufacturers strive to achieve. In the pursuit of providing consumers with the most simple and user-friendly experience in using these new technological devices, manufacturers have resorted to setting default passwords to avoid the hassle of having to change the passwords for users.

A simple search online for default passwords on connected DVR devices showed the webpage showing the DVR series number along with the default password and (vague) instructions on how to change and enable the passwords (Figure 2). The U.S. Computer Emergency Readiness Team (US-CERT) has issued an alert (TA13-175A) to address the risk and impact of not changing passwords. US-CERT has identified that "attackers can easily obtain default passwords and identify internet-connected target systems" and that exposed systems can be identified using "search engines like Shodan" to conduct their attacks on vulnerable systems.[11] One simple solution to decreasing the attack surface in connected devices would be to prompt consumers to reset their password after an initial start or factory reset. This would force consumers to reset default passwords to prevent systems being open to attacks by hackers.

International Effort to Create Internet of Things Security Framework Certification

Compliance to international frameworks and attainment of certifications by businesses are mainly done to show the customers that the business is providing the best standard of products and services. The most common and well-known certification is the Payment Card Industry Data Security Standard (PCI-DSS) certification which is a "widely accepted set of policies and procedures intended to optimize the security of credit, debit and cash card transactions and protect cardholders against misuse of their personal information."[12] Businesses will seek to become PCI-DSS compliant for their own benefits to prevent data compromise of sensitive financial information of customers, but also customers who have an understanding of PCI compliance will want to see that the business that they are interacting with is PCI-DSS compliant to have a sense of confidence that their data will be secure.

Like the credit card industry, there is a need for an increase in emphasis for manufacturers of connected devices to show that the devices that they are producing are compliant with international standards as a secure device. A consumer who buys a closed-circuit television expects that there are security controls in place to prevent potential hackers from watching them and their family. The domains for the proposed Internet of Things Compliance Framework should incorporate the common families and domains as seen in established frameworks such as the NIST 800-53 Rev 4: Security and Privacy Controls and the NIST Cybersecurity Framework. Alongside these domains, the working group should refer to research by well-known vulnerabilities research groups like OWASP to determine what are some of the greatest concerns. The "OWASP Top IoT Vulnerabilities," published in 2014, cite insecure web interface and insufficient authentication/authorization at the top of the list for vulnerabilities in connected devices.[13] Using the research that is continuously being conducted on the possible points of weakness, a security compliance framework should be created and implemented across the industry.

Recently, the IoT Security Foundation released the "IoT Security Compliance Framework." This framework divides the compliance into different compliance classes that focus on security objectives for confidentiality, integrity, and availability. This framework works more like a checklist that asks the questions of whether the manufacturer or consumer has met the list of requirements on their compliance framework. Upon analysis of this specific framework, the requirements are vague and do not focus on connected devices but rather the business practices. For example, Requirement 2.3.1.4 states, "the company follows industry standard cyber security recommendations (e.g. UK Cyber Essentials, NIST Cybersecurity Framework, etc.)."[14] Merely asking whether the manufacturer is implementing other cyber security recommendations does not provide clear expectations of a strong security posture. The difference between checklists and frameworks is that checklists often creates a sense of complacency by the organization using it because the certificate can be attained by showing how the company meets each requirement whereas frameworks tend to have procedures and guidelines to help guide and interpret the business to be at its desired security posture.

Despite some need for revision and improvement, the efforts by the IoT Security Foundation should serve as a model for the international community to contribute in the efforts of regulating and controlling the security of connected devices. As connected devices increase in its impact on daily lives, it is only a matter of time before connected devices are considered a critical infrastructure of the U.S. and across the world.

But Wait... Compliance Does Not Equal Security

Though creating frameworks and promoting compliance is beneficial in creating an awareness and a security-first attitude, compliance does not equal security. Former CEO of Target Gregg Steinhafel said "Target was certified as meeting the standard for the payment card industry in September 2013. Nonetheless, we suffered a data breach."[15] Security professionals will all agree that compliance to a set of rules or a framework is not enough. While the frameworks illustrate a set of rules and procedures that professionals have agreed upon as best practice, without an investment in blending the policy and the technology, data breaches can never be completed prevented.

Compliance to frameworks is the foundation for more secure systems. The creation for an Internet of Things Compliance Framework is a call for the blend of policy and technology. Businesses must be willing to incorporate compliance frameworks to set the first step in motivating consumers to start understanding the changing threat environment. After establishing this baseline, consumers must be more aware of the "default effect" and try to adhere to the using the technology to help create a more secure environment. The 'default effect' by consumers is a psychological effect that reflects a natural acceptance of default settings because of three reasons: "(1) Effort: choosing the default option requires no physical action. (2) Implied endorsement: decision-makers may infer a default has been preselected due to its merit. (3) Defaults may result from reference dependence: the default option may represent a reference point which colors the evaluation of other may represent a reference point which colors the evaluation of other options as gains or losses."[16]

It is understandable that even with the best compliance framework and cooperation by manufacturers of connected devices, consumers must gain a better understanding of why simple controls such as changing default passwords to complicated password lengths are important. This education in cybersecurity is very like what is seen in healthcare. The goal of physicians is to make sure that their patients remain healthy enough so that the patients do not have to come visit them as much. Security professionals are just the same: they strive to create a system that is protected from data breaches so that the business runs smoothly. Physicians follow best practices of preventative medicine by suggesting vaccinations, exercise, and healthy lifestyles to their patients. Security professionals promote "cyber health" by suggesting strong passwords, encryption of hardware, and understanding of basic Internet behavior to the users. Despite the efforts of these professionals, not everyone is 100 percent healthy both in a physical and cybersecurity sense. However, because there are these controls and awareness in place, there is a reduced number of people who become ill and systems being breached. This must be the motivating factor for organizations to adhere to the compliance frameworks for Internet of Things devices. The blend of policy and technology is critical in the formation of a more secure connected device environment.

---

[1] Noler, C. "Timeline: A Brief History of the Internet of Things (Infographic)". The Street. 18 Oct. 2016. Web. 26 Jan. 2017.

[2] Postscapes. "Internet of Things (IoT) History". Postscapes.com.

[3] Waring, J. "Number of devices to hit 4.3 per person by 2020 – a report". Mobile World Live. 16 Oct. 2014. Web. 26 Jan. 2017.

[4] Schneier, B. "Lessons from the Dyn DDoS Attack". Security Intelligence. 1 Nov. 2016. Web. 30 Jan. 2017.

[5] Accenture. "The Internet of Things: The Future of Consumer Adoption". Accenture Interactive. 2014. Print. 7 Feb. 2017.

[6] Higgins, K. "DDoS on Dyn Used Malicious TCP, UDP traffic". Dark Reading. 26 Oct. 2016. Web. 8 Feb. 2017.

[7] Bekerman, D., Herzberg, B., Zeifman, I. "Breaking down Mirai: An IoT DDoS Botnet Analysis". Incapsula.com. 26 Oct. 2016. Web. 8 Feb. 2017

[8] Khandelwal, S. "New Windows Trojan Spreads MIRAI Malware to Have More IoT Devices". The Hacker News. 9 Feb. 2017. Web. 21 Feb. 2017.

[9] Block, C. "What does NIST 800-160 Mean for Quantification, FAIR, and IoT?". Linkedin Pulse. 16 Dec. 2016. Web 23 Feb. 2017.

[10] OWASP. "OWASP Internet of Things Project". 15 Feb. 2017. Web. 23 Feb. 2017.

[11] US-CERT. "Alert (TA13-175A): Risks of Default Passwords on the Internet". US-CERT. 7 Oct. 2016. Web 26 Feb. 2017.

[12] Rouse, M. "PCI DSS: Definition". Techtarget.com. May 2009. Web. 26 Feb. 2017.

[13] OWASP. "Top IoT Vulnerabilities". OWASP.com. 18 May 2016. Web. 27 Feb. 2017.

[14] IoT Security Foundation. "IoT Security Compliance Framework". IoT Security Foundation. 6 Dec. 2016 Web 27 Feb. 2017.

[15] Mello, J. "Target Breach Lesson: PCI Compliance isn't enough". Technewsworld.com. 18 Mar. 2014. Web. 26 Feb. 2017.

---

[16] Dinner, I., Goldstein, D., Johnson, E., Liu, K. "Partitioning Default Effects: Why People Choose Not to Choose". Journal of Experimental Psychology. Vol. 17. No. 4. 2011.

New Age of Cybersecurity

Cory Shyu
Publication Month: October 2016

Abstract: The Internet of Things (IoT) has transformed the technology sector profoundly. While companies are rushing to reap benefits from increased productivity and automation by adopting more agile technology solutions, privacy and security issues have risen at an alarming rate. With recent high-profile data breaches across multiple industries, specifically the government, healthcare, retail, and financial services, companies have reprioritized security as a top objective. This paper addresses the key areas in which companies should rethink cybersecurity strategies and develop appropriate roadmaps to achieve security objectives.

Introduction

Cyber-attack used to be a foreign concept and viewed as an extremely rare event. The network sharing protocols were originally designed under the assumption of trust a few decades ago. Not long ago, cases of high profile data breaches have started to dominate headlines and people started to be conscious of the consequences of the lack of security in the Internet era. External hackers caused over a third of data breaches in 2013.[1] The magnitude of breaches has been astronomical, costing millions of dollars in legal damages and loss in revenues. According to a research note by Gartner,[2] companies are more concerned about cybersecurity than ever before due to recent threats facing organizations including Target, Home Depot, and JP Morgan. The large-scale data breaches were wake-up calls for top executives to reprioritize cybersecurity initiatives. Janice Newell, CIO of Providence Health & Services,[3] mentioned that it is no longer a challenge to obtain budgets on strengthening security capabilities. Companies are contemplating the adoption of more resilient security systems. Gartner predicts "by 2018, 40 percent of large enterprises will have formal plans to address aggressive cybersecurity business disruption attacks, up from 0 percent in 2015."[4]

Key Security Objectives

- Protect intellectual properties: Data theft is a source of major risk. Cyberattacks from China often target at security vulnerabilities to steal intellectual properties. Companies with large IP portfolios need to safeguard their intellectual properties against theft.

- Protect personal information: Employee and customer data are highly sensitive. According to Jenny Durkan Global Chair of the Cyber Law and Privacy Group at Quinn Emanuel Urquhart & Sullivan LLP, one hacker organization has allegedly stolen more than 100 million personal records. Identity theft is a growing concern in the healthcare industry.

- Protect financial information: Financial records often contain highly confidential competitive information. Companies face the risk of losing such information to competitors. The FBI's Cyber Division estimated that more than 500 million financial records have been stolen.[5]

- Protect key operational data: Companies that process large volumes of transactions are sensitive to the risk of operational disruption. A halt in business operation can cost millions of dollars economic loss.

The Rise Of Advanced Persistent Threats (APT)[6]

Security practitioners recognize the growing APT incidents that are more targeted, malicious, and often bypass traditional security controls. The scale and scope of security compromises from APTs are much more disruptive to business operations. The advent of APT requires companies to think beyond traditional security strategies and calls for security innovations.

New Challenges In The Cybersecurity Landscape

Compass Intelligence points out the major trends in IoT that have significantly impacted the challenges in cybersecurity.[7]

- Exponential growth in number devices and heterogeneity of vendor sources: The increased complexity arisen from the proliferation of devices has a major impact on the access control protocols and security deployments because devices come from a variety of vendors with different hardware and security standards.

- Obsolescence of security standard and guidelines: Security and privacy standards are absent in the age of IoT. Most IoT devices were already in the market without proper security measures and new devices are introduced constantly. Policies and standards have not been in pace with the rapid changes in technologies.

- Higher vulnerability and increased response time: The increased adoption of big data infrastructure such as cloud has resulted in new challenges in data privacy and security. The data being handled often contain highly sensitive information such as intellectual property, password, and personal and financial information. The extent and scope of potential damages have grown exponentially. The consequences of data compromises are much damaging. This results in long lags between data breach and company response time. According to Center for Strategic & International Studies (CSIS), "85 percent of breaches took months to be discovered," and the average time is five months.[8]

- Increased sophistication of hacker techniques: The digital age has introduced advanced techniques. Hackers have taken advantage of advanced tools to disrupt critical business operations. According to Kirk Bailey, CISO of University of Washington, there is a clear gap between company preparedness and hacker capabilities.

- Trade-off between security and automation: The utilization of cloud computing platforms can be a source of competitive advantage. However, the use of third-party platforms and software introduces new security risks. Companies often ignore the implications of critical liability clauses and access controls in service contracts. Fortune 500 IT leaders often cite this issue as a major source of risk.

Regulations

As data breach became more prevalent, policymakers have raised standards and mandated disclosure requirements. Most notably, the SEC required proper disclosure on data breaches in 2011. The costs associated with increased scrutiny and auditing can be expensive for large public companies. While federal regulatory requirement on data breaches has still been in development, state-level regulations are likely to be in effect in the upcoming years.[9] Joseph Lindstrom, GM of Information Security and Risk Management at Microsoft said that it's a matter of "when" cybersecurity becomes a regulation issue.

Current State Of Cybersecurity Practices

- Gap between perception and execution: According to a research surveying more than 500 C-level executives, 90 to 95 percent stated that they saw values in investing in security infrastructures, but less than 50 percent of them stated that they were actively involved.[10] A CSIS survey showed that 45 percent of the surveyed companies believed they did well, however only 10 percent were taking adequate steps.[11]

- Absence of threat detection programs: According to GISS surveys conducted by Ernst & Young in 2014,[12] 36 percent of respondents did not have a threat intelligence program; further 26 percent stated that their data protection policies were "ad-hoc" or "informal". In addition, 56 percent stated that it is unlikely their organization could detect sophisticated attack; 63 percent of organizations would take more than an hour to detect an attack.[13]

- A surge in adoption of cybersecurity insurance: "According to the Ponemon Institute, the adoption rate for cyber insurance more than doubled from 10 percent to 26 percent. over the past year."[14] A further study by Gartner showed that 33 percent of the companies plan to purchase cyberinsurance in the next 12 months.[15] While cyberinsurance can mitigate the magnitude of potential risks, it does not address the fundamental issues. Cyberinsurance should be used to address unavoidable risks in combination with building solid internal security infrastructure.

Rethink Security Strategies And Implementations

As mentioned previously, the rapid changes in the technology landscape have introduced new challenges to information security. The majority of companies have not been able to keep their policies and procedures up-to-date. To get started, companies should reexamine their security practices as follows:

- Assess and prioritize company information assets: The first question to address is, what are the most sensitive data and where are they located[16]? And most importantly, what is the risk appetite for potential breaches? Survey shows that only 29 percent of companies have a complete inventory of data they own, and the percentage is declining due to the explosion of data volume.[17] A seemingly simple question can be a challenge to answer. Companies should consider the cost of losing data, regulation, and the nature of data and develop a priority list based on the assessments.

- Reassess existing policy and procedures for handling critical business data: New tools continue to be created and are often adopted too fast. Data security risks should be reassessed in pace with adoption of new technologies. Companies should rethink the trade-off between speed and security, then ask themselves which data should be automated and which shouldn't. There are thousands of technology solution vendors, each with different policies and standards on security. The consequences of mishandling data can be serious and should be reevaluated frequently.

- Reevaluate bring your own device (BYOD) policies: In the digital age, employees often bring their own devices to work. 57% of companies consider employees to be the most likely source of attack.[18] This fosters the need for tightened endpoint control. Companies should develop clear guidelines on the use of personal devices.

- Strengthen security control procedures: Having an effective patch management process is the foremost important control according to Gartner.[19] "96 percent of successful breaches could have been avoided if the victim had put in place simple or intermediate controls."[20] The research findings are astonishing, indicating common weaknesses in existing security controls. Most companies fail even at the basic level. The fundamental controls such as patch, monitoring, and whitelisting applications should not be ignored.

- Implement routine company-wide security training programs: During the "Business in the Age of Cyber Threats" conference at the University of Washington, senior security executives all emphasized the importance of changing attitude toward security – specially, security should be treated as an operational issue. Security hygiene should be routine and needs company-wide awareness. Appropriate data security policy training programs should be in place and update-to-date.

- Develop threat detection and response programs: Instead of being reactive to cyber-attacks, companies should explore advanced detection techniques and designate response teams to handle incidents timely. The team that handles incidents should develop proper response plans.

The Five Security Operations Center Models (SOC)[21]

To implement a sound security practice, companies need to consider building proper SOCs. The primary objective of an SOC is to manage threat detection, response and prevention capabilities with centralized security operations functions and to ensure continuous monitoring of previously mentioned key security implementations. Gartner predicts that "by 2019, 50 percent of all security operations work in large and midsize enterprises will be conducted out of an owned or a shared security operations center, up from 15 percent in 2015." Gartner suggests 5 models of SOC to fit different organizational needs:

- Virtual SOC: A virtual SOC has no dedicated facility with only part-time team members and is reactive in nature. This model is the least mature among all SOC models and may be suitable for small businesses that expect infrequent incidents. This model can also be adopted as an interim approach for transitioning into more dedicated SOC model.

- Multifunctional SOC: A multifunctional SOC has dedicated facility and team members to perform security and other critical 24/7 IT operations. This model may be suitable for small, midsize and low-risk large enterprises when the respective functions are already performed by the same team members. While this model can does not require large capital outlay compared to some other dedicated models, the primary risks with this model is that politics, budget, process maturity levels can hinder execution.

- Distributed SOC: This model has dedicated and semi-dedicated team members which typically run during business hours. It is co-managed by managed security service providers (MSSP). This model may be suitable for small to midsize businesses. The primary driver for the adoption of this model are talent shortage, budget restrictions, and the considerable cost of 24/7 operations. Thus, having an in-house 5x8 operation with an MSSP covering non-business hours is a popular choice for larger organizations.

- Dedicated SOC: This model has a fully in-house dedicated facility and team that runs 24/7. A dedicated SOC is self-contained and possesses continuous day-to-day security operations. The team is typically composed of in-house security engineers, security analysts and a SOC manager. This model is typically used by large enterprises, service providers, and high-risk organizations with multiple business units and geographically dispersed locations. This model is much more expensive than the other models due to higher personnel costs.

- Command SOC: This SOC model coordinates other SOCs and provides threat intelligence expertise. When an organization has multiple SOCs, there is a need to designate a command SOC that coordinates and manages other SOCs hierarchically. This model may be suitable for very large enterprises and service providers, governments, and military.

Other Considerations

- Cost-benefit assessment: No system is perfect and it is impossible to protect every asset. The use of advanced cybersecurity technologies can only mitigate, but not eliminate risks. Also, there is a trade-off between increased security and individual privacy as well as the speed of getting work done. When tightening controls, the two get compromised and the right balance should be considered.

- Silo management: The silos between network control systems and endpoint are primary challenges for organizations to respond to advanced attacks effectively. When organizations move from a less centralized SOC toward a more centralized SOC model, there should be proper changes in process, policy, and organization structures.

Recommendations

Satya Nadella said, cybersecurity is like going to the gym and must be exercised daily. Cybersecurity is no longer an IT issue, but requires company-wide awareness and appropriate implementation. Recent large-scale targeted attacks have prompted numerous conversations among top-executives regarding where they should start. I recommend a six-step action plan to rethink and address potential cybersecurity risks:

1. Develop priority list for key assets: Companies need to identify the key areas with the least risk tolerance and prioritize asset protection mechanisms in the event of attack.

2. Reevaluate policy and procedures: Employee BYOD and third-party vendor management are among the top security concerns among security executives. Vendor service agreement and liability sharing clauses are the primary source of dispute when data security is compromised. Companies need to reevaluate the potential vulnerabilities and current policies and procedures.

3. Analyze current gaps: After reassessment of current policies and procedures, the next step is gap analysis. Companies need to ask what needs to be done and how to bridge the gaps.

4. Strengthen security controls: Security hygiene can mitigate more 90 percent of potential data breaches. Companies should conduct routine re-examination and audit of existing security practices.

5. Enforce company-wide security trainings: Data breaches can come from a variety of sources. Given that hackers can easily search for vulnerabilities, breaches can happen anywhere in an organization. Therefore, companies must conduct up-to-date security trainings to all employees.

6. Develop implantation plans for threat detection and response programs: The implementation of SOC is critical to ensuring continuous monitoring of security controls. This is especially an important step to become proactive rather than reactive. Companies should consider the costs and benefits of the different SOC models and select the most appropriate one to meet their specific needs.

APPENDIX

Gap Between Perception And Reality [22,23]

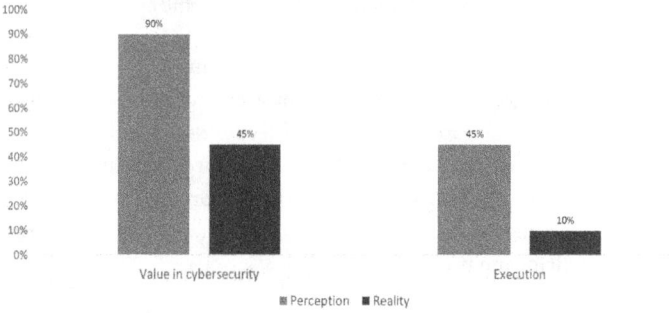

Perception ■ Reality

Absence Of Threat Detection Programs [24]

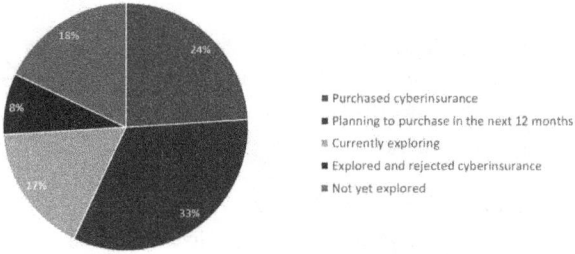

■ Purchased cyberinsurance
■ Planning to purchase in the next 12 months
■ Currently exploring
■ Explored and rejected cyberinsurance
■ Not yet explored

Status Of Cyberinsurance Adoption [25]

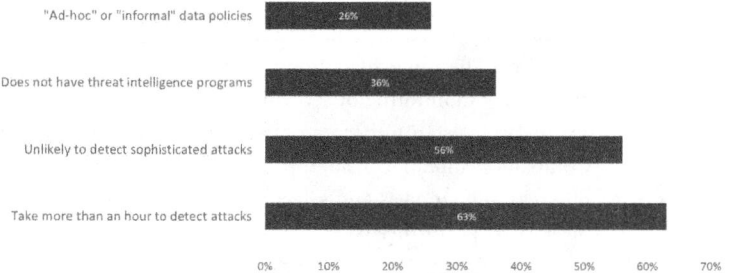

[1] Biswas, Ritam. "Data Center Security: Global Market." BCC Research. Nov 2015. Accessed <www.bccresearch.com>.

[2] Procter, Paul E., et al. "Attack on Sony Pictures Is a Digital Game Changer." Gartner. 9 Feb. 2015. Accessed <www.gartner.com>.

[3] "Business in the Age of Cyber Threats." Conference. 8 Dec. 2015. Foster School of Business, University of Washington.

[4] Procter, Paul E. et al.

[5] *2015 Second Annual Data Breach Industry Forecast*. Experian. 11 Feb. 2015. Accessed <www.experian.com>.

[6] Pingree, Lawrence and Neil MacDonald. "Best Practices for Detecting and Mitigating Advanced Persistent Threats." Gartner.18 Jan. 2012. Accessed <www.gartner.com>.

[7] "Security and Privacy in the Internet of Things (IoT) Challenges, Market Opportunities and Forecast 2015 – 2020." Compass Intelligence. Aug. 2015. Accessed <www.compassintelligence.com>.

[8] Lewis, James, "Raising the Bar for Cybersecurity." 14 Feb 2013. Center for Strategic & International Studies. Accessed <www.csis.org>.

[9] *2015 Second Annual Data Breach Industry Forecast*.

[10] "Business in the Age of Cyber Threats."

[11] Lewis, James.

[12] "Cyber Threat Intelligence – How To Get Ahead Of Cybercrime." Ernst & Young. Nov. 2014. Accessed <www.ey.com>.

[13] Ibid.

[14] "The Aftermath of a Data Breach: Consumer Sentiment." Ponemon Institute LLC. Apr. 2014. Accessed <www.ponemon.org>.

[15] Wheeler, John A. "Understanding When and How to Use Cyberinsurance Effectively." Gartner. 12 Mar. 2015. Accessed <www.gartner.com>.

[16] Lobel, Mark and Gary Loveland. "Cybersecurity the New Business Priority." PWC (PriceWaterhouseCoopers). 2012. Accessed <www.pwc.com>.

[17] Lewis, James.

[18] "Cyber Threat Intelligence – How To Get Ahead Of Cybercrime."

[19] Wheeler, John A.

[20] Lewis, James.

[21] Rochford, Lawson, "The Five Models of Security Operation Centers." Gartner. 22 Oct. 2015. Accessed <www.gartner.com>.

[22] "Business in the Age of Cyber Threats."

[23] Lewis, James.

[24] "Cyber Threat Intelligence – How To Get Ahead Of Cybercrime."

[25] Wheeler, John A.

Ashley Madison and Managing a Risky Business

Kevin Rawls

Publication Month: January 2016

Abstract: Cheating is risky business – when your business model is built upon cheating, it adds an entirely new level of risk. The website Ashley Madison is a now notorious website built around enabling married people to have extramarital affairs, that in 2015 experienced a very severe data breach of its customers' data. This paper explores some of the heightened levels of internal and external risks faced by a business that operates in a legally sound but morally compromised space.

Introduction

Ashley Madison considers itself the world's leading married dating service for "discreet encounters." What that means in plain English is that it is a website to help married people cheat on their spouses. While not illegal, Ashley Madison has gotten a lot of recent attention for providing such a morally dubious service. Attention that is understandably negative and from many people who feel compelled to fight back against a company whose slogan is "Life is short, have an affair."[i] In an enterprise rooted in such a morally questionable foundation and with millions of users, lots of media attention, and vast amounts of highly sensitive data, risk management is extremely important for their success. However, with this high risk comes many potential control failures, the most threatening of which include internal events and external events.

Internal Events

Internal events at Ashley Madison could and have proven to be extremely dangerous to their enterprise. For example, in 2012 the company was sued by former employee Doriana Silva. She claimed that she had suffered a wrist injury from being overworked on a project involving creating thousands of female bots for their website.[i] Why was

---

[i] www.ashleymadison.com

she creating so many bots? The stark truth of their website is that only approximately 12,000 of their 5.5 million users are female, less than one percent.[2] At the same time, Ashley Madison offers their customers a "guarantee"[3] that users will find a match by using their service. To compensate for this very high discrepancy the company has reportedly made over 70,000 bots, some 3,000 of which were tasked to Silva over a three week period in preparation for their new Portuguese website. In 2015, the Ontario Superior Court dismissed the case leaving the company reportedly "very pleased."[4] Ashley Madison also alleged that Silva had kept confidential documents and sought to retrieve them.

It is clear from these reports that their internal workings are sometimes harsh and shady, which is understandable given the nature of their business. However, this creates a very large potential for control failure by unhappy and disgruntled employees. It is enough that their work is considered morally wrong by most societies, and that they are often the recipients of criticism and judgment. Ashley Madison as a company then adds on to this, working their employees to the point of lawsuit, whether the lawsuits are successful or not. This undoubtedly fosters an internal culture of unhappy employees, employees who have access to highly sensitive data that could potentially tarnish the already negative reputation of their company. This ticking time bomb of an internal working environment is undoubtedly a risk management nightmare that could easily start a domino effect ending in disaster. A potential control failure in this aspect of the company is a crucial thing to consider when evaluating risk for Ashley Madison.

In terms of managing internal risk, they could do many things differently. They could start by giving their employees better working conditions and not working them to the point of injury. In a business where the employees are doing work that could potentially risk the reputation and safety of a company, it would be a prudent to treat them well - particularly when they have access to highly sensitive documents that could damage the company if leaked. A more delicate approach to administration might do wonders for managing the risk of internal events at Ashley Madison.

External Events

While internal events are a massive risk management concern, it is clear that their largest potential for control failure lies in external events. The uncontested best example of this is the massive data breach that occurred in July of 2015, where over 60 gigabytes of data containing user details were leaked. This attack was orchestrated by a group calling themselves "The Impact Team" on July 15th 2015.[5] After the breach, The Impact Team threatened Ashley Madison's parent company Avid Life Media (ALM), saying they would release user data if they did not shut down AshleyMadison.com and its sister site EstablishedMen.com. ALM did not back down and on August 18th a 10 gigabyte compressed archive confirmed by experts was leaked to the Internet with user profile information from AshleyMadison.com. ALM promptly responded by calling out The Impact Team, saying, "This event is not an act of hacktivism, it is an act of criminality. It is an illegal action against the individual members of AshleyMadison.com, as well as any freethinking people who choose to engage in fully lawful online activities."[6] Two days later, a second and even larger data dump was leaked (12.7GB) including the email of ALM CEO Noel Biderman. A week later Biderman stepped down from his position as CEO.[7]

The Ashley Madison data breach was a massive blow to the reputation of an already unpopular company but the final nail in the coffin came in the form of a failed promise uncovered in the data. The attack was allegedly fueled by the company's guarantee that if customers wanted to, they could pay a $19 dollar fee and have all of their information permanently deleted from their site, an option that earned the company more than $1.7 million dollars.[8] This was determined to be a lie when the hackers leaked data from accounts that had paid to have the data deleted. This caused massive outrage among customers and ended in a $576 million dollar class action lawsuit against the company.[9]

Risk Management

The data breach highlights how catastrophic a control failure in the security from outside events can be for a company like Ashley Madison. Data security should be the highest priority for an enterprise with a business model so widely considered to be morally wrong, and as

Match.com co-founder Trish McDermott puts it, "a business built on the back of broken hearts, ruined marriages, and damaged families."[10] The highly sensitive environment of their company was clearly not taken into enough consideration and after what can only be described as a complete and utter failure in control, they were left with a tarnished reputation and millions of dollars in loss.

There are numerous things Ashley Madison could have done to prevent - or at least lessen the blow of - the data breach. They could have taken the time to consider just how sensitive their data is, not just for the reputation of their company but also for the personal lives of their customers. More resources, money, and time could have been invested in the security of their data rather than other expenses, such as an attempted super bowl ad in 2009.[11]

Another example and one of the biggest things Ashley Madison failed to do which could have greatly alleviated the situation was encrypt their data. The data that they promised would be deleted through their "full delete" option, was not only not deleted, it was not encrypted at all. This meant the hackers had to go through very little effort to expose all the secrets in those files. A higher level of attention to critical details such as encryption and care to cover all the security basics might have gone a very long way in controlling these risks.

Conclusion

Ashley Madison is a company that provides a very risky service, but ironically has failed in controlling their own risks. Some might consider it poetic that a website intended to help people cheat on their spouses was taken down in the way that they were. Nevertheless, the site was not completely taken down, and today anyone can still go on AshleyMadison.com and make an account. The data breach showed not only the business but the world how necessary managing risky business can be. The only way Ashley Madison can bounce back from this catastrophe is to invest significantly much more time, money, and effort into risk management.

1 "Woman Hurt Typing Fake Profiles for Dating Site, $20M Suit Alleges."
    CityNews. 10 Nov. 2013. Accessed Dec. 2015 <www.citynews.ca>.
2 Reed, Brad. "The Most Hilarious Revelation about the Ashley Madison Hack
    Yet." *Yahoo Tech*. 27 Aug. 2015. Accessed Dec. 2015 <www.yahoo.com/tech>.
3 "The Ashley Madison Affair Guarantee Program." Ashley Madison. N.D.
    Accessed Dec. 2015 <www.ashleymadison.com>.
4 Loriggio, Paola. "Lawsuit Against Dating Site for Married People Seeking
    Affairs Dismissed." *The Globe and Mail*. 18 Jan. 2015. Accessed Dec. 2015
    <www.theglobeandmail.com>.
5 "Online Cheating Site AshleyMadison Hacked." *Krebs On Security*. 15 Jul. 2015.
    Accessed Dec. 2015 <www.krebsonsecurity.com>.
6 Zetter, Kim. "Hackers Finally Post Stolen Ashley Madison Data." *Wired*. 18
    Aug. 2015. Accessed Dec. 2015 <www.wired.com>.
7 Perlroth, Nicole. "Ashley Madison Chief Steps Down After Data Breach." *The
    New York Times*. 28 Aug. 2015. Accessed Dec. 2015 <www.nytimes.com>.
8 Welch, Chris. "Ashley Madison's $19 'Full Delete' Option made the Company
    Millions." *The Verge*. 19 Aug. 2015. Accessed Dec. 2015
    <www.theverge.com>.
9 Loriggio, Paola.
10 Farrell, Paul. "Ashley Madison Hacked: 5 Fast Facts You Need to Know."
    Heavy. 20 Jul. 2015. Accessed Dec. 2015 <www.heavy.com>.
11 Hill, Catey. "Banned! These Ads Are Too Racy for the Super Bowl." *Daily
    News*. 29 Jan. 2009. Accessed Dec. 2015 <www.nydailynews.com>.

Cybersecurity in the U.S. Private Sector

Mark Tchao

Publication Month: March 2016

Abstract: Despite its perpetual resurfacing in the media, the prevalence of cyber-attacks on American companies is no grounds to excuse them– data breaches affect the privacy and financial security of millions of people, disrupts economic prosperity, and are arguably the largest threat to national security. While massive retailers or utility providers never imagined being liable for the well being of an entire country, reality proves otherwise. Incentivizing companies to invest in top cybersecurity measures in the profit-driven market continues to be a challenge and government compliance can be illusory, but without decisive changes in the landscape of matters, things may only get worse.

The State of Affairs

"There are two kinds of big companies in the U.S. There are those who've been hacked by the Chinese and those who don't know they've been hacked by the Chinese," said FBI Director James Comey in an interview with CBS "60 Minutes."[1] But the threat of hackers extends beyond just the Chinese– criminal organizations and nation-state actors across the globe are increasingly targeting the Western private sector, hoping to capitalize from stolen personal information intellectual property, and even attempt to control infrastructural systems.[2] While it may be consoling to believe that the public sector is solely responsible for the security of its people– online or otherwise– the truth is that it is simply not the case. It is largely within the chaotic realm of the private sector that our privacy, our finances, and our safety lies.

Data breaches involving personal customer information tend to receive the most publicity, with high-profile incidents involving large corporations making headline news. Major companies such as Target, Home Depot, JPMorgan Chase, and Anthem have all experienced massive data breaches leading to the compromising of hundreds of millions of personal records. In the Target hack alone, 70 million records of its customers were stolen, including 40 million credit and debit card numbers.[3] In the JPMorgan Chase hack, 76 million households and 7 million small businesses were impacted, making it one of the largest data breaches in the finance industry.[4]

The list of companies goes on: Home Depot had 109 million records involving credit card numbers compromised, Ebay had 145 million records involving login credentials and addresses stolen, Anthem had personally identifiable information (PII) involving social security numbers for 80 million people stolen– and these are just the significant breaches.[5] Virtually every major business in the U.S. has experienced a data breach, whether they are aware of it or not, leaving millions of people vulnerable to fraud and theft.

Data breaches involving intellectual property and trade secrets tend to receive less public attention, though devastating nonetheless. One high-profile example, however, is the Sony hack where business information as well as plans and copies of unreleased films were compromised. But Sony, along with virtually every other major technology firm, and many companies within the pharmaceutical and manufacturing industries have experienced hacks involving intellectual property.[6] Often times these attacks are perpetrated by Chinese hackers who sell the stolen information to companies, who then, due to strong production capabilities and lack of regulation in China, introduce these products into the market before the original creators do.

This can be devastating for a company, as seen with the bankruptcy of Nortel, which was once a leading multinational telecommunications and network equipment manufacturer based in Canada, having once controlled 40% of the telecommunications infrastructure in the U.S.[7] For almost ten years, Chinese hackers exfiltrated critical intelligence, including research and development (R&D) reports, business plans, and technical documents. After continually losing profits and being forced to lay off employees, Nortel filed for bankruptcy in 2009; all the while Chinese competitors concurrently burgeoned.[8] There is no clear indication as to whether the Chinese competitors themselves compromised the data or whether Nortel's bankruptcy was caused by this corporate espionage, the correlation is hard to ignore. Cyber theft of intellectual property can be a national security concern as well, such as when Chinese hackers stole critical secrets from Lockheed Martin regarding information on their F-35 Lightning II stealth fighter jet, allowing the Chinese government to replicate a stealth fighter of their own.[9]

Yet a more crucial though often overlooked victim of cyber attacks within the private sector is infrastructural and public safety control systems. With 85 percent of the U.S.'s critical infrastructure being privately-owned, it is important for the safety of the country that the companies that run the critical infrastructure prevent malicious attackers from gaining access to these systems.[10] And the risk of cyber attacks to infrastructure is completely feasible– demonstrated in examples such as the Saudi Aramco hacks, which severely disrupted oil production in Saudi Arabia, and Stuxnet, which targeted Iranian uranium enrichment facilities.[11] The Stuxnet hack serves to be an especially ominous case as it had the full capacity and sophistication to cause a nuclear meltdown, and yet it opted for a more discreet intent to slowly degrade the centrifuges within the enrichment facilities.[12] If advanced hostile nation-states desired to cause massive damages and loss of life by target nuclear facilities within the U.S., it is completely within the realm of possibility to do so– even by simply taking Stuxnet's code and weaponizing it.

In recent news, ISIS has been attempting to attack the United State's power grid, and though currently unsuccessful in causing damage, antiquated security controls within the energy infrastructure are not difficult to find.[13] And this risk to public safety extends beyond infrastructural systems. A group of researchers demonstrated that they could remotely killed the brakes on a Jeep Cherokee while it was driving down a highway, revealing the possibility of malicious actors threatening public safety on the streets.[14] Though it is unclear how tangible of a threat vehicle hacking will be in the future, to ignore the risk is a luxury we cannot afford.

The Cost of Insecurity

The cumulation of cyber criminal activity costs both businesses and consumers substantial amounts of money. A study conducted by the Ponemon Institute of Cyber Crime indicated that cyber breaches cost each average American firm about \$15.4 million every year.[15] This average is double the average for firms outside of the U.S. The study also estimated that about \$160 billion worth of intellectual property is stolen from Western companies every year.[16] Overall, cyber criminal activity costs both businesses and consumers \$400 billion a year, and one fourth of this total is believed to be from the U.S. alone. A report by McAfee estimated that over 500,000 American jobs have been lost due to cyber attacks since the report was published in 2013.[17] So in addition to the damages to privacy of personal information, business continuity, and public safety, an insecure private sector becomes a significant financial burden to both businesses and consumers alike.

Yet despite of these facts, most companies are not impelled to invest in premium security systems and practices due to a lack of a financial incentive.[18] Investing in cybersecurity controls can be a multimillion-dollar expense, and researchers at the Pardee Center for International Futures believe that by 2019, the cost for security systems will outweigh its actual benefits.[19] The business leaders in the private sector are often unwilling to spend large amounts of money on security for what they believe is a chance that their companies would get hacked. And for many companies, the cost of a data breach does not even outweigh the continuous significant investment in security systems in the first place. "You can spend an infinite amount on security," says Robert Carr, CEO of Heartland Payment Systems Inc., "Where do you draw the line?"

It is within this obscure assumption of adequacy that leads business leaders to place their full confidence in complying to government security standards and regulations. However, compliance to government initiated standards are widely considered to be mere an illusion of security, and may often conflict with ideal security goals.[20] Furthermore, the government has an equally poor track record of an inability to keep secrets, with examples like the Chelsea Manning leak, the Edward Snowden leak, the OPM breach, the Pentagon breach, and other incidents. In order to foster innovation and encourage businesses to improve security beyond the bare minimum, there needs to be fundamental and collaborative changes within both the private and public sectors.

Changing the Landscape

Regarding changes within the private sector, insurance companies should underwrite rates based on cyber risk assessments. Because all publicly traded companies are required to invest in cybersecurity insurance, the insurance companies have the ability to incentivize businesses to reduce their security risk in order to save more money on insurance. Continual risk-based assessments will accumulate a good understanding of safe security practices, in which they could share and recommend with other companies who are assessed as high risk.

Also, businesses should focus on providing white hat incentives for uncovering security vulnerabilities within their systems. United Airlines rewarded a hacker one million air miles for responsibly notifying United Airlines of a critical zero-day Remote Code Execution (RCE) exploit within their systems, as well as other risks.[21] Rewarding hackers for uncovering security flaws is much cheaper than implementing and maintaining multimillion dollar security systems and tends to succinct. Instead of relying on blanket security controls, organizations are able to discover precise vulnerabilities within their systems. Businesses can also potentially deter black hat hackers from illegally profiting off of the company's vulnerabilities and instead turn in these discoveries for a guaranteed reward, all without breaking the law.

Additionally, companies should be endorsed for innovating practices in cybersecurity. Target experienced a 46 percent drop in profits after the 2013 hack, therefore it can be presumed that consumers are wary of the risks of data breaches and would prefer to shop where they feel their information will be safe. If market research firms like J.D. Power and Associates were to publicly reward companies for striving for the best security practices, it would reassure customers and strengthen brand value for businesses.

Regarding changes within the public sector, the government must end the war on encryption, and encryption should instead be encouraged as a common practice within business and consumers. When the National Security Agency (NSA) forced major technology firms to install crypto backdoors into their systems and products, it lead to massive vulnerabilities like FREAK (Factoring attack on RSA-EXPORT Keys).[22]

A group of security researchers demonstrated that with "$104 and 8 hours of Amazon's cloud computing power" they could exploit the FREAK vulnerability to hack into the NSA's website using a Man-in-the-Middle (MITM) attack.[23] The government's fear of encryption technology and its struggle to control its implementation is not only futile– it threatens the security of everyone.

Furthermore, the government should establish an agency that moderates communication among the private sector for sharing security information. This agency should accumulate data about cyber activity and work with companies to develop better security standards and regulations, and give recommendations for top-tier security practices. With their expertise, this agency can work closely with local law enforcement to track malicious actors, and can lead investigations involving cybercrime.

Lastly, businesses should be fined more strictly for not complying to cybersecurity standards so that business leaders no longer consider data breaches to be a small financial risk. Companies should be strictly fined for data breaches, and this money should be distributed to victims as indemnities. These businesses are responsible for securing the data of its customers; therefore businesses must make amends to its consumers rather than disregard their failures.

Overall, it should not be acceptable that tens of millions of Americans have their online information compromised every year, or that businesses lose millions of dollars to cyber espionage, or that we tolerate the threat of cyber attacks causing real-world damages. Though the commonality of data breaches make them appear like a normal cost of doing business, they are a serious concern to the well-being and security of the U.S. In order to better protect everyone in both the cyber and physical world, the public and private sectors must take redesigning measures to not just meet or enforce bare security requirements, but to strive for the best security practices attainable.

---

[1] Pelley, Scott. "FBI Director on Threat of ISIS, Cybercrime." *CBS News*. 05 Oct. 2014. Accessed Dec. 2015 <www.cbsnews.com>.

[2] Jortiz. "Government Needs the Private Sector to Improve Cybersecurity." *TaaSera*. Accessed Dec. 2015. <www.taasera.com>.

[3] Krebs, Brian. "The Target Breach, By the Numbers." *Krebs on Security*. 14 May 2014. Accessed Dec. 2015. <krebsonsecurity.com>.

[4] Tobias, Sharone. "2014: The Year in Cyberattacks." *Newsweek*. 31 Dec. 2014. Accessed Dec. 2015. <www.newsweek.com>.

[5] Collins, Keith. "A Quick Guide to the Worst Corporate Hack Attacks." *Bloomberg*. 18 Mar. 2015. Accessed Dec. 2015. <www.bloomberg.com>.

[6] Perez, Evan. "Security Firm: Chinese Hackers Tried to Steal Tech and Drug Companies' Secrets." *CNN Money*. 9 Oct. 2015. Accessed Dec. 2015. <money.cnn.com>.

[7] Leyden, John. "Whistleblower: Decade-long Nortel Hack 'traced to China'" *The Register*. 15 Feb. 2012. Accessed Dec. 2015. <www.theregister.co.uk>.

[8] Kehoe, John. "How Chinese Hacking Felled Telecommunication Giant Nortel." *Financial Review*. 26 May 2014. Accessed Dec. 2015. <www.afr.com>.

[9] Gertz, Bill. "Top Gun Takeover: Stolen F-35 Secrets Showing up in China's Stealth Fighter." *The Washington Times*. 13 Mar. 2014. Accessed Dec. 2015. <www.washingtontimes.com>.

[10] "Critical Infrastructure and Key Resources." *Information Sharing Environment*. 4 Feb. 2015. Accessed Dec. 2015. <www.ise.gov>.

[11] Pagliery, Jose. "The Inside Story of the Biggest Hack in History." *CNN Money*. 5 Aug. 2015. Accessed Dec. 2015. <money.cnn.com>.

[12] Kelley, Michael B. "The Stuxnet Attack On Iran's Nuclear Plant Was 'Far More Dangerous' Than Previously Thought." *Business Insider*. 20 Nov. 2013. Accessed Dec. 2015. <www.businessinsider.com>.

[13] Bender, Jeremy. "'They'd Love to Do Damage': The FBI Says ISIS Wants to Go after One of America's Biggest Vulnerabilities." *Business Insider*. 19 Oct. 2015. Accessed Dec. 2015. <www.businessinsider.com>.

[14] Greenberg, Andy. "Hackers Remotely Kill a Jeep on the Highway-With Me in It." *Wired*. 21 July 2015. Accessed Dec. 2015. <www.wired.com>.

[15] Griffiths, James. "Cybercrime Costs the Average U.S. Firm $15 Million a Year." *CNN Money*. 8 Oct. 2015. Accessed Dec. 2015. <money.cnn.com>.

[16] Lawrence, Dune. "The Global Cost of Cybercrime: More Than $400 Billion Per Year." *Reuters*. 09 June 2014. Accessed Dec. 2015. <www.reuters.com>.

[17] Kirchheimer, Sid. "Cybercrime Costs 508,000 U.S. Jobs." *AARP*. 25 July 2013. Accessed Dec. 2015. <blog.aarp.org>.

[18] Pasquali, Valentina. "Cover: The Untold Cost of Cybersecurity." *Global Finance*. 2 May 2013. Accessed Dec. 2015. <www.gfmag.com>.

[19] Chabrow, Eric. "Assessing the Cost of Cybersecurity." *BankInfoSecurity*. 10 Sept. 2015. Accessed Dec. 2015. <www.bankinfosecurity.com>.

[20] Miller, Wes. "How Compliance and Security Requirements May Conflict." *TechNet*. June 2008. Accessed Dec. 2015. <technet.microsoft.com>.

[21] Dastin, Jeffery. "United Airlines Awards Hackers Millions of Miles for Revealing Risks." *Reuters*. 16 July 2015. Accessed Dec. 2015. <www.reuters.com>.

[22] Abel, Jennifer. "NSA "backdoor" Mandates Lead to a Computer-security FREAK Show." *ConsumerAffairs*. 6 Mar. 2015. Accessed Dec. 2015. <www.consumeraffairs.com>.

[23] Paganini, Pierluigi. "Just $104 to Exploit the FREAK Flaw and Hit the NSA Website." *Security Affairs*. 07 Mar. 2015. Accessed Dec. 2015. <securityaffairs.co>.

Mandatory Cybersecurity Risk Management Framework in the Healthcare Sector

Andy Herman
Publication Month: December 2016

Abstract: This paper explores the gap in the current healthcare cybersecurity approach – that there is no mandatory risk management framework for healthcare organizations. The current method of control for protection of patient information has been through the enforcement of Title 2 of the HIPAA governance. The author suggests introducing a mandatory implementation of a full cybersecurity framework with monitoring systems before receiving the incentives guaranteed by the meaningful use clause associated with electronic health records. While recognizing that the healthcare sector is already burdened with heavy compliance requirements, the key point is that a cybersecurity framework should be considered an operational necessity, not simply a voluntary option.

Breaches in the continuously evolving cyberspace atmosphere have contributed to financial and reputational loss for many organizations across all industries. Of the sixteen critical infrastructure sectors, the healthcare sector has become a sector of increasing interest by both cybersecurity professionals and hackers trying to protect and gain access to the valuable patient health information. Stolen healthcare information including personal identifiable information and insurance numbers has led to identity thefts and painful problems for victims. Research has shown that stolen electronic patient health information is sold on the black market at a rate of $50 per record.[1] Though healthcare data breaches in 2014 were primarily caused by the negligence of physicians (losing devices containing personal identifiable information), "98 percent of data breaches in healthcare in 2015 were a result of hacking and other IT-related incidents."[2] Improvement and maintenance of cybersecurity is one of the main Healthcare and Public Health sector goals. It is imperative to determine the root cause of the breaches and develop mitigation plans to minimize the damage. There are many possible reasons to explain the increase in data breaches this past year, but I feel that the Meaningful Use clause, part of the American Recover and Reinvestment Act of 2009 (ARRA), has contributed the most to creating an atmosphere where hospitals are unprepared. The clause "promises stimulus incentives to physicians using EMR/ medical practice software that meet some still *unspecified* criteria," which exposes them to potential data breaches in the pursuit of compliance driven by a desire for financial gains.[3] The HITECH Act proposed incentive payments to accelerate "the adoption of HIT and use of qualified EHR."[4] The intent of the massive overhaul to electronic health records was to improve the quality of care that physicians could provide patients. Though the benefits of shifting to new technology increases the potential for improved quality of care, there are vulnerabilities with the implementation of this program that creates a risk to one of the most important infrastructures in our country. Therefore, the sector would benefit from an additional requirement for electronic health records - meaningful use (EHR-MU) requiring that institutions under HIPAA implement a cybersecurity program that uses the NIST Cybersecurity Framework. Understanding that healthcare organizations are already under a lot of pressure to maintain compliance to HIPAA, mandatory cybersecurity risk assessment programs should be considered if the goal of the EHR-MU is to improve the quality of care.

The Office of the National Coordinator of Health Information Technology (ONC) is located within the Office of Secretary of the U.S. Department of Health and Human Services (HHS). One of the missions of the ONC is to "[coordinate] nationwide efforts to implement and use the most advanced health information technology and the electronic exchange of health information."[5] The ONC should be concerned about this issue of cybersecurity because of the risk for loss of electronic health records, which pose an operational risk to the mission of healthcare organizations. The ONC recommends that healthcare organizations conduct a risk assessment to reduce the likelihood of these events happening.[6] They provide a toolkit that is not required by the HIPAA security rule, but provides a method of being vigilant and compliant with the guidelines of HIPAA. Furthermore, the ONC's program (SRA Tool) asks 156 Boolean logic questions that align with HIPAA requirements.[7] The SRA Tool provides merely a statistical outline of what areas are currently at risk but does not offer controls and metrics to monitor improvement. The ONC has published and released numerous flyers and information packets to help healthcare organizations become more informed about healthcare cybersecurity. The ONC has done a great job in increasing awareness of cybersecurity. The next step is to implement health information technology with the proper establishment of cybersecurity frameworks and mitigation plans *before* the complete transition by hospitals to electronic health records in both private and public sectors of healthcare.

Another government entity whose operational risk can be mitigated by the proper implementation of a mandatory cybersecurity framework is the Center for Disease Control (CDC). The CDC and the ONC have collaborated to modernize medicine through the implementation of electronic health records (EMR). They have spearheaded the movement towards ERM adoption and have held workshops to inform and create awareness about the benefits that ERM can provide to the healthcare sector. In 2007, the CDC and ONC held their first EMR workshop. At this event, they stated that "privacy, security, medical legal issues, cultural change, and workforce" would be relevant issues to the topic of "improving health-care statistics through EMR and health information exchange."[8] This initiative by the CDC illustrates that the CDC and ONC were concerned about the security of the electronic patient information gathered in the pursuit of increased quality of care. Unfortunately, an analysis of the events at the EMR workshop showed no further evidence that addressed how organizations could secure information or what protocols should be considered. The CDC has worked with other organizations to continue to increase participation of healthcare organizations in the transition to electronic health records. On October 16, 2012, the CDC collaborated with the Association of Public Health Laboratories to publish the "Clarification Document for EHR Technology Certification." This document is intended to document the requirements to be considered properly certified as an ELR (Electronic Lab Record) compliant technology.[9] While scanning this document, it became evident that there is no clarification on this document regarding the requirements for a risk assessment or mitigation plan to protect health information. Recall the mission of the HITECH ACT was to improve the quality of care by implementing technology to make the delivery of healthcare efficient. The lack of emphasis on the implementation of a cybersecurity framework as an important aspect of the transition to electronic health records will act as an operational risk because the potential for breaches that threaten personal identifiable information of patients. This operational risk could potentially lead to the decrease in the quality of care.

The current method of control for protection of patient information has been through the enforcement of Title 2 of the HIPAA governance. Title 2 of HIPAA has five rules: Privacy Rule, Security Rule, Transactions and Code Set Rules, the Unique Identifiers Rule, and the Enforcement Rule. The Privacy and Security rule will be the focus points of this paper, particularly as it relates to protecting electronic healthcare information. The Privacy Rule establishes the standards that are associated with "giving patients the right to access and request amendment of their PHI [Protected Health Information] as well as requesting restrictions on the use or disclosure of such information."[10] The Security Rule sets a "national set of security standards for the confidentiality, integrity and availability of EPHI."[11] The HIPAA provides a guideline, rules, and regulation for healthcare organizations to follow to ensure patient information is protected. Cybersecurity compliance to these rules and regulations can be generally met using the cybersecurity frameworks established by NIST. Hospitals generally adapt the cybersecurity framework as the foundations to their cybersecurity programs before adapting parts of the program to fit the needs of their own organization.[12]

Another control that is currently in place is the Executive Order 13636, "Improving Critical Infrastructure Cybersecurity," which was signed by President Obama on February 12, 2013.[13] This executive order was established to address the concerns of our nation's cyber infrastructure. It consists of three main areas: "(1) information sharing, (2) privacy, (3) the adoption of cybersecurity practices."[14] The President tasked the Department of Homeland Security to develop a voluntary program to help promote the cybersecurity framework that NIST was ultimately able to create. This voluntary program is called the "C³ Voluntary Program." C³ Voluntary Program was launched in 2014 alongside the final version of the NIST cybersecurity framework.

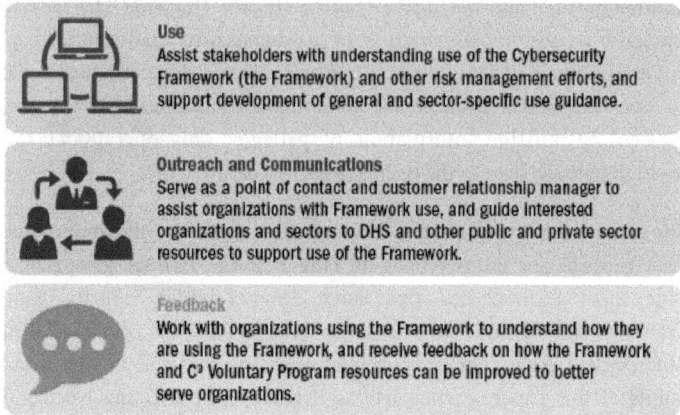

Figure 1: C3 Voluntary Program Graphic
Source: U.S. Computer Emergency Readiness Team

The purpose of the C³ Voluntary Program is to "assist stakeholders with understanding use of the [Cybersecurity] Framework and other cyber risk management efforts, and support the development of general and sector-specific guidance for framework implementation."[15] The benefits of having a voluntary range from less pressure and more flexibility, but the disadvantages of a voluntary implementation of a cybersecurity framework is the potential for a lackadaisical attitude towards security. Organizations will see the word "voluntary" and it may suggest a lower importance in implementing. In 2014, the Healthcare Information and Management Systems Society (HIMSS) has been noted as accurately saying that "HIPAA compliance is not equal to security" and that the NIST cybersecurity framework is critical in the bridging of the gap between compliance and security.[16] The irony is that though HIMSS understood the importance of security of healthcare information, they recently wrote a letter to NIST to request that the NIST Cybersecurity Framework remain voluntary. HIMSS "acknowledges that healthcare organizations can benefit from improving their risk management process and better address cybersecurity risks."[17] However, the argument for the necessity of the cybersecurity framework to be voluntary was based on the following reason:

> *"To 'prevent duplication of regulatory processes and prevent conflict with or superseding of regulatory requirements, mandatory standards, and related processes' as required by the Cybersecurity Enhancement Act of 2014, the NIST Cybersecurity Framework should continue to be voluntary, consistent with Section 405 of CSA."[18]*

This helped me understand the argument presented by HIMSS to allow the NIST cybersecurity to remain voluntary. Since the healthcare sector is already burdened with having to comply with HIPAA and HITECH Act, it is understandable that they may not want to be forced into compliance with another form of governance. However, it is important to understand that the mandatory cybersecurity framework should not be seen as a nuisance and especially if the physicians are seeking to gain some financial incentives through the EHR–MU incentive program, it is imperative that the organizations are prepared to protect the patients.

The EHR-MU is currently divided into three stages: stage 1, stage 2, and stage 3. Stage 1 requires that the provider meet a set of fifteen core requirements and five from the optional list to receive the incentives that "range from \$44,000 (through Medicare) to \$63,750 (through Medicaid)."[19] The organization must be in each stage for at least two calendar years before they can qualify for the next stage. Upon reading through a detailed core requirements form, there were no mentions of the voluntary cybersecurity framework. The requirements did mention the use of EHR certified technology. If the hospital could prove that they were able to use the EHR certified technology they were considered to have fulfilled the requirements for that task. As mentioned earlier, even the process of certification of the EHR-enabled technology does not include a clear procedure to ensure cybersecurity.

An example of when the lack of proper implementation of cybersecurity in the public sector of healthcare had negative effects can be demonstrated by one of the biggest HIPAA violations at St. Joseph Health System in Bryan, Texas. On December 2013, St. Joseph Health System "experienced a three-day long data security attack" which resulted in hackers gaining access to the protected health information of 405,000 patients at the hospital.[20] The technology that was used at St.

Joseph Health System was "certified EHR technology" using the guidelines provided by the CDC. Furthermore, a review of the financial statements showed that the St. Joseph Health System received $1,954,000 in 2013 and $5,103,000 in 2014 upon "demonstration of compliance with the criteria for meaningful use incentives" from the Centers for Medicare and Medicaid Services.[21] The evidence revealed in the financial reports indicated that St. Joseph's Health System is participating in Stage 1 of the Meaningful Use Incentive program. Furthermore, this meant that the core objectives were being met. Though there was evidence of an electronic system to maintain patient information, an analysis of the organizational chart of the hospital indicated that the management of this system was not by a CISO but the only IT staff member who carried the title of "site director." [22] From this example, we can see the risks that are associated with the promotion of Meaningful Use Incentive Program without proper implementation of cybersecurity can potentially lead to huge breaches. It is difficult to jump to conclusions that a better cybersecurity program will have prevented this information breach, however, when looking at the history of third-party hackers gaining unauthorized access to servers, some of these cases can be deterred by a simple implementation of a cybersecurity framework.

There are many hazards that are associated the rush that physicians are going through to gain financial incentives of the meaningful use clause. Rushing to fulfill the meaningful use clause of the ARRA, which "promises stimulus incentives to physicians using EMR/ Medical practice software that meet some still unspecified criteria" can result in negligence in security of valuable information.[23] Dr. Steven Waldren, an information technology expert from the American Academy of Family Physicians, proposed that "the meaningful-use program [has] pushed some medical practices to implement EHRs even though they weren't exactly ready to."[24] As we saw with the example of St. Joseph Health System, the incentive program can present huge operational risk because the lack of controls and preparedness to handle the security of EHRs. Financial gains are often the critical factor in leading to negligence and overlooking the importance of preparing the proper infrastructure and cybersecurity environment before implementation. Acknowledging that there is great potential for improvement of the quality of care with a well-organized electronic health records system, I have proposed the idea of having a "Step 0" which would remove the *voluntary* cybersecurity framework implementation suggestion and *enforce* the implementation of a full cybersecurity framework with monitoring systems before receiving the incentives guaranteed by the EHR-MU. As mentioned by HIMSS, mere compliance to governance such as HIPAA will never guarantee complete security. Having electronic health record systems that merely comply with the rules and standards for HIPAA should not be the minimum requirement to increase the use of IT systems in healthcare. I believe it is critical to not lose focus on the importance of improvement of quality of care over the opportunity for financial gains. From my personal experience being with physicians, this distinction is frequently overlooked.

In conclusion, when comparing the impact that this mandatory emphasis on cybersecurity has on healthcare with other critical infrastructure sectors in the U.S., we will be able to observe the overall improvement in safety across the different sectors. In this increasingly technologically dependent society, it is important to increase the awareness of the importance of cybersecurity. Cyber crimes and breaches to databases across all industries lead to President Obama signing the Executive Order 13636 to improve critical infrastructure cybersecurity.[25] Estimates from various economic studies have stated that cyber crime "costs the global economy over $400 billion per year."[26] The Executive Order 13636 did not want to make the implementation a mandatory process because the government does not want to be accused of pressuring private sectors into more regulatory laws. The meaningful use clause of the American Recovery and Reinvestment Act hopes to contribute to the improvement of the integration of health information technology for the overall increase in quality of care. This should not be rushed and careful consideration for the NIST cybersecurity framework as a mandatory aspect should be considered. In a field as expansive as healthcare, the successful implementation of a cybersecurity framework has the potential to act as a catalyst for other sectors to follow suit to maintain their security and potentially reduce the number of breaches.

---

1 Lowe, H. "Stolen EHR Charts Sell for $50 Each on Black Market". Medscape Medical News, 2014.

2 Landi, Heather. "Hacking Accounted for 98 Percent of Healthcare Data Breaches in 2015, Report Says - Dolbey Systems, Inc." Dolbey Systems Inc. Healthcare Informatics, 04 Feb. 2016. Web. 14 Feb. 2016.

3 Needle, Sheldon. "How Much Should Doctors Worry About 'Meaningful Use'?" (CTS Medical Blog, December 1, 2012)

4 Federal Registrer. "Medicare and Medicaid Programs; Electronic Health Record Incentive Program; Final Rule". Department of Health and Human Services. 28, July 2010.

5 "About ONC", HealthIT.gov, August 11, 2014.

6 Ibid.

7 Health IT. "Security Risk Assessment." Security Risk Assessment Tool. 26 June 2015. Web. 15 Feb. 2016.

8 Center for Disease Control and Prevention. "Improving Health-Care Statistics Through Electronic Medical Records and Health Information Exchange". EMR Workshop. 29 May 2007. Web. 23 Feb. 2016

9 Centers for Disease Control and Prevention, Association of Public Health Laboratories. "ELR 2.5.1 Clarification Document for EHR Technology Certification". 16 October 2012.

10 "Cybersecurity: A Shared Responsibility", HealthIT.gov, (January 12, 2015).

11 Ibid.

12 Ewell, Cris V., "Foundations of Organizational Information Assurance." IMT 551A Lecture. University of Washington, Seattle. 5 Oct. 2015.

13 "Foreign Policy Cyber Security Executive Order 13636." The White House President Barack Obama. 12 Feb. 2013. Accessed 02 Mar. 2016 <www.obamawhitehouse.archives.gov>.

14 Ibid.

15 "Critical Infrastructure Cyber Community C³ Voluntary Program." U.S. Department of Homeland Security. 14 Oct. 2015. Accessed 18 Feb. 2016 <www.dhs.gov>.

16 Hall, Susan D. "HIMSS Seeks Specific Guidance from NIST on Cybersecurity Framework." *FierceHealthIT*. 14 Oct. 2014. Accessed 18 Feb. 2016 <www.fiercehealthit.com>.

17 Monegain, Bernie. "HIMSS Presses NIST to Keep Cybersecurity Framework Voluntary for Organizations." Healthcare IT News. 10 Feb. 2016. Web. 03 Mar. 2016.

18 Ibid.

19 HealthIT.gov. "EHR Incentives & Certification." Information about EHR Incentives and EHR Certification. 4 Apr. 2014. Web. 04 Mar. 2016.

20 McCann, Erin. "Hackers Swipe Health Data of 405K." Healthcare IT News. 05 Feb. 2014. Web. 25 Feb. 2016.

21 Ernst & Young LLP. Consolidated Financial Statements and Supplementary Information. Rep. Irvine: Ernst & Young LLP, 2014. Print. (Page 27)

22 St. Joseph Health. "Leadership and Governance." Leadership and Governance. 2016. Web. 26 Feb. 2016.

23 Needle, Sheldon. "How Much Should Doctors Worry About 'Meaningful Use'?" (CTS Medical Blog, December 1, 2012)

24 Lowe, H. "Stolen EHR Charts Sell for $50 Each on Black Market". Medscape Medical News, 2014.

25 The White House. "Foreign Policy Cyber Security Executive Order 13636." The White House. The White House, 12 Feb. 2013. Web. 02 Mar. 2016.

26 Gabel, Detlav, Bertrad Liard, and Daren Orzechowski. "Cyber Risk: Why Cyber Security Is Important." Cyber Risk: Why Cyber Security Is Important. 1 July 2015. Accessed Mar. 2016.

Chapter II
Critical Infrastructure

Dam Operational Risk

Ross Braine
Publication Month: May 2016

Abstract: The purpose of this examination of the U.S. Dams Sector was to identify potential control failures and identify the best path for mitigation, specifically in terms of energy. The author used internal audits of the Homeland Security system, combined with best practices pulled from both the "Dams Sector-Specific Plan" and "Operational Risk Management" written by Philippa X. Girling. Findings show that the dams sector has a multitude of process and system exposures with some identified remedies and clear steps leadership can take to strengthen their sector. At the end of this paper, the author discusses potential solutions and illustrates the steps the Dams Sector could take in order to shore up cyber defenses.

Introduction

The purpose of this paper is to identify and discuss one of the sixteen critical infrastructure sector[2] identified by the Department of Homeland Security.[1] Since many of the sectors identified are interdependent, this paper will touch on two closely related sectors. The main sector identified and discussed is the Dams Sector in regards to dam ability as electricity producers, which also affects the Energy Sector.

I have spent all my years either fishing or visiting dams throughout the western U.S. and thought that it was surprising to find that the "Dams Sector" was listed on the official website of the Department of Homeland Security. This should not have been surprising since these large structures are very visible, hold back large volumes of water, produce low cost amounts of energy, and are consistently in the media. I was very interested in the removal of the Elwha and Glines Canyon Dams as a scientific experiment and as an insider to the workings of the

---

2 Chemical, Commercial Facilities, Communications, Critical Manufacturing, Dams, Defense Industrial Base, Emergency Services, Energy, Financial Services, Food and Agriculture, Government Facilities, Healthcare and Public Health, Information Technology, Nuclear Reactors, Materials, and Waste, Transportation Systems, and Water and Wastewater Systems

process. For those who are unaware of the project, the Elwha and Glines Canyon dams were built by private companies in the early 1900s to produce electricity. In 2000, the U.S. Department of the Interior, Bureau of Reclamation purchased them for removal. The two dams produced about 40 percent of the energy requirements for the Diashowa American paper mill in Port Angeles.[2] With the removal of the dams, there is a restored salmon run and a loss of electrical production in the area.

This is an exciting subject to write about, because I find the infrastructure of the U.S. intriguing, especially with the increased risk of online security. This paper will aim to discuss a few of the physical and technological operational risks of the Dams Sector in both the government and private sectors along the Columbia River in Washington and Oregon.

Background

The Department of Homeland Security "Dams Sector compromises dam projects, navigation locks, levees, hurricane barriers, mine tailings, impoundments, and other similar water retention and or control facilities."[3] According to the Dams Sector overview, the "sector is a vital part of the nation's infrastructure and provides a wide range of economic, environmental, and social benefits, including hydroelectric power, river navigation, water supply, wildlife habitat, waste management, flood control, and recreation."[4] In addition, of the roughly 87,000 dams, approximately 65 percent are privately owned and state dams' safety offices regulate more than 77 percent.

Along the mainstream of the Columbia River, there are 11 dams that are both governmentally and privately held as illustrated in Table 1.[5]

Dam Name	Owner
Grand Coulee	U.S. Department of the Interior, Bureau of Reclamation
Chief Joseph	U.S. Army Corps of Engineers
Wells	Douglas County Public Utility District
Rocky Reach	Chelan County Public Utility District
Rock Island	Chelan County Public Utility District
Wanapum	Grant County Public Utility District
Priest Rapids	Grant County Public Utility District
McNary	U.S. Army Corps of Engineers
John Day	U.S. Army Corps of Engineers
The Dalles	U.S. Army Corps of Engineers
Bonneville	U.S. Army Corps of Engineers

Table 1: Dams along Mainstream of the Columbia River

Table 1 is very clear on who the U.S. owners are, however, the Public Utility Districts (PUDs) are not that clear. PUDs are nonprofit, community-owned and governed held utilities that pay bondholders and investors who vote on policy much like stockholders in a private corporation. Grant County PUD is managed by "a five-member board of commissioners made up of local citizens elected on a nonpartisan basis by the people of Grant County. Commissioners set policy, review operations and approve budget expenditures."[6] In essence, these PUDs are private corporations who own dams and sell the electricity for income.

Key Risks

According to the Dams Sector-Specific Plan, Annex to the National Infrastructure Protection Plan created by the U.S. Department of Homeland Security, "from the security perspective, risk is defined as a function of three parameters: (1) threat, the likelihood of an attack being attempted against a target, (2) vulnerability, the susceptibility of a target to being compromised by an attack, and (3) consequence, the set of undesirable impacts of the attack, if successful."[7]

According to Girling, there are seven operational risk events categories: 1) Internal Fraud, 2) External Fraud, 3) Employment Practices and Workplace Safety, 4) Clients, Products, and Business Practices, 5)

Damage to Physical Assets, 6) Business Disruption and System Failures, 7) Execution, Delivery, and Process Management.[8]

I was granted an interview with a high level person in the U.S. Bureau of Reclamation and that person told me there 3 threats that the bureau has identified and they include hacking, infrastructural shutdown, and terror threats.[9]

Hacking is the buzzword of the moment, especially with the large public issues in Target and Home Depot. Users are scared to have their personal information stolen and with current high-speed media, it is a constant scare factor in the news reports. Hacking in the dams sector can cause more than just user information lost, it can result in loss of life. Dams have a modern program called STADA, which is a computerized remote control system. Dams use this system because they have to be constantly adjusted because of demands on power, both high usage as well as low usage. The problem with this remote access is that there is a way for hackers to get into the system and destroy the facility. One worry is that the turbines could be overspun which would cause them to burn out and shutdown permanently. There was one large virus that the Israelis and Americans used to over-spin the centrifuges in Iran and that virus is Stuxnet. The fact that we have used a virus to destroy the capabilities of a fifth of Iran's nuclear centrifuges shows that this threat is very real and very possible. Other things that hackers could hijack are the gates. The gates are what hold the water back and where the water flows when there is a need for more electricity, more water downstream, or to lower the reservoirs. If a hacker was able to open the gates completely, the consequences would be severe as town and cities would be flooded and electricity would cut off.

Infrastructural shutdowns are also a major risk in the dams sector. When a power plant loses all the energy and goes empty, it takes energy to restart the whole system. The only power plants that can start on their own are hydroelectric plants. "In the northwest, Grand Coulee Dam is the largest single generation station and is the single most important power structure."[10] It would be the only plant that could restart any of the other plants in the whole northwest. In fact, it is so valuable and integral to the northwest that it is the only dam with a dedicated armed security force on site and on call at all times. Now that generation has been discussed, there needs to be some time taken to talk about transmission of all this energy. In order to make sure that the power is flowing to users, there is one commission that monitors all the power generation and transmission and that is the North American Electric Reliability Corporation – Western Electricity Coordination Council (NERC-WECC). The NERC-WECC enforces reliability with audits and establishes standards for both federal and non-federally run dams. The attempt is to reduce the risk of operation errors and show the threat if a dam is not in compliance. The danger in noncompliance is that the system could fail.

Finally, terror threats to the dams sector. While hacking could be done by terrorists, some of them are also done by lone wolf individuals or groups. Not every hacking threat is due to terrorism; sometimes hackers see the system as a challenge and do it just for the thrill. Terror threats in this paper address physical damage to property. If a terror group were to disable or destroy a dam, there would be a ripple effect throughout the sector and region. For example, if the Grand Coulee Dam was to be destroyed, the power created by it would end, floods would destroy homes, and crops would fail. The power created by Grand Coulee produces enough electricity to light 2.3 million homes and serves as the main factor in controlling floods on the Columbia River.[11] Needless to say, it seems that the Grand Coulee is in fact the single most important structure along the Columbia and in the northwest. As I interviewed the executive in the Bureau, I was unable to get how many individuals are in the protective unit stationed at the site due to homeland security directives. These individuals are trained in anti-terror methods and are fully capable of protecting the site for an extended period of time. Again, this is the only dam in the northwest with a fully dedicated armed security force, which makes me wonder how we protect those other dams along the Columbia and throughout the U.S.

Recommendations

Now that the Key Risks have been identified using the Dams Sector-Specific Plan, Annex to the National Infrastructure Protection Plan created by the U.S. Department of Homeland Security of threat, vulnerability, and consequence as well as interviewing the high-level executive, there are some recommendations to create a plan.

First, upon reviewing the Dams Sector-Specific Plan, it is very clear that the teams have created a very comprehensive plan with multiple guides and handbooks. The plan also talks about the cost-benefit plan to determine how much money to invest in a certain aspect and acknowledges that there is not a one-size-fits-all program. My recommendations are based on what I did not clearly see in the 136-page plan.

Threat

The news outlets would make it seem that we are under constant attack and after taking the IMT 556 class in the University of Washington (UW) Information School, these threats seem very real. The biggest revelation was the visit from the Chief Information Security Officer to the UW. He told us that there are constant threats to the security of the UW and if there is that much trouble at the UW, I can only imagine what other threats there are to our other infrastructures.

The best recommendation that I can make on this subject is to hire more people to work in the security office. We need to hire the best of the best in order to keep the security intact and keep us moving forward. However, there is a huge shortage of security specialists and we need to start training more folks. Universities and the government need to collaborate and start more Internet security programs like the one current running in the UW iSchool.

Vulnerability

It is very scary how vulnerable the dams sector truly is. According to a Business Insider article, more than 500,000 potentials targets were identified in power plant systems, water treatment centers, and traffic controls.[12]

As stated earlier in the paper, the Stuxnet virus was able to successfully destroy one fifth of Iran's nuclear power sector. The virus was entered into the system with a minor thumb drive and was able to replicate throughout the system. A second version of the virus was added later and it was only then that it was discovered, however, much of the damage was already done. The Business Insider article showed that whenever an employee sets up a wireless access point to connect to the system without encryption, there is a huge infrastructure exposure.

In order to ease some of this exposure, I would recommend that the networks require encryption and not allow non-recognized users to connect. This is not a popular suggestion since we all need our connectivity to run our smartphones, tablets, and laptops but this practice must be exercised throughout the dams sector.

Consequences

The consequences of a total shutdown in the Grand Coulee dam power plant alone would be a major hit to the northwest and would ripple throughout the region. If the electricity was to cut off, there would be over 2.3 million homes affected and the northwest would be unable to restart any other power plants because of the amount of energy required to restart systems. The same would be said if the turbines were turned on full force and overspun causing them to break down. If the infrastructure was not ready for this major power surge, there would be a blackout and most of the system would be fried.

The consequences if the dam was to be destroyed physically would be the same as above with blackouts and the flooding below the dam would drown many towns and potentially destroy crops who rely on the irrigation system connected to the Columbia River project.

Conclusion

Like most issues in the government and private sectors, money is always at the front of every conversation. Currently, the government is not spending enough money to train security officers at a high enough rate and the income levels are lower than those offers in the private sector. The government needs to make sure that cybersecurity is on the list as an "electronic WMD" in order for it to get the attention that it must have and maintain higher levels of funding.

It appears that the commissions and committee have done an exhaustive review of the processes in the Dams Sector-Specific Plan. If I were to compare this plan to what I have learned in the IMT 556 class, I would consider this a Risk and Control Self-Assessment (RCSA). A well-designed RCSA program provides insight into risk that exist in the firm, regardless of whether they have occurred before."[13] However, the fact that we still have these vulnerabilities is shocking and eye opening. The government and private dams need to work together with universities to train security specialists. This means more funds, more outreach, and more transparency to the issues, especially the fact that we are so open to attack.

I believe that senior leadership for both government and private businesses need to take the handbooks very seriously and create a mitigation plan for every aspect of their sector. The teams that put together the Dams Sector-Specific Plan was made up of both government and private sector representatives and so this plan works across sectors. However, with most sectors, there is not a one-size-fits-all approach and to leaders need to figure out how they plan to implement this plan. The NERC guidelines help the groups make those better-informed decisions and people like the person I interviewed truly believe in this sector and should be supported.

This sector is so vastly important to the infrastructure of the US and it needs to buff up its security measures and protection. The biggest threat appears to be online activity, we need to have more security officers, and I am hopeful that more people realize the importance of the Dams Sector, I certainly have.

---

[1] "Critical Infrastructure Sectors." Department of Homeland Security. 2014. Accessed Mar. 2015 <www.dhs.gov>.

[2] "Elwha and Glines Canyon Dams, Elwha River near Port Angeles, Washington." Bureau of Reclamation, U.S. Department of Interior. N.D. Accessed Mar. 2015 <www.usbr.gov>.

[3] "Critical Infrastructure Sectors."

---

[4] "Dams Sector." U.S. Department of Homeland Security. N.D. Accessed Mar. 2015 <www.dhs.gov>.

[5] Confidential Interview with US. Bureau of Reclamation, conducted by Ross Braine. Mar. 2015.

[6] "What is a PUD?" Public Utility District No. 2 of Grant County, Washington. N.D. Accessed Mar. 2015 <www.grantpud.org>.

[7] Dams Sector-Specific Plan: An Annex to the National Infrastructure Protection Plan. U.S. Department of Homeland Security. 2010. Accessed Mar. 2015 <www.dhs.gov>.

[8] Girling, Philippa X. *Operational Risk Management: A Complete Guide to a Successful Operational Risk Framework.* Oct. 2013. Wiley.

[9] Confidential Interview.

[10] Ibid.

[11] "Grand Coulee Dam Statistics and Facts." Bureau of Reclamation, U.S. Department of the Interior. Mar. 2015 Accessed Mar. 2015 <www.usbr.gov>.

[12] Ingersoll, Georffrey and Michael B. Kelley. "There's Only One Thing Stopping Enemy Nations From Smashing America's Power Grid." *Business Insider.* 1 Mar. 2013. Accessed Mar. 2015 <www.businessinsider.com>.

[13] Girling, Philippa.

Energy Sector Risk Assessment

Colin Andrade
Publication Month: February 2017

Abstract: This paper identifies the key risks the U.S. government and private energy-related corporations face within the Energy Sector. Specifically, the author examines the current risk strategies and controls within the Energy Sector, and then concludes with recommendations about how key stakeholders can improve resiliency.

Critical infrastructure has long been a major source of concern for the U.S. in wartime and in peace. Keeping our nation's financial, transportation, and energy systems up and running at all times is integral to economic and societal success. The landscape of risk associated with our critical infrastructure runs everywhere thanks to the growing interconnectivity of systems in the modern age. For example, without our Communications infrastructure running smoothly, our Finance and Transportation sectors would be unable to function effectively and likely collapse. While all sixteen of the infrastructure sectors our Department of Homeland Security (DHS) defines as "critical" are key to this country's stability, there is one in particular that acts as the bedrock of them all – the Energy sector.[1]

The DHS divides the Energy sector into three interrelated categories: electricity, oil, and natural gas.[2] The U.S. has more than 6,413 power plants spread across the country being powered by combustible coal, nuclear power, and natural gas.[3] Due to the integrated nature of the Energy sector, the DHS has labeled it "uniquely critical because it provides an 'enabling function' across all critical infrastructure sectors."[4] Despite the fact that 80 percent of the country's energy infrastructure is owned by the private sector, it remains a major source of concern for our government.[5] Any malfunction or attack on this infrastructure has the potential to shut down our country abruptly and make even the simplest day-to-day tasks impossible for citizens. This paper will look to identify the key risks our government and private energy-related corporations face moving forward, their current risk strategies and controls, and concludes with recommendations about how key stakeholders can improve resiliency.

On the federal government side, the U.S. Department of Energy (DOE) oversees the Energy sector and is responsible for general risk management duties. In the 2015 annual report written in conjunction with the Department of Homeland Security (DHS), the DOE lays out a number of key tasks for the agency moving forward. These tasks include:

"Strengthening the resilience of supply chains, enhancing cyber and physical security, examining interdependencies within the Energy Sector and across other sectors, enhancing climate resilience, addressing the risk associated with aging infrastructure and workforce, and developing meaningful metrics to assess the sector's progress toward security and resilience."[6]

All it takes is a quick scan of this list to see that risk mitigation is the main priority for the DOE. Clearly, the DOE recognizes the importance of the energy sector (and related infrastructure) and is focusing its attention on risk prevention and the mitigation of negative risk events. The two risks the paper will focus on from the government perspective are 1) the interdependencies within the energy sector and 2) the reliance on private sector partners to help keep critical infrastructure up and running.

The Energy sector is incredibly complicated and diverse thanks to critical infrastructure that spans city, county, and state boundaries. The DOE must fully understand and map out all of these interdependencies in order to properly protect and control critical assets. Their annual report discusses the technology advancements of the 20th century as a catalyst for reliance on interdependencies between systems and stakeholders.[7] The energy-sector infrastructure in the U.S. is tied into the communication, information technology, transportation, and even financial service infrastructures. The following table from the DOE report gives a visual example of these infrastructure interdependencies:

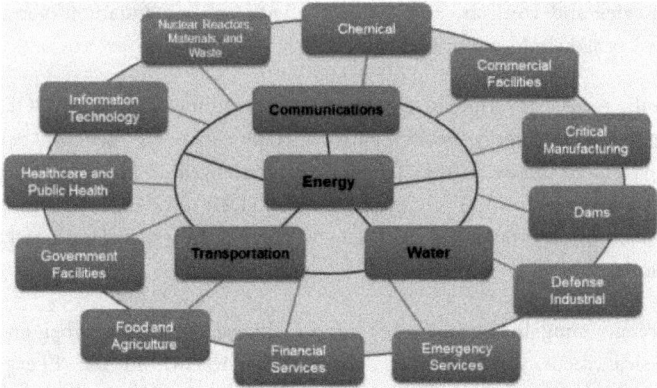

Source: U.S. Department of Energy 2015 Energy-Specific Report[8]

This becomes important in the event of a disruption of one form or another. The connectivity of the system means that any disruption has the potential to cause wide spread effects on our country.

Hypothetical Scenario

Let us walk through a hypothetical scenario in which a simple attack on a power grid in California could have devastating effects on the biggest financial firms located across the country in New York City. Imagine a malicious hacker, be it a cyberterrorist or just a common "computer nerd" trying out a new method, gets into California's electrical grid control system and shuts down power to the Los Angeles basin. The resulting blackout could possibly decommission the communication networks that connect the Los Angeles-based financial institutions to their colleagues in New York City. Critical cross-country networks could be affected and investment management firms attempting to complete trades on the New York Stock Exchange would be unable to get orders filled. This could potentially result in millions of dollars of losses depending on how financial markets reacted to the news of a major blackout in the country's second largest city. Information technology companies based in Silicon Valley could also feel the effects of sweeping blackouts if they were not prepared with backup servers in locations far enough away to not be effected. Business could come to a halt resulting in loss of revenues and plunging stock prices.

While this may seem like a scene from a movie, it is not entirely out of the realm of possibility. Earlier this year, Ukraine's power grid was completely shut down by hackers. The country was without power for an extended period before engineers could restart the system manually at substations.[9] Closer to home, a study by the Federal Energy Commission (FEC) noted that an attack on just nine critical substations scattered across the country would likely cause a national power outage that would last weeks or months.[10] The ever-increasing interconnectivity of our critical infrastructure will make events like this more common going forward and the DOE must put a special emphasis on preparing for risk events that can potentially permeate to other critical infrastructure sectors.

Accomplishing this goal will require the cooperation of the private sector – a majority owner of the physical energy infrastructure in this country. Managing the private sector and the way private corporations operate and secure their physical energy infrastructure presents a second formidable risk to the DOE. As private corporations must deal with third-party risk from vendors and suppliers, the U.S. federal government must effectively manage third-party risk associated with the owners of our critical energy infrastructure. PwC, a consulting firm, recommends applying a stratification process to third-party risk management in which firms identify third parties that carry the most potential risk and then prioritize accordingly.[11] Though this recommendation is meant for the private sector, it would translate nicely to the DOE's oversight of private corporations under their mandate as well as their general risk management process. Ultimately, private corporations have a much narrower view of the risks associated with their infrastructure and it is up to the U.S. government and the DOE to provide oversight and monitoring in order to protect our country on a wider scale.

Private Sector Risks

As private corporations make up 80 percent of the ownership of energy infrastructure in this country, it is important to touch on the risks associated with these businesses. This paper will focus on two companies, FirstEnergy and Florida Power and Light; both of which have firsthand experience with the large-scale ramifications of improper risk controls.

FirstEnergy is an Akron, Ohio-based diversified energy company, and touts itself as one of the largest investor-owned electric systems in the country. They operate more than 240,000 transmission lines in the Midwest and Mid-Atlantic regions.[12] In 2003, poor weather led to falling trees and sagging power lines that eventually found themselves tangled up. Almost immediately, customers began calling FirstEnergy to let them know they had weak power and tripping transmission lines. At the time, FirstEnergy did have an emergency alert system in place, but due to a system error, FirstEnergy controllers failed to notice any of the issues. They disregarded the customer complaints and assumed the poor electricity distribution was a competitor's fault. Not long after the complaints began, the FirstEnergy control room went dark, and the system controllers realized they had a major issue.[13] It was eventually determined that the malfunction in FirstEnergy's control systems was due to a bug in their computer code. Spokesperson Ralph DiNicola said at the time that the "fault was so deeply embedded, it took [developers] weeks of poring through millions of lines of code and data to find it."[14] The cascading effect of the blackout that could not be controlled (in large part due to the lack of early awareness from FirstEnergy) led to 50 million people in eight states and Canada being left without electricity.[15]

The example of FirstEnergy points to the importance of controlling system risks in the Energy sector. As much (if not all) of the critical infrastructure in the sector is controlled by computers, there must be a tight risk management controls in place to assure 99.9999 percent uptime of all systems. There should also be backup systems in place that, at the very least, can help prevent blackouts from spreading through the electrical system. Making a mistake in one line out of millions of code is one thing; not having a workaround that allows you to prevent further damage is another.

In fairness to FirstEnergy, they do acknowledge the risk involved in operating complex systems in their 10K reports. They mention the risk surrounding their infrastructure due to aging equipment and weather related events. They also refer to the interconnected nature of the business and how this potentially poses risks to system functionality.[16] It seems safe to assume that the 2003 incident was a wake up call for the company, and subsequently their risk management (including the acknowledgement of potential risk) has improved over the last decade.

Our second victim of poor risk management in the private energy sector is Florida Power and Light (FP&L). Much like FirstEnergy, FP&L is a large electricity provider responsible for nearly 4.8 million customers in Florida.[17] The company has a very good track record of providing excellent service to customers and has been ranked in the top ten of Fortune's "World's Most Admired Companies" list.[18] With such an impressive resume, it would be easy to assume that FP&L's risk management function has performed flawlessly. As the following example will show, however, even the smallest oversight by a single employee can lead to widespread outages in the energy sector. It will also prove the importance of forcing employees to adhere strictly to the processes put in place in order to mitigate risk.

In February of 2008, a FP&L engineer was investigating a malfunctioning switch at one of the company's electricity substations in West Miami. In order to diagnose the issue with the switch, he disabled two levels of relay protection – a practice that was frowned upon by his employer.[19] Protective relays are "safety devices that monitor changes in the grid and are responsible for tripping breakers if conditions enter a danger zone that could harm transmission lines."[20] In disabling the relay protection, he opened up the possibility of any potential issue at that particular substation to radiate out and effect a large portion of the grid. Unfortunately for the engineer and FP&L, a fault happened to occur while the relay protection was disabled and caused an outage affecting 26 transmission lines and 38 substations. In all, 584,000 customers were left without power.[21] Immediately after the incident, FP&L President Armando Olivera was forced to issue an apology and assured the public that they were implementing "interim changes governing relay protections to prevent a recurrence."[22]

This incident is a prime example of how the threat of "people risk" constantly hovers over a business. Despite having a strict policy in place that prevents both levels of protection from being disabled, the engineer went ahead anyway and removed the protections. Whether it was negligence or lack of procedural knowledge that prompted the engineer to disable the protections, the point remains the same – private corporations are constantly at risk of losing customers, money, and reputation due to the follies of individual employees. In this particular instance, FP&L could have prevented this issue with two very simple steps: 1) better oversight of their employees in the field and 2) better training on how and when engineers are allowed to disable mission critical safety devices.

Recommendations

So far, this paper has discussed a number of specific risk management recommendations for each of the energy related entities discussed thus far. This section presents two general recommendations for the sector as a whole. The first recommendation would be for greater segmentation of the U.S. energy infrastructure. As the system currently stands, it is far too easy for internal or external events to bring large portions of our energy infrastructure to its knees. Much like the President and Vice President never fly on the same plane, the energy sector's infrastructure should be kept segmented in the off chance that a dramatic risk event does take place and a need arises for alternate electricity to get the country up and running again. Corporations who rely on electricity to power mission critical technology would feel safer knowing that if one electric grid goes down, it would not affect their backup technologies in different locations. Admittedly, more segmentation may create certain inefficiencies in the system and lead to extra costs. However, these extra financial costs are unlikely to match the monetary and social costs of an event that shuts down our county's entire electrical grid.

The second recommendation would be the improvement and evolution of cybersecurity defenses in the sector. While this is certainly not a novel idea and is already a major focus for the DOE, the importance of preventing cyber attacks on our energy infrastructure cannot be overstated. It is common knowledge that cyber warfare is fast overtaking physical warfare across the globe. As the U.S. energy infrastructure continues to become increasingly computer driven, it will also become a more prominent target for foreign countries with a vendetta. Critical infrastructure in the U.S> has historically been safe thanks to the geographical distance between the country and its enemies. Cyber warfare greatly reduces that advantage.[23] Thanks to the release of information about events like Stuxnet, the computer virus that helped slow down the Iranian nuclear program, it is known that these types of attacks are already occurring. The DOE must find a way to incentivize the brightest cybersecurity minds to come work for them and the private companies the DOE watches over. If that means hiring brilliantly skilled individuals with coding and hacking abilities who typically would not fit into a corporate or government environment (think high school drop-outs), so be it.

Conclusion

It must be understood that the risks associated with the country's energy sector are far too great to go unnoticed. Electrical grids, gas, and nuclear power provide the backbone for the U.S. and allow its other critical infrastructure to operate successfully. The DOE has an incredibly important role in overseeing and closely monitoring the private companies that operate underneath them. Without an evolving risk management strategy, the DOE runs the risk of allowing major security holes to open up in an increasingly hostile world. The U.S. government already has a policy of using "all means necessary" to respond to a digital attack on a U.S. operated electrical grid (including physical retaliation), but prevention and risk mitigation should clearly be favored over hostile retaliatory actions.[24] By mandating better segmentation of systems and bulking up cybersecurity defenses, the DOE would be announcing to the world that the U.S. takes security of its critical infrastructure very seriously and may just focus the spotlight on the sector long enough to attract the next generation of great minds to solve the country's most important problems.

---

[1] Department of Homeland Security. (27 Oct. 2015). "Critical Infrastructure Sectors." Retrieved 15 Feb. 2016 from <http://www.dhs.gov/critical-infrastructure-sectors>

[2] Department of Homeland Security. (19 Jan. 2016). "Energy Sector." Retrieved 15 Feb. 2016 from <http://www.dhs.gov/energy-sector#>

[3] Ibid

[4] Ibid

[5] Ibid

[6] Department of Homeland Security. (2015) "Energy Sector-Specific Plan." Retrieved 15 Feb. 2016 from <http://www.dhs.gov/sites/default/files/publications/nipp-ssp-energy-2015-508.pdf>

[7] Ibid

[8] Ibid

[9] Kuchler, H. & Buckley, N. (5 Jan. 2016). "Hackers Shut Down Ukraine Power Grid." Retrieved 20 Feb. 2016 from <http://www.ft.com/intl/cms/s/0/0cfffe1e-b3cd-11e5-8358-9a82b43f6b2f.html#axzz40eqLeOj4>

[10] Smith, R. (12 Mar. 2014). "U.S. Risks National Blackout from Small-Scale Attack." Retrieved 20 Feb. 2016 from <http://www.wsj.com/articles/SB10001424052702304020104579433670284061220>

[11] PricewaterhouseCoopers. (Nov. 2013). "Significant Others: How Companies can Manage the Risks of Vendor Relationships." Retrieved 22 Feb. 2016 from <https://www.pwc.com/us/en/risk-assurance-services/assets/pwc-viewpoint-vendor-risk-management.pdf>

[12] FirstEnergy. (12 Feb. 2016). "About Us." Retrieved 20 Feb. 2016 from <https://www.firstenergycorp.com/about.html>

[13] Zetter, K. (2014). *Countdown to Zero Day*. New York, NY: Broadway Books. Pg. 159

[14] Poulsen, K. (11 Feb. 2004). "Software Bug Contributed to Blackout." Retrieved 22 Feb. 2016 from <http://www.securityfocus.com/news/8016>

[15] Ibid

[16] FirstEnergy. (2015). "FirstEnergy 2015 10K." Retrieved 22 Feb. 2016 from <https://www.firstenergycorp.com/content/dam/investor/files/10-K/2014-10K.pdf>

[17] Florida Power and Light. (2016). "Company Profile." Retrieved 23 Feb. 2016 from <https://www.fpl.com/about/company-profile.html>

[18] Ibid

[19] Florida Power and Light Newsroom. (29 Feb. 2008). "FPL Announces Preliminary Findings of Outage Investigation." Retrieved 23 Feb. 2016 from <http://newsroom.fpl.com/news-releases?item=101775>

[20] Zetter, K. (2014). *Countdown to Zero Day*. New York, NY: Broadway Books. Pg. 161

[21] Florida Power and Light Newsroom. (29 Feb. 2008). "FPL Announces Preliminary Findings of Outage Investigation." Retrieved 23 Feb. 2016 from <http://newsroom.fpl.com/news-releases?item=101775>

[22] Ibid

---

[23] Zetter, K. (2014). *Countdown to Zero Day*. New York, NY: Broadway Books. Pg. 377

[24] Ibid. Pg. 398

The Runaway Train

Kenny Lee
Publication Month: November 2015

Abstract: The oil boom in America and the extensive use of tank-car trains to transport crude oil has ushered into an era when oil-train derailments and the resulting spills have skyrocketed 900% in just two years from 2010 to 2012. At the heart of the problem is the common tank cars used by freight train companies known as DOT-111, which has multiple design flaws and are ill equipped to protect crude oil in an accident. NTSB has made multiple recommendations over the years to the Pipeline and Hazardous Materials Safety Administration (PHMSA), which regulates the freight-train industry, and saw little action. So much so that the Association of American Railroads (AAR), in an effort to speed up the process, adopted its own CPC-1232 standards. Finally, PHMSA acted in May 2015 with the issuance of the new DOT-117 standard, which comes with multiple improvements over the DOT-111 as recommended by the NTSB. However, the risk to the community around the train tracks remains as train companies have three to 10 years to retrofit the existing fleets.

Introduction

It was a beautiful summer night in a population 6,000[1] town east of Montreal, Quebec called Lac-Mégantic. Christian Lafontaine and his wife Melanie - along with Christian's two brothers and a few friends - were having a good time at the Musi-Café located in the heart of the town. Although it was after midnight, the café was still buzzing with three dozen or so patrons enjoying their company eating and drinking complete with the smooth jazz music played in the background by the on-site band. Several miles to the west up on the hill in the town of Nantes, a series of events had caused a 74-car unmanned oil freight train with close to 2 million gallons of oil to roll downhill toward Lac-Mégantic at a speed of up to 62mph. At 1:14AM, as Christian and his wife were getting ready to leave, they felt the earth shake and Christian turned and looked at his wife and asked, "Did you feel that? It felt like an earthquake" Before Melanie had a chance to respond, they felt another jolt, only much stronger this time. Then the restaurant turned pitch black, immediately followed by bright flashing orange lights reflected from the nearby tall buildings. Inside the bar, someone yelled "Fire!" and that was when Christian grabbed his wife's hand and pulled her out through the front door. As they exited the front door and looked to their right, they could see a wall of fire and smoke 15 to 20 stories high hurling toward them at a high rate of speed. They turned and ran in the opposite direction with all the power and strength they could exert. They were among the last to get out of Musi-Café alive.[2]

Forty-seven people perished that early morning of July 6th, 2013, thirty of in the Musi-Café[3] as a result of the oil train derailment right behind the popular restaurant. The train had made a stop in Nantes a few hours before and the lone train engineer left the train for the night after leaving an engine running to operate the pneumatic or compressed-air operated brakes to keep the train stationary. As fate would have it, the running engine caught on fire somehow and firefighters were dispatched to the scene. In the course of putting out the fire, the firefighters shut off the engine to prevent the fire from reoccuring, probably not knowing that it was needed for the brakes to function. The brakes then slowly lost air pressure and the train started rolling downhill toward Lac-Mégantic. Musi-Café is located next to the train track where it starts to curve which caused the unmanned train to derail.

A total of 1.5 million gallons of oil out of nearly 2 million gallons aboard the ill-fated train were spilled or burned. The accident economically paralyzed the entire Lac-Mégantic with 115 companies destroyed and hundreds others at risk of bankruptcy due to the oil clean-up effort, combined with the shutdown of the major artery of transportation.[4] It cost $195 million dollars for the cleanup alone.[5] The final environmental impact and the economic toll will probably not be known until years later. It took a year's worth of cleanup before the areas were declared safe for residents to return;[6] both the namesake lake and the Chaudière River have been polluted by the spilled oil; the byproducts and residues of burned crude oil are toxic and could remain in the soil and waterways for years to come.[7]

Emerging Risk

The incident in Lac-Mégantic ushered in a new era in which the increasing use of freight trains to transport crude oil introduced a safety and environmental risks for the communities near the train tracks. The advance in the development of hydraulic fracturing technique, also known as fracking, to extract oil and natural gas economically has turn North America, particularly the U.S., into the biggest oil producing country in the world.[8] Most of the oil extractions occurred in North Dakota[9] and surrounding states where few pipelines are available,[10] so oil-tank trains have become the transportation of choice for its flexibility and geographic reach. Trains also allow oil companies to ship the cargos to places that are far from oil pipelines and refineries where oil prices typically command higher premiums, which mean more profits for the producers.[11] As the oil production grows, weekly rail deliveries of U.S. oil has jumped from 7,000 carloads in 2011 to 16,000 in 2014, an increase of a whopping 129 percent in just three years, according to the U.S. Energy Information Administration.[12] With the increase in delivery of oil by rails, accidents have skyrocketed from less than 10 cases in 2010 to almost 90 in 2012.[13]

The growing needs for crude-oil trains and the frequency of accidents have raised concerns for safety and put the industry under scrutiny. Many accidents have occurred since the Lac-Mégantic incident. A train carrying oil and gas derailed and burned in Gainford, Alberta, in October 2013; Oil continued to float on swamp waters near Aliceville, Alabama months after the November 2013 oil train crash; large explosions can be seen from miles away after an oil train derailed in Casselton, North Dakota, in December 2013. The list goes on.[14] Unfortunately, the rate of occurrences has not slowed down in recent months. In just a 30-day timeframe from mid-February to mid-March of 2015, four oil-tanker trains have crashed and burned in the United States and Canada.[15] States such as Montana and North Dakota where most of the oil productions take place have become ground zero for oil train safety and put many residents near the railways on edge.[16]

Tank Car Design and Regulations

Why are oil trains prone to accidents and explosions? At the heart of the matter, according to National Transportation Safety Board (NTSB), is the popular tank cars used to transport oil and gas known as DOT-111 being unsafe to carry flammable liquids.[17] According to NTSB, DOT-111, a type of unpressurized tank cars, have multiple design flaws with respect to the tank heads, shells, and fittings that allow hazardous liquids to leak in an accident resulting in fires and explosions. With more than 170,000 DOT-111 cars[18] being used to transport hazardous materials, catastrophic accidents will all but certain to reoccur if history is any indication if improvements to the design are not made in time.

As early as 1991, NTSB had examined the safety performance of DOT-111 tank cars and concluded that the tank cars "have a high incidence of failure when involved in accidents"[19]. NTSB recommended the Pipeline and Hazardous Materials Safety Administration (PHMSA), which regulates the industry, to work with other public agencies and private organizations to identify a list of hazardous materials that "should be transported only in pressure tank cars with head shield protection and thermal protection if needed", but stopped short of recommending improvements to the DOT-111 standards. It was not until after another fatal train derailment in 2009 in Cherry Valley, Illinois where rail cars loaded with thousands of gallons of ethanol ignited in flames after the derailment, before NTSB recommended PHMSA to require newly manufactured and existing tank cars for hazardous materials to "have enhanced tank head and shell puncture-resistance systems and top fittings protection that exceeds existing design requirements for DOT-111 tank cars", as well as improvements to the bottom outlet valves and center sills.[20]

Over the ensuing years, PHMSA however did not act on the recommendations despite urging by NTSB and industry associations such as the Association of American Railroads (AAR). In an effort to speed up the process, a new CPC-1232 standards, which call for thicker tank shell, rollover protection, and head shields, were issued by AAR and submitted to PHMSA for approval in 2012. No approval has been received thus far. As of early 2015, improving the legacy DOT-111 tank cars remains on NTSB's "Most Wanted" list.[21]

Meanwhile, some railway companies are hesitant to invest in the new CPC-1232 tank cars lest PHMSA deems the proposed standards inadequate resulting in additional investments to retrofit the already more-expensive tank cars. Yet other companies forged ahead and started buying CPC-1232 compliant tank cars for transporting hazardous materials.

In a twist of fate, new questions are being raised after a couple incidents in which CPC-1232 compliant tank cars derailed and caught on fire.[22] This prompted NTSB to call for even stronger tanker-car design recommending PHMSA in April 2015 to require tank cars be equipped with thermal protection systems that meet or exceed the requirements of Title 49 CFR 179.18(a),[23] which stipulates tank cars to withstand (1) a pool fire for 100 minutes and (2) a torch fire for 30 minutes. NTSB went on to recommend PHMSA to require pressure relief devices, an aggressive milestone schedule for retrofitting the existing tank cars and annual reporting. This time, PHMSA responded aggressively. On May 1st, 2015, PHMSA announced new rules for the enhanced tank car standards adopting most of NTSB's recommendations.[24] The new rules require high-hazard flammable unit trains to (1) install an electronically controlled pneumatic braking system, (2) adopt the new DOT-117 design for newly manufactured tank cars and retrofit legacy cars to meet the same specifications, (3) reduce operating speeds to no faster than 50 mph or 40 mph in high-threat urban areas, (4) have more accurate classification of unrefined petroleum-based products, (5) conduct risk assessment considering at a minimum 27 safety and security factors, and (6) notify State, local, and tribal officials to discuss routing decisions and provide appropriate contact information in the events information related to routing of hazardous materials through their jurisdictions.[25]

Budget Shortfall

A recent Amtrak derailment in Philadelphia on May 12th, 2015, in which eight people were killed and dozens hospitalized, has highlighted another risk of the train industry—budget shortfall that causes delay and neglect of upgrading and maintaining the U.S. ailing transportation infrastructure. While the Philadelphia accident does not involve freight trains or oil tank cars, passenger trains run on more than 22,000 miles of track that are also used by freight trains.[26] The "interdependency of freight and passenger rail infrastructure – including common bridges, tunnels, and tracks – also increases the likelihood that incidents affecting highly critical assets could affect the entire railroad system."[27] While the cause of the Philadelphia accident is under investigation, it has been widely reported that the train was traveling twice the 50 mph speed limit. If it is indeed the case, a technology called Positive Train Control (PTC) safety systems, which likely could have prevented the Philadelphia accident by overriding the control and slowing down the train.[28] For no particular reason other than meeting a spending cap, the House of Representatives with Republicans as the majority voted to cut Amtrak's budget by $251 million the day after the accident[29] while the investigations of the root cause are still ongoing. This move of Congress exemplifies the extreme polarity of ideology over reasoning on the part of GOP without regard to scientific data and analyses. According to American Enterprise Institute, a public policy research community, between 2004 and 2013, United States train safety records are far behind those of the European developing countries with one reported passenger injury per 75,000 passenger miles on average, comparable to the records of a country like Lithuania. Many European countries experienced one injury per 250,000 to 470,000 passenger miles, much lower than the United States[30]. Yet, railroad management agencies such as the Northeast Corridor Infrastructure and Operations Advisory Commission, which manages the Northeast Corridor multi-states passenger railways including the one on which the Amtrak train crashed in Philadelphia expected to receive only 68% of requested funding for fiscal year 2015 if federal funding remains consistent with that of fiscal year 2014.[31]

By the same token, America's overall infrastructure does not fare any better. In the 2013 Report Card for America's Infrastructure, the America's Society of Civil Engineers gave the U.S. infrastructure a D+ grade,[32] and the country will need $3.6 trillion dollars to fix the problems as compared with only $1.3 trillion had we approved the funding in 2001.[33] The transportation critical infrastructure is also known to have been targeted by foreign adversary such as Iran.[34] It is important for the U.S. government to act more than ever to protect this critical infrastructure. President Obama proposed an infrastructure spending back in 2012 in his State of the Union address, yet it has been delayed by Congress and even used as a bargaining chip in recent months by the Republican Chairman of the Committee on Transportation and Infrastructure, Bill Shuster (R-PA), in exchange for the President's approval of the Keystone XL pipeline project. Evidently, the White House did not budge.

Conclusion

What can we do now that we have learned that the oil tank cars are not up to snuff; the regulations have not evolved quick enough with the rapid changes; the railroads and infrastructure are badly in need of cash infusion to upgrade and maintain for safety?

The Department of Transportation (DOT) Rule Summary issued on May 1st, 2015[35] stipulates new tank cars manufactured after October 1st, 2015 to meet the new requirements is a good start. It also issues the required timetables for existing DOT-111 and CPC-1232 to be retrofitted with the most vulnerable non-jacketed DOT-111 to be completed by May 1st, 2017 and others to be completed between March 2018 to May 2025. These will come at a cost to the freight train companies and it is unclear at this point what the reception of the new law by these companies would be. We can only hope that the transition would not be an issue for the industry judging from the aggressiveness exerted in the past to retrofit and improve the safety of the tank cars while waiting for PHMSA to come up with the new regulations.

While the new DOT rule for now resolves the design flaws of the legacy tank cars, it does not address other aspects of oil train accidents. Recently, several Democratic Senators including Maria Cantwell (D-WA), Patty Murray (D-WA), Tammy Baldwin (D-WI), and Dianne Feinstein (D-CA) have introduced the Crude-By-Rail Safety Act of 2015 that, if passed, will require PHMSA to enact new regulations to address among others, (1) resources for first responders on training programs, emergency response plan, and notification procedures, (2) requirements for rail carriers on emergency response plans and (3) sharing information with State Response Commissions and Local Emergency Planning Committees along the rail routes on crude-by-rail shipments.[36]

Congress and the President must work together to provide the badly needed upgrades to the transportation infrastructure from roads to bridges to tunnels with high assurance of safety. Humans make mistakes and will continue to make mistakes. This is where technology can be deployed to compensate for the human shortcomings such as the mentioned Positive Train Control Safety System that automatically slows down trains if found to be speeding.

Carrying millions of gallons of flammable materials that endanger human and wildlife lives and environments can never be a good solution. Transporting oil using pipelines will reduce the risk since pipelines themselves do not move and can be built to avoid populous areas, but they are expensive and take years to build assuming all the local, tribal, state and federal authorities, as well as environmentalists can come to an agreement. As an example, the proposed Keystone XL pipeline that would have duplicated the phase I route from Hardisty, Canada to Steele City, Nebraska except with a shorter and direct route started in 2008 and took years of negotiations and political wrangling, only to be rejected twice by the Executive Branch, once in 2012 and another in 2014. Currently, the plan has been on-hold indefinitely citing ongoing litigation.[37]

The stalling of the Keystone XL pipeline proposal also reflects the attitudes of Americans including those of President Obama toward reducing the greenhouse effect, which experts believe has contributed to the current climate change and extreme weather. In 2012 alone, natural disasters have cost the United States $110 billion dollars making it the second costliest in history.[38] However, a balance needs to be struck between oil independence before a viable alternative energy source can be found and reducing greenhouse gas by moving away from fossil fuels. As such, investing in expensive pipelines would be counterproductive to the environmental policy established by the hard work of many. Given the pro-environment policy that is the White House, it is unlikely that large expansion of pipeline projects would be approved as long as Democrats have a say in the decision making process. One can find the hints in Obama's plan to combat climate change announced in June 2013 that singles out "heavy-duty vehicles (commercial trucks, vans, and buses) are currently the second largest source of greenhouse gas pollution within the transportation sector."[39] The same plan also calls for a reduction in greenhouse gas emission.

The best strategy to reduce the risk associated with oil trains has to involve replacing fossil fuels with clean energy to knock out both problems at once – reducing the risk of train accidents and cutting down greenhouse gas to help the environments. Building more pipelines, while possibly helping reducing oil train accidents, cannot be a long-term and sustainable solution. The last thing we want is to make oil so inexpensive that makes it much more difficult to move away from and adopt clean energy. We know that progress toward clean energy conversion is difficult and expensive to make (think buying an electric car, which is more expensive than a traditional gas-engine one, or using solar panels instead of grid power), so we cannot allow the momentum toward green energy to go the opposite direction by adding "incentives" to fossil fuels. The short term could be painful, but the long-term returns will be worth it.

In the meantime, oil trains are here to stay and the risk to the communities around the train tracks remain. As for the railroad industry, it now has an additional risk on its hand in addition to the risk brought about by train accidents—compliance to the PHMSA's new DOT-117 standards. The events that led to the industry where it is today highlight the important roles of risk management and its oversights in the boardroom. Board members should raise the bar by asking the executives the right questions; look across the industry, such as the lessons learned from the Lac-Mégantic incident to see how risk can be mitigated to protect the interest of the shareholders; and finally consider the "black swan" or outliers in the risk management strategy.[40] Train accidents should not be a foreign concept to railroad executives, and the fact of the matter is that using corn-syrup grade tank cars to haul flammable liquids is simply "pushing the envelope" and exposes the company to grave risks. MMA, the operator of the train derailed in Lac-Mégantic, filed for bankruptcy[41] shortly after the incident after facing multiple lawsuits and may end up footing part of the proposed $200 million settlement.[42]

---

[1] City-Data. "Population Lac-Mégantic - Ville, Quebec, Canada." Statistics Canada. 24 Oct. 2012. Accessed Jun. 2015 <www.city-data.com>.

[2] Giovanetti, Justin. "Last Moments of Lac-Mégantic: Survivors Share Their Stories." *The Globe and Mail*. 19 Aug. 2014. Accessed Jun. 2015 <www.theglobeandmail.com>.

[3] Seminoff, Corinne. "Musi-Café Reopening in Lac-Mégantic a Big Boost to Town's Recovery." *CBC News*. 15 Dec. 2014. Accessed Jun. 2015 <www.cbc.ca>.

[4] "Lac-Mégantic : la relocalisation des commerces se fait pressante | Tragédie à Lac-Mégantic." *Radio-Canada News*. 29 Jul. 2013. Accessed Jun. 2015 <www.ici.radio-canada.ca>.

[5] Mas, Susana. "Lac-Mégantic Cleanup to Get as Much as $95M from Ottawa." *CBC News*. 21 Nov. 2013. Accessed Jun. 2015 <www.cbc.ca>.

[6] Lac-Mégantic : pas de retour à la maison avant un an." *Radio-Canada*. 3 Aug. 2013. Accessed Jun. 2015 <wwww.ici.radio-canada.ca>.

[7] Kovac, Adam. "Lac-Mégantic: Environmental Impact Impossible to Predict." *Montreal Gazette*. 6 Jul. 2013. Accessed Jun. 2015 <www.montrealgazette.com>.

[8] "U.S. Surges Past Saudis to Become World's Top Oil Supplier -PIRA." *Reuters*. 15 Oct. 2013. Accessed Jun. 2015 <www.reuters.com>.

[9] LaGesse, 02, and 2012, "Oil Train Revival."

[10] "United States Pipelines Map." Theodora. 2008. Accessed Jun. 2015 <www.theodora.com>.

[11] LaGesse, David. "Oil Train Revival: Booming North Dakota Relies on Rail to Deliver Its Crude." *National Geographic News*. 2 Dec. 2012. Accessed 19 May 2015 <news.nationalgeographic.com>.

[12] "Rail Deliveries of U.S. Oil Continue to Increase in 2014." U.S. Energy Information Administration. 28 Aug. 2014. Accessed Jun. 2015 <www.eia.gov>.

[13] Soraghan, Mike. "Oil Spills: Crude Mishaps on Trains Spike as Rail Carries More Oil." *Environment & Energy Publishing*. 17 Jul. 2013. Accessed Jun. 2015 <www.eenews.net>.

[14] "Recent Oil Tanker Accidents." *CNN*. 7 May 2015. Accessed Jun. 2015 <www.cnn.com>.

[15] Bergquist, Lee. "Safety Concerns Grow along Paths of Oil Tanker Train Traffic." *Milwaukee Wisconsin Journal Sentinel*. 15 Mar. 2015. Accessed Jun. 2015 <www.jsonline.com>.

[16] Krauss, Clifford, and Jad Mouawad. "Accidents Surge as Oil Industry Takes the Train." *The New York Times*. 25 Jan. 2014. Accessed Jun. 2015 <www.nytimes.com>.

[17] "Derailment of CN Freight Train U70691-18 With Subsequent Hazardous Materials Release and Fire Cherry Valley, Illinois." National Transportation Safety Board. 19 Jun. 2009. Accessed Jun. 2015 <www.ntsb.gov>.

[18] Simpson, Thomas. "PHMSA-2012-0082 (HM-251), Hazardous Materials: Rail Petitions and Recommendations to Improve the Safety of Railroad Tank Car Transportation." Railway Supply Institute. 5 Dec. 2013. Accessed Jun. 2015 <www.rsiweb.org>.

[19] "Derailment of CN Freight Train U70691-18."

[20] Ibid.

[21] "NTSB 2015 Most Wanted." National Transportation Safety Board. Jan. 2015. Accessed Jun. 2015 <www.ntsb.gov>.

[22] "Tanker Cars under Scrutiny after Spilling Oil in Recent Derailments." *CBC News*. 18 Feb. 2015. Accessed Jun. 2015 <www.cbc.ca>.

[23] "Safety Recommendation." National Transportation Safety Board. 13 Apr. 2015. Accessed Jun. 2015 <www.ntsb.gov>.

[24] "Rule Summary: Enhanced Tank Car Standards and Operational Controls for High-Hazard Flammable Trains." U.S. Department of Transportation. 30 Apr. 2015. Accessed Jun. 2015 <www.dot.gov>.

[25] Ibid.

[26] "Transportation Systems Sector-Specific Plan." U.S. Department of Homeland Security. 2010. Accessed Jun. 2015 <www.dhs.gov>.

[27] Ibid.

[28] Taylor, Andrew. "House GOP Approves Cuts to Amtrak Budget Despite Crash - US News." *U.S. News & World Report*. 13 May 2015. Accessed Jun. 2015 <www.usnews.com>.

[29] Caygle, Heather. "House Panel Votes to Cut Amtrak Budget Hours after Deadly Crash." *Politico*. 13 May 2015. Accessed Jun. 2015 <www.politico.com>.

[30] Hassett, Kevin. "Mind the Gap: U.S. and European Train Safety." American Enterprise Institute. 17 Mar. 2015. Accessed Jun. 2015 <www.aei.org>.

[31] "Northeast Corridor Five-Year Capital Needs Assessment Fiscal Years 2015 to 2019." Northeast Corridor Infrastructure and Operations Advisory Commission.16 Sep. 2014. Accessed Jun. 2015 <www.nec-commission.com>.

[32] "2013 Report Card for America's Infrastructure." American Society of Civil Engineers. N.D. Accessed Jun. 2015 <www.infrastructurereportcard.org>.

[33] Ibid.

[34] Clapper, James. "Worldwide Threat Assessment of the U.S. Intelligence Community." Office of National Intelligence. 26 Feb. 2015. Accessed Jun. 2015 www.dni.gov>.

[35] "Rule Summary: Enhanced Tank Car Standards and Operational Controls for High-Hazard Flammable Trains."

[36] Cantwell, Maria. "Cantwell Joins Fire Chiefs, King County Leaders to Address Oil Train Risks." Cantwell. 7 Apr. 2015. Accessed Jun. 2015 <www.cantwell.senate.gov>.

[37] Epstein, Reid J. "The Keystone XL Pipeline Timeline." *The Wall Street Journal.* 24 Apr. 2014. Accessed Jun. 2015 <blogs.wsj.com>.

[38] "2014 United States Climate Action Report." U.S. Department of State. 30 Apr. 2014. Accessed Jun. 2015 <www.state.gov.

[39] "President Obama's Plan to Fight Climate Change." The White House. 25 Jun. 2013. Accessed Jun. 2015 <www.whitehouse.gov>.

[40] Searle, Annie. "Dear Member of the Board." *Shared Assessments.* 24 Feb. 2015. Accessed Jun. 2015 <www.sharedassessments.org>.

[41] Phillips, Jack. "MMA Bankruptcy: Montreal, Maine & Atlantic Was Behind Lac-Megantic Derailment." *Epoch Times.* 7 Aug. 2013. Accessed Jun. 2015 <www.theepochtimes.com>.

[42] "Lac-Mégantic Rail Disaster: $200M Proposed Settlement Reached." *CBC News.* 9 Jan. 2015. Accessed Jun. 2015 <www.cbc.ca>.

The American Health Care System

Divya Kothari
Publication Month: June 2016

Abstract: This paper delves into the complex and most recent evolution of the American Health Care system, and the subsequently evolving risks associated with the Patient Protection and Affordable Care Act of 2010. The growing complexities of this critical sector have added to the existing risks of an already complicated landscape.

As the world's strongest economy continues to boast strong growth, one of the sectors that continues to be fraught with issues is the Health Care & Services sector. Even with President Obama's last successful campaign centered on establishing a robust health insurance exchange platform, the effectiveness of its implementation remains debatable till date.

Without further ado, let us look at the new stakeholders in the system, and analyze the vulnerabilities and concerns for each of these. With the recently implemented Patient Protection and Affordable Care Act of 2010 ("ACA"),[3] the health care landscape changed dramatically. We shall discuss the evolution of this sector to understand the new landscape and examining the inherent risks and how to mitigate them.

By the late 2000s the American health care system was essentially managed by the states themselves, bifurcating into specific divisions for different services offered. Each state had its own DHHS that would be responsible for supporting recipients in the low-income bracket, in need of medical assistance.[4] Each state would identify its own metrics of aid categories and then decide the eligibility of members for coverage under this Medicaid program. Recipients qualified under these programs would often go to doctors of their choice and the bills (also known as 'claims processing') would be submitted directly to state government.[1]

---

[3] Also referred to as "Obama Care"
[4] More commonly grouped under the umbrella term of 'Medicaid'

As the economy went through turbulent times during the 2005 housing bubble and shortly thereafter, the sub-prime mortgage recession in late 2007-2008, a far larger population emerged that was unable to pay their medical bills as jobs were lost and more recipients increasingly kept getting qualified for Medicaid.[2] The year of 2008 highlighted the difficulty of the 'fee for service' model that the state governments had adopted as state budget deficits skyrocketed with medical coverage costs.[3] The need for an overhaul of the entire framework became transparent. The private healthcare insurers were very much cognizant of these changing times and offered a great solution - the government could allow recipients to pick a 'private health plan'. These health plans would be designed in such a way that they would negotiate subsidized fee contracts with doctors, clinics, hospitals etc. in exchange for offering a higher volume of patients/clients for a subsidized fee that the health insurer would pay the doctor/clinic. The health care service providers were happy with timely payments unlike state governments that became notorious for late payments under increased financial pressure.[4]

The model worked. Across the country, state governments scrambled to allow recipients to be enrolled into health care plans. This was by no means a small initiative. Numerous factors that come into play, which unknowingly paved the way for further risks. Despite technology advancing at a pace far beyond our imagination, the government continued with legacy and ancient mainframe systems to determine eligibility for members with ever changing eligibility/ demographic data/healthcare details. To aid them in the process, separate independent entities were appointed by State governments to enable recipients to independently choose a health plan with far more sophisticated technologies posing for inevitable systems and processes risks due to integration and several other issues.

While the model seemed extremely promising, the inherent need for each state government to implement, maintain and run their own independent systems was overkill.[5] President Obama convinced Congress to establish a central 'Federal Exchange' that allowed State governments to replace their systems and integrate them with the Federal Exchange which would then administer Medicaid programs. The scale at which the Federal Exchange was planned was extensive, including multiple programs such as Medicare (for senior citizens), CHIP (Children Health Insurance Program), LTSS (Long Term Services & Supports), insurance claims processing etc.[6] The ACA broadened the coverage for Medicaid up to 133 percent of the poverty line, and also extended the coverage to a larger segment of the populace through federal government subsidies.

While being widely hailed as a great solution, the ACA turned out to be double-edged sword in itself. As a federal program it allowed States some breathing room, as they would be able to sway federal subsidies. However, on the flip side, it took away the autonomy of the States to administer health care for themselves. So with this evolution in the last few years, we are at a stage where we have grown from two stakeholders, the 'doctor/clinic' and the 'patient' to one where we have four key players, 'the service providers', 'the insurance companies', 'the government' and 'the recipient'.[7] The ACA framework has its own significance and risks for each of these entities, which we will eventually look to mitigate.

For a capitalist economy trying to wade its way out of recession, amassing capital in order to reform a struggling health care system (an estimated 50 million uninsured citizens before President Obama took office)[8] would of course be a challenge. Given the extent to which the Affordable Care Act was extending the Medicaid program, the financial hit of funding this program was considerably large. For the year of 2015, the net cost of the ACA was $76 billion.[9] Even a resurgent and strong economy like the U.S. can be weighed down by heavy deficits and debts.

The next and natural step to fund these deficits was by imposing higher taxation. The first winners to higher taxes were high-income individuals. The next big fish for the government was the pharmaceutical industry. When the Affordable Care Act was initially rolled out, it was done with the support of the pharmaceutical industry. But with government deficits widening unendingly, the next step of raising taxes for specialty drugs, was quite like a boomerang. Something waiting to hit the system back. With the government wanting to increase its revenue to offset deficits, the pharmaceutical industry decided to continue growing by pursuing a policy of higher drug pricing.[10] And that is what you see happening today which can be categorized as another operational risk is bordering on financial instability. In fact, these extra 'Obama Care taxes' will in all probability, eventually lead to increasing the overall end costs for health care. A short term fix, certainly. A long-term cure? Not.

Even as the government passed a 1,000-pages long ACA the actual implementation was no mean feat. The sheer scale of this effort was unprecedented and continues to remain a work in progress as the government learns the lessons of risk management the hard way. After a grand launch in October 2013, the first week of being operational, the website had enrollments for only one percent of the estimated population target.[11] There were issues with enrollments as health plans that received forms through the portal were missing necessary information to complete the job of enrollment. The response time of the website was publicly criticized since it was agonizingly slow. Officials later released reports saying the actual web traffic was closer to 250,000 simultaneous users against an earlier estimate of 50,000 users.[12]

First impressions are worth millions. And the implementation of ACA did not exactly leave the best one. The system development costs were initially charted out to be around $600 million[13] split between several information technology ("IT") firms. The lack of coordination and planning between these agencies is another classic example of a systemic risk which resulting into a complete website failure. Ignoring technology as a crucial component is a people risk. Even though some of these firms were relieved of their duty (e.g. CGI Federal),[14] the lesson was learnt the hard way. It is estimated that the actual cost of implementing the website[15] through 2014 was closer to $2.1 billion against the $800 million estimated initially by the Department of Health and Human Services ("DHHS").[16] This also highlights the fact that no sector can function entirely on its own. The Health Care sector is extremely reliant on several other critical sectors for continuity of operations and service delivery, including: Communications, Emergency Services, Energy, Food and Agriculture, Information Technology, Transportation Systems, and Water and Wastewater Systems.[17] In our present study we focus on the dependency on the IT sector and how management must always factor this as a key point in their decision-making.

While some of the concerns have been identified, there are several additional risks that continue to plague the system. The system established in the Affordable Care Act in essence is facilitating enrollments into private health plans. Since recipient data and conditions continue to keep changing, the continuous evaluation and determination of eligibility is a big risk. There continue to be cases where wrong eligibility determinations have led to early/late plan coverage enrollments/terminations. As a recipient of health care benefits this is not the kind of problem you'd want to be worrying about during a health problem.

Handling of health care related data in America is governed by the Health Insurance Portability and Accountability Act, 1996 ("HIPAA"). Even as initial concerns of the exchange website not being HIPPA complaint were addressed,[18] the inherent nature of making such sensitive data available at this scale through the web has significant security risks. Whether there is one platform i.e. the Federal Exchange, or State-owned systems for the 17 states that decided *not* to be part of the Affordable Care Act implementation, it is essential to make these systems resilient and robust towards any kind of cyber warfare.

Even as the government continues to evolve and make slow but steady progress, the private health insurance companies face their own risks and challenges. And some of these risks are exactly opposite in nature. They are similar to the ones that generally accompany an activity associated with fast growth and rising expenses. As health plans see a growing influx of recipients, the overall cost of medical care for the population has also constantly been rising across the board. Since premiums negotiated with the government have been stagnant, numerous reports indicate that health plans are offsetting their rising expenses with an increase for private health care coverage. This introduces an inherent risk of attrition within health plans. The churn in itself is not an issue, but it is a huge blow to a recipient at the end of the day who may have to keep switching providers.

Another risk introduced with health plans is the dependence on insurance. The days where we could walk into a health care clinic are long gone and the days of being unable to afford health care with insurance continue to mar the horizon. The extension of the Medicaid populace helped add coverage to a new subset of individuals. But the rise in cost of healthcare is creating additional risk for the individuals who could have previously been able to afford their own health care. The deductibles for insurance is increasing despite Obama Care's subsidized plans and has reached levels of up to $5,000 for certain plans.[19] The argument being that health plans run the risk of pricing themselves out of affordability for an average American, and losing a large chunk of their current subscribed users base.

Just the way we have systems risks associated with the government, there's a similar risk for private health insurers. Especially in cases where squeezed IT budgets are made to accommodate highly available systems and interfaces with external clients and vendors like the governments (state and federal), claim processors (typically independent third party processors for regulatory reasons), pharmaceutical partners etc.

All this change is meaningless without the right health care providers backing up the new evolving systems. Health care professionals deal with patients and this is the most crucial part of the process - making sure people are treated with the best possible care and treatment available. Unlike the past, with liberal Medicaid coverage checks from the government, health care is now very closely monitored by health care insurance companies. So when health care providers submit claims for processing it often involves instances of microscopic scrutiny. When doctors and medical professionals are retrospectively probed for the justification of their suggested treatments or diagnosis, it can become problematic. After all there's a fine line between precaution and need, which may not necessarily be best assessed by a claims processor. This makes the system vulnerable to lots of ambiguity. It also involves long financial cycles in many cases, often resulting in arbitration disputes.

Lastly, the most important stakeholders in the health care services are the recipients of medical care. The underlying principle of all health care service is to arrange for quality medical care. This problem is still not completely addressed and is actually one of the biggest risks to the entire health care services industry.[20] With an increasing focus to enroll with independent health plans, recipients are forced to 'pick' healthcare/medical plans instead of having freedom of going to the best medical practitioner. This fundamental change in how this profession now aligns medical care to a plan rather than a medical professional for a recipient is a fundamental change. This is a major obstacle in cases where a recipient needs to go see different specialists who may not be part of the same health plan.

Going back to BASEL II's definition of 'Operational Risk' as the risk of a change in value caused by the fact that actual losses, incurred for inadequate or failed internal processes, people and systems, or from external events (including legal risk), differ from the expected losses[21] - all the risks identified above fall within the ambit of this definition. Moreover, they have been well summarized by Deloitte as these three: (1) regulatory uncertainty, (2) implementation across various stakeholders and (3) resource availability.[22] As far as a risk mitigation plan is concerned, in 2010 the Department of Homeland Security ("DHS") issued an Annex to the National Infrastructure Protection Plan[23] that aims to measure effectiveness by proposing 'Risk Mitigation Activities' along with Appendix Five[24] that together put forward an excellent structure with well laid out steps:

- Identification of different entities, associations and their relationships with each other. Who are the primary organizations, the intermediaries and their contractual obligations with one another? Which institution responsible for the information supply chain?
- Prioritization of critical assets as the key supporting infrastructure within a particular jurisdiction and using a consistent criteria for such evaluation. Also keeping in mind infrastructure belonging to dependent sectors that could have national impact (e.g. IT, Communications, etc.).
- Conducting period hazard vulnerability assessments in a structured and disciplined manner. Thereafter, matching the risks thus found with the protection goals and objectives. Also

charting out impact probability maps and risk cards for dissemination of this information.

- Developing a robust and resilient strategy to be adopted in times of crises. This extensive strategy must be prepared taking into consideration the viewpoints of all stakeholder representatives as well as internal employees in different departments. An important component of this strategy shall be continuous research & development that keeps tabulating all sorts of potential risks that the establishment may face in future and continuously reworks on its crisis management plan.
- Last but not the least, the element of communication must be woven into all the above-mentioned steps. Setting a tone of transparency and accountability, especially in financial disclosures and public grievances can go a long way for an institution's working as well as reputation.

The entire process of moving recipients from a 'fee for service' model to enrollment into private health insurance plans mandated coming up with a well-constructed plan which could be flawlessly implemented, along with a plan for incident management and disaster recovery in case something goes haywire, which it did. Let us hope it does not happen again.

---

[1] Kronke C. & White R. "The Modern Health Care Maze Development and Effects of the Four-Party System" The Independent Institute, 2009. Accessed 2nd March 2016 < https://www.independent.org>

[2] Gilmore G. "An Analysis of The Great Recession's Effect on Health Care Expenditure Growth Rates in the United States" Georgetown University Washington DC. Accessed 3rd March 2016 < www.econ-jobs.com>

[3] "Fee-for-Service." Medicaid.gov. N.D. Accessed 4th March 2016 <www.medicaid.gov>

[4] Kronke C. & White R. "The Modern Health Care Maze Development and Effects of the Four-Party System" The Independent Institute. 2009. Accessed 2nd March 2016 <www.independent.org>

[5] "Report of the Working Group on Challenges to the Employment-Based Healthcare System" United States Department of Labor. Accessed 2nd March 2016 <www.dol.gov>

[6] Supra.

[7] Kronke C. & White R. "The Modern Health Care Maze Development and Effects of the Four-Party System" The Independent Institute, 2009. Accessed 2nd March 2016 < https://www.independent.org>

[8] Miller J. "Thirty Million Uninsured" Fact Check, 16th September 2009. Accessed 5th March 2016 < www.factcheck.org>.

[9] Shabad R. "CBO projects deficit to fall to $468B in 2015" The Hill, 26th January 2015. Accessed 6th March 2016 <http://thehill.com>.

[10] Kronke C. & White R. "The Modern Health Care Maze Development and Effects of the Four-Party System" The Independent Institute, 2009. Accessed 2nd March 2016 < https://www.independent.org>

[11] Pace M., "A Bleak First Week: 99.6% of Healthcare.gov Visitors Did NOT Enroll in Obamacare" Compete, 15th October 2013. Accessed 6th March 2016 <https://blog.compete.com>.

[12] Mullaney T. "Obama Adviser: Demand Overwhelmed HealthCare.gov" USA Today, 6th October 2013. Accessed 5th March, 2016<http://www.usatoday.com>.

[13] Boehlert E. "The Myth of the $634 Million Obamacare Website" Media Matters, 24th October 2013. Accessed 6th March 2016 <http://mediamatters.org>.

[14] Eilperin J. & Goldstein A. "Obama administration to end contract with CGI Federal, company behind HealthCare.gov" The Washington Post, 10th January 2014. Accessed on 7th March 2016 <https://www.washingtonpost.com>.

[15] Health Care. Centers for Medicare & Medicaid Services. N.D. Accessed <www.healthcare.gov>

[16] Rugy V. "How Much Did HealthCare.gov Really Cost? More Than The Administration Tells Us" National Review, 1st October 2014. Accessed 7th March 2016 <http://www.nationalreview.com>.

[17] Department of Homeland Security Website <https://www.dhs.gov/healthcare-and-public-health-sector>

[18] Kuranda S. "Obamacare Site: Not HIPAA Compliant, Doesn't Need To Be" CRN, 25th October, 2013. Accessed 8th March, 2016 <http://www.crn.com>

[19] Davis E., "Out-of-Pocket Maximum – How it works and Why to Beware" About, 24th August, 2015. Accessed on 8th March 2016 <http://healthinsurance.about.com>

[20] Kronke C. & White R. "The Modern Health Care Maze Development and Effects of the Four-Party System" The Independent Institute, 2009. Accessed 2nd March 2016 < https://www.independent.org/pdf/tir/tir_14_01_3_kroncke.pdf>

[21] "Basel II: Revised international capital framework" Retrieved 2013-06-06 <bis.org>

[22] "Risk Management for Health Care Reform Programs: A Health Plan Perspective" Deloitte Consulting LLP, 2014. Accessed on 8th March 2016 < http://www.pmi.org>

[23] "Annex to the National Infrastructure Protection Plan" DHHS & DHS. Accessed on 8th March, 2016 <https://www.dhs.gov>

[24] Supra, pg. 67

American Dams

Risk Analysis and Recommendations

Courtney Harris
Publication Month: August 2016

Abstract: This paper examines dams across the U.S and the risks they impose on the American people. In particular, this paper focuses on the increasing threats to the sector from inconsistent governance, lacking emergency action plans, and growing concerns about the environmental and cultural impact of dams.

Executive Summary

American dams are a rich part of this country's history, and supply a renewable source of energy in many areas, particularly the Pacific Northwest. However, a lack of maintenance on dams and growing concern of dams' impact on our environmental health have brought public scrutiny and a demand for dams to be made safer and "greener" or, for some, to be removed all together. This paper examines some of the major risks that American dams impose upon individuals, businesses and different aspects of our government.

The 20th century saw incredible growth in the number of dams built in the U.S. as rivers across the country were dammed for irrigation, hydroelectric energy, inland navigation and water storage. While these dams were built with the best technology available at the time, many do not meet current regulations and in fact, pose a higher risk due to growing populations and widespread development than originally anticipated.

There are many challenges facing our dams today, and the risks within those challenges are worrisome. At an average age of 52 years old, American dams have seen great changes in their surroundings and in the weather conditions they must face. The mistake of planning for current conditions, 50 years ago, has led to peoples' lives being put in danger, as the conditions in those exact locations are vastly different today.

Inconsistency in governance and Emergency Action Planning poses a significant risk to the safety of American citizens, but also to other aspects of our infrastructure, such as railways, roads and power lines. Resource shortages are an issue that many entities face, but given the dire situation of our dams, it is a risk that must be addressed.

Finally, public opinion of dams has soured in the last few decades, with demand for the removal of dams that are particularly harmful to the environment or simply no longer useful. These are expensive undertakings for an already resource starved sector, and action must be taken to appease the public and also ensure that every dollar spent repairing older dams and/or building new dams is well thought out and will survive the scrutiny of environmental groups and indigenous people.

Introduction

There are four key reasons that dams are built in the U.S.: to control flooding, to provide irrigation for farmland, municipal water supply, and hydroelectric power.[1] This last reason was a particularly influential driver behind the incredible pace at which dams have been built in our country. The first hydroelectric plants were built in the 1880's to power specific buildings or companies, with little to no regulation.[2] It would be less than 50 years and many dams later when construction would begin on the Hoover Dam – the largest dam in the world upon its completion, and what is still considered the second tallest dam in the U.S.[3]

Today, there are approximately 87,000 dams in the U.S., and they impound nearly 600,000 of the country's 3.5 million miles of river. Of these dams, two-thirds are privately owned and the remaining one-third is split between federal, local, state and "unknown" ownership.[4] In this paper, we will look at assessments made by the American Society of Civil Engineers and the U.S. Army Corp of Engineers to identify the risks that American dams impose on both the government (financially, politically and related to infrastructure) and the private sector (loss of lives and businesses).

In the Homeland Security's, Dam Sector-Specific Plan, a classification system is presented for the dam system:

Hazard Potential Classification	Loss of Human Life	Economic, Environmental or Lifeline Losses
Low	None Expected	Low, Limited to owner
Significant	None Expected	Yes
High	Probable, one or more expected	Yes

"The dam isn't the problem, it's the maintenance that's the problem." –
Kim Kalama

There are many concerns today regarding the health of American dams, and the environmental impact that they are having on the planet. The average age of an American dam is 52 years old, and their structural integrity is being questioned – not necessarily because of age, but due to a lack of maintenance. In particular, dams that were previously classified as "Low Hazard Potential" or as "Significant Hazard Potential" are being reassessed due to the development of the land surrounding the dam and our ever-increasing population.[5] These dams that once only risked flooding farmland, now risk taking lives, should they fail. According to the American Society of Civil Engineers (ASCE), there were 4,000 deficient dams in 2013, and half of those were "High Hazard Potential" – which means that human lives are at stake.

The ASCE gave American dams a D+ grade in their 2013 Infrastructure Report which, given our dependency on these dams for energy, water,

U.S. Dams Hazard Potention

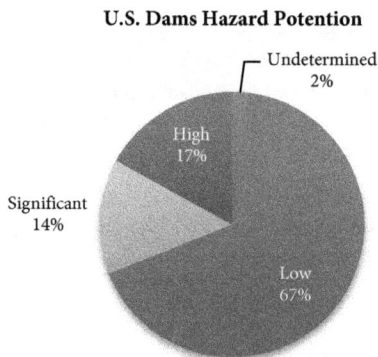

food and personal safety, should be considered unacceptable. This unsettling fact begs the question: what is the plan, should one of these dams fail? What processes are set into place to reduce the loss of life and damages as much as possible? As with any system that carries risk, many dams have an Emergency Action Plan, or an EAP. "The purpose of an EAP is to facilitate and organize employer and employee actions during workplace emergencies."[6] This written document is meant to guide people during an emergency and, hopefully, save their lives and the lives of others. Naturally, you might assume that all dams would have an EAP in place. That assumption would be false.

The figure to the right shows the percentage of dams by Hazard Potential Classification. As you can see, 67 percent of dams in the U.S. are considered a low hazard potential, and another 14 percent are considered a significant hazard potential. Only 17 percent of dams in this country risk human life, should they fail.[7] So, can we assume that these 17 percent of dams have an EAP? Unfortunately, to assume that would also be wrong.

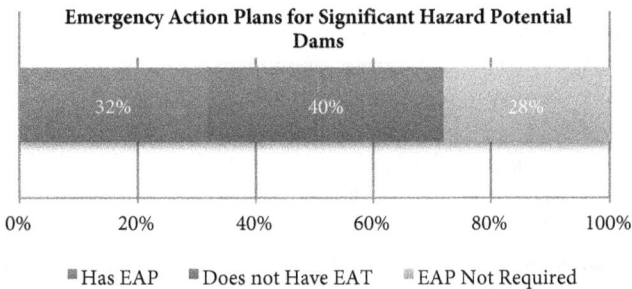

Emergency Action Plans for Significant Hazard Potential Dams

32%	40%	28%

0%   20%   40%   60%   80%   100%

■ Has EAP   ■ Does not Have EAT   ▨ EAP Not Required

Only 32 percent (or roughly 4,000 of the 12,500 dams) that are considered a significant hazard potential have an Emergency Action Plan. The remaining 8,500 dams are not required to have an EAP, or they simply do not have one.

In this paper, we're going to take a look at the risks that we face due to our aging dams and the seemingly flippant attitude towards preparing citizens, businesses and our government for their likely decline, both in usefulness and in structural integrity. But before that, let's examine which other sectors rely upon our dams.

Dependencies

What other sectors of American infrastructure depend on our dams functioning properly?

Energy

Per the Department of Energy, hydropower is responsible for producing 7 percent of the U.S.' electric generation in 2013.[8] However, in the Pacific Northwest, that percentage is much higher. According to the Foundation for Water & Energy Education, the PNW has hydropower to thank for up to 80 percent of its electricity generation each year.[9] Obviously, should our dams fails, we risk the loss of a major source of cleaner, renewable energy. It is worth noting here, however, that less than 3 percent of the 87,000 dams in our country generate hydroelectric power. And while the Pacific Northwest would certainly feel the impact of an electricity-generating dam failing, the rest of the country would be far less affected.

Food and Agriculture

As mentioned earlier in this paper, another reason for building a dam is to provide irrigation for farmland that would otherwise be too dry to successfully yield crops. In fact, 48 percent of dams are built and used for the sole purpose of irrigation.[10] Per the Association of State Dam Safety Officials, "Ten percent of American cropland is irrigated using water stored behind dams."[11] In areas like California and Colorado, where drought can (and does) destroy entire crops, the water that dams store is incredibly important. Our ever changing climate and increasingly extreme seasons are an issue that we can assume to deal with for generations to come – having water stored in dams for irritation will keep farms producing fruits, vegetables and grains and weather through periods of no rain.

Water

While it is unclear exactly how much of our drinking water comes from the reservoirs created by dams, it is well known that at least a portion of American's clean, drinking water is a direct result of dams. With water already being a scarce resource in many parts of our country, the importance of this water supply has never been greater.

Transportation Systems

Dams help to make rivers more navigable for large barges that carry food, supplies, materials and more through our country. Through lock systems, otherwise treacherous river routes are tamed and large ships with heavy loads can enjoy a smooth ride. While this is an important aspect of dams, navigation and transportation account for less than 1 percent of their overall role.[12]

Operational Risks

James Lam defines operational risk as "...the risk of direct or indirect loss resulting from inadequate or failed internal processes, people and systems or from external events."[13] He goes on to describe people risk, process risk, system risk and event risk. This is the framework that will be used to describe the operational risks of American dams as they stand today.

Planning for Current Conditions, not Future Conditions – Process Risk, System Rick and People Risk

It seems obvious that deficient dams are a risk – but why? How could so many dams (over 4,400) deteriorate to the point that the structural and hydraulic deficiencies make them so susceptible to failure?[14]

Dams were built with the most advanced technology and sophisticated engineering practices at the time – but that was, for the average dam, 50 years ago. Today's standards are far stricter and we have seen more extreme weather patterns that they must face. However, the process of updating a dam and incorporating new building standards is not as simple or financially realistic as updating a piece of software. The Association of Dam Safety Officials estimates that cost approximately $21 billion to just repair the high hazard dams that have been declared deficient.[15] This would be funded by both the public sector (tax payer money) and the private sector (the private owners of dams) and would span over the 15 years.

The number of deficient dams that could lead to a loss of life is startling – and part of this is due to a lack of thinking through the changes that a dam could bring to a region. Many dams were built for irrigation and, as such, were classified as low hazard potential. Low hazard dams adhered to less stringent requirements, as their failure would simply result in farmland flooding and not much else. However, as the land became usable and more people came to live and work in these areas, the hazard classification was upgraded and the standards to which the dam was built were no longer sufficient to adequately protect the people in its shadow.

Not only do the risks exist for human life, but also for businesses that are based in the areas near the dams. Dams, by nature, hold back a river and create a reservoir – these are typically referred to as lakes. These lakes are popular places to build homes, recreational businesses, restaurants, stores, etc. Upon failure, not only could people be injured or killed, the economy could take a hit as homes and businesses are washed away.

Recommendations

It is recommended for any new dams being built and existing dams that a projected lifespan of the dam be built out. This would essentially be a risk management exercise, where an external source would create a series of "what if" scenarios regarding the region in which the dam exists. What if oil is discovered 10 miles from here and the entire area booms with development of houses and business? Is the dam sturdy enough to protect those lives and businesses? What is the likelihood that the hazard potential classification changes to something more or less significant? With an exercise like this, hopefully the issue of building dams to existing conditions without considering how that dam would affect the area and its inhabitants would be eliminated.

Policies should be built around the kinds of analysis to be done for any future dam builds and for any repairs to be conducted on existing dams. The cost of repairing a dam is incredibly high – not only would thinking ahead save tax payers and dam owners' money, it could also save lives.

Inconsistency in Dam Governance

As was mentioned earlier, no one entity owns the American dam system – there exist a wide variety, from private owners, to non-profits and the federal government. It takes a village to operate these dams – but there is no standardization amongst these villages. The government and publically owned dams, in particular, lack the resources to staff their dams with enough qualified employees. As with any business, a lack of resources means that some things will be neglected – and for a 50-year-old dam, built according to 50-year-old science in the face of current environmental challenges, there is little room for error or neglect.

Individual states have dam safety programs that cover 77 percent of American dams that "...permit, inspect, and enforce regulations for about 77 percent of U.S. dams."[16] However, these are run by individual states, without an overarching governing body to enforce consistence regulations across the country.

Recommendation

Resources will likely be an issue for any sector, and the dam system is no different. Even if a dam location is short staffed or has a less tenured work force, there should be strict policies for monitoring, operating and maintaining the dams. These would likely vary slightly, as each dam is built for the river it is containing and the geography in which it is housed – but there should be a standard set of best practices from which all policies are derived to ensure that each and every dam is being operated at the highest level of excellence that it can. Private and public groups will need to work together, which they currently do on many issues, to create a persistent set of standards that they all agree to adhere to.

Lack of Emergency Action Planning

It was mentioned earlier that only 32 percent of the dams that, upon failure, would risk human life have an Emergency Action Plan. This is unacceptable. Dams contain rivers – they house massive bodies of water in, oftentimes, remote locations. This means that it may take a significant amount of time before an emergency response team is able to get to the dam location, should something go wrong. Without a required EAP, it is not guaranteed that documentation exists for an employee who needs to alert someone about a dam breach or failure. It is not a sure thing that documentation exists for a new or inexperience employee that walks them through what to do in an emergency to prevent further damage to the dam or the surrounding area.

Recommendation

The recommendation is that every single dam in this country has some sort of documented Emergency Action Plan. Even the low hazard potential dams should have clear instructions for what to do during a dam breach or failure, written in a language that an inexperience dam worker could comprehend in an emergency situation.

In particular, deficient dams should be required to have an EAP that is reviewed on an ongoing basis to ensure that any new developments in the area, changes in geography or weather conditions are taken into account. Given the higher risk of failure, it is essential that the employees of this dam be well versed on what to do in an emergency and participate in practice drills.

Growing Concern over Environmental/Cultural Impact

Not only are dams receiving scrutiny due to their aging structures, lack of planning and high-risk profile, but also many of them are currently being assessed for future usefulness. If the 20th century was the "Era of the Dam", the beginning of the 21st century most certainly marked the end of that era. If a dam has a reputation for being anything less than safe and useful and non-destructive to the environment, it is likely that someone will start pushing for its destruction.

When a portion of a river is dammed, the geology of that ecosystem is completely altered. In recent years, the Pacific Northwest has seen a 90 percent decrease in the number of salmon running up the rivers, as the dams block the route that these fish are genetically wired to take.[17] Ladders and steps aren't working and several salmon species have been placed on the endangered species list. Having barges transport spawning salmon to spawning pools, and then transporting the newly hatched fish back through the dam wastes resources. Hatcheries are able to harvest eggs and hatch new fish, but there is very little genetic diversity and, often, these hatchery fish die before every coming back to spawn.

Lastly, many of the populations that suffer the most when a river is dammed are indigenous people. In particular, a small fishing and trading village existed along the Columbia River, right on the border of Washington and Oregon for over 15,000 years. Up until 1957, it was the "oldest continuously inhabited community on the North American continent."[18] In order to harness the power of the Columbia, the government built The Dalles Dam, which flooded the falls and blocked the salmon from reaching the small village.

When a dam is built, the water must be stored somewhere, and typically, something is lost in the flooding, whether it is 15,000-year-old village or decades old artifacts left behind by a tribe long ago. With our ever-decreasing supply of national treasures, more and more people are looking at dams less as helpful feats of engineering, and more as environmentally and culturally destructive.

Recommendation

There is a strong push to dismantle dams in this country today. The era of the dam has passed and the rate at which new dams are being built is a mere fraction of what it was 40 years ago. Dams that no longer serve a purpose should be taken down and the river freed. This is done in a controlled way today, and has been done upwards of 1,200 times since 1912, with approximately 850 removals occurring in the past 20 years.[19] To remove a dam purposefully and intentionally is far better than the dam failing because it couldn't undergo repairs soon enough.

Any consideration for a new dam should heavily take into account the impact on the environment and any group of people. By ignoring these two important factors, the government or a private body could build something that creates such a controversy; it may not be long before millions of dollars are being spent taking the dam back down.

For those dams that are still necessary, it is pivotal that they be repaired as soon as possible, and any changes that can be made to lessen its impact on the environment should be considered. Environmental groups are gaining strength in their efforts to dismantle dams and if a dam isn't built well, and/or doesn't provide enough benefit to outweigh the consequences, odds are fairly good that it will be coming down in the next decade or so. If the government or a private owner doesn't want to pay for removing a dam, they need to make sure that any dollars put into it are making it better for this new, very environmentally aware generation.

Conclusion

As we can see, there is significant work to be done on both the private and public side when it comes to our nation's dams. Currently, the dams and their owners face every kind of operational risk that exists – resource shortages lead to people making mistakes or being improperly trained, insufficient systems and designs are leading to compromised structural integrity and an increased risk of dam failure, dams have lost that "golden" reputation and are under intense scrutiny by the public for their harm to salmon runs, indigenous people and national treasures.

With better-documented and more rigorously requited Emergency Action Plans, as well as a transparent and thorough assessment of the best dams to repair and the best dams to dismantle, it is possible that the funds allocated to the Dam Sector could decrease the overall level of risk the sector is facing, compared to its current bombardment of risks.

---

[1] Why Build a Dam?" *DamNation*. 2016. Accessed Mar. 2016 <www.damnationfilm.com>.

[2] "Hydropower Program." U.S. Bureau of Reclamation. 2. Feb. 2016. Accessed Mar. 2016 <www.usbr.gov>.

[3] "Hoover Dam." U.S. Bureau of Reclamation. 12. Mar. 2015. Accessed Mar. 2016 <www.usbr.gov>.

[4] "Dams Sector Specific Plan." U.S. Department of Homeland Security. Nov. 2015. Accessed Mar. 2016 <www.dhs.gov>.

[5] "Dams: 2013 Report Card for America's Infrastructure." American Society of Civil Engineers. Mar. 2013. Accessed Mar. 2016 <www.infrastructurereportcard.org>.

[6] "Emergency Action Plan." Occupational Safety & Health Administration, U.S. Department of Labor. N.D. Accessed Mar. 2016 <www.osha.gov>.

[7] "Dams Sector Specific Plan."

[8] "Frequently Asked Questions." National Hydropower Association. 2013. Accessed Mar. 2016 <www.hydro.org>.

[9] "Overview of Hydropower in the Pacific Northwest." Foundation for Water & Energy Education. 2016. Accessed Mar. 2016 <www.fwee.org>.

[10] "Role of Dams." International Commission on Large Dams. N.D. Accessed Mar. 2016 <www.icold- cigb.org>.

[11] "Dams Are a Vital Part of the National Infrastructure." Association of State Dam Safety Officials. 2016. Accessed Mar. 2016 <www.damsafety.org>.

[12] "Roles of Dams."

[13] Lam, J. "Enterprise Risk Management: From Incentives to Controls." Elsevier, Inc. 2016.

[14] "Dam Safety 101" Association of State Dam Safety Officials. 2016. Accessed Mar. 2016 <www.damsafety.org>.

[15] "Dams: 2013 Report Card."

[16] "Dams Sector Specific Plan."

[17] "When Salmon are Dammed." Pacific States Marine Fisheries Commission and the Oregon Fisheries Congress. 4 Apr. 1997. Accessed Mar.2016 <www.psmfc.org>.

[18] John, F. "Columbia River was a Wild, Frothy, Dangerous Place, Once." *Offbeat Oregon History*. 6 Sep. 2010. Accessed Mar. 2016 <www.offbeatoregon.com>.

[19] "2013 Dam Removals." American Rivers. N.D. Accessed Mar. 2016 <www.americanrivers.org>.

Food for Energy or Energy for Food

A Chemical Dependency

Jeffrey B. Seward

Publication Month: November 2016

Abstract: This paper explores the risks and the long-term impact of the Oil and Gas Sector on the Food and Agriculture Sector. Agriculture needs the Oil and Gas Sector in order to produce at current levels. If oil and gas were eliminated overnight, our very ability to produce food crops would be gone along with it. One of the most important risks to look at is need to eat versus need consume oil and gas. The relationship between these two critical infrastructure sectors will have implications on American commerce and the country's food supply.

"Energy cannot be created or destroyed; rather, it transforms from one form to another." – Law of Conservation of Energy

Energy surrounds us from the sun shining above, to the chemical stores harvested beneath the ground. We, not unlike other plants and animals, consume energy, transform it for our purposes, and release the byproducts of those transformations. Just as we followed the cycle of sun energy to plants, up to our end consumption of food that makes us able to function from day to day, energy influences us in ways that are truly hard to comprehend. However, it takes energy to make energy. Centuries ago, farming took animal and manpower weeks, months even, to bring bounties of crops from seed sown in the ground to seed harvested for our consumption. With the advent of modern technology, we moved from manpower to machine power, thus enabling each farmer to plant more acres and harvest more crops. Those machines were powered by coal-fired steam engines, then combustible fuels like gasoline and diesel. Even getting those crops to storage facilities, manufacturing sites, and end production takes millions of gallons of fuel. The Energy Sector, specifically the oil and gas sector, is what helps America's famers ensure that crops will have the energy stores necessary to plant, tend, and harvest those crops. However, what happens when the necessity of one sector threatens the survival of another sector, and may even be at odds with that sector? I will examine the risk and impact of the Oil and Gas Sector on the Food and Agriculture Sector and what that means for us in terms of commerce and our ability to feed others and ourselves.

The Oil and Gas sector employed almost 180,000 people in extraction in February of 2016.[1] While this is a smaller subsector of the mining, quarrying, and oil and gas extraction, the necessity of this sector to keep the country running is no doubt crucial. In fact, without the Oil and Gas sector, it becomes impossible for agriculture to take place at the level allowed currently by technology. To illustrate this dependency, let us look at a small farm case for their production and usage to understand how necessary oil and gas is to ensure food production.

One farm in eastern Montana planted 4,000 acres, or 6.25 square miles, of land into wheat production for the 2015 harvest year. This farm utilizes some of the latest technologies for minimizing fuel usage such as updated machinery and GPS tracking of vehicles and equipment to minimize overlap, thus increasing coverage and decreasing fuel expended due to double coverage of areas. This farm had a final harvest of 140,000 bushels of wheat, working out to a harvest of 35 bushels per acre. This yield would feed approximately 84,000 people if the entire crop were dedicated to food production. However, if that seed were dedicated to being planted, given a 92% germination rate of seed, there is the potential to use that crop to feed 1.5 million people in the next year.

Seems impressive, but now let us look at the expenses of that farm for the same year. That farm spent $24,600 on fuel for tractors, combines, and trucks that carried out operations of hauling equipment, seed for planting, and harvested seed for storage and sale. That same 6.25 square miles also requires $109,000 in chemicals to treat the crops to reduce losses and $207,200 in fertilizer to ensure proper growing conditions to maximize yield. When all is said and done, the operation expenses for that farm alone work out to be $340,800. This means that just to cover the operation costs given the yield of the farm, the price of wheat needs to be $2.43. This does not cover any taxes, land payments, machinery payments that would also potentially need to be made.

Now to factor in what that fuel consumption does to the environment, the very thing agricultural production depends upon. Using the average price of fuel in 2015, one can estimate that at total fuel cost of $24,600 and an average diesel price of $2.12 per gallon, the farm in eastern Montana used approximately 11,600 gallons of diesel fuel. Using calculation from the U.S. Energy Information Administration,[2] each gallon of fuel burned created 22.38 pounds of carbon dioxide, making for a total of almost 260,000 pounds of carbon dioxide put into the air during a single farming season. While there are studies that show wheat yields benefit from increased carbon dioxide in the air,[3] it is also noted that there is a tipping point in which that no longer becomes the case. Unfortunately, at the time of writing this document, there was no information that could be found on how much carbon sequestering wheat is capable to offset the amount of carbon production during the planting cycle.

The sheer amount of CO_2 created by one small farm in eastern Montana is truly incredible; however, in the grand scale of that production, agriculture only accounts for 9 percent of CO_2 emissions [4] while the transportation industry accounts for 26 percent. Electrical generation creates 30 percent of CO_2 emissions. It is run on a mixture of coal and natural gas. For this paper, I am focusing on the oil and gas sector alone. There would be an element of the electrical generation side that would need to be investigated to determine how much electrical generation is done through natural gas, as it is a significant source of heating and electrical power generation.

The impact that the oil and gas sector has had on CO_2 outputs is impressive in that it does account for the 26 percent of emissions that come from the transportation sector. Given that it is also source of CO_2 generation that has only existed in the last 110 years, it is clear the kind of impact it has in conjunction with the amount of CO_2 generated with each gallon of diesel and gasoline.[5] The climbing rate of CO_2 has been a source of concern for scientists with concentrations rising significantly since the start of measurements on Mauna Loa.[6] As stated previously, increased CO_2 does help increase yield in wheat,[7] that limit can be reached very easily. That part alone would stifle crop production, even lending to production to fall significantly before the discussion of other environmental impacts takes place.

Agriculture needs the Oil and Gas Sector in order to produce at current levels. Even for that small farm, planting, fertilizing, spraying, harvesting, and transporting crops over for production that takes place on 6.25 square miles would be impossible without the power of oil and gas. It is part of what allows our country to have the lowest expenses in terms of disposable income used to buy food. However, when it comes to reaching threshold CO_2 levels and crop production, we find ourselves in a conundrum that may force us to define who we are. Agriculture's dependence on oil and gas is like that of a chemical dependency. There is the need for it to be able to function at current capacities. If oil and gas were eliminated overnight, our very ability to produce food crops would be gone along with it. To say that it would be like going back to the days before powered machinery would be an understatement. Currently, there are no all-electric farm machinery options available. The power requirements of food and agriculture need oil and gas in order to assure production. Until companies like John Deere, Case International, and Caterpillar develop more hybrid or all electric options, and power storage for electrical vehicles improve, agriculture will have to maintain its status quo for powering itself.

One of the most important elements to look at is what Food and Agriculture views as risks versus what the Energy sector, specifically Oil and Gas views as risks. Food and Agriculture says in their risks that, "Climate change poses a major challenge to U.S. agriculture because of the critical dependence of the agricultural system on climate and the complex role that agriculture plays in rural and national social and economic systems.[8]" The Oil and Gas sector does not admit to climate change being part of its risk profile, coming closest with its risk assessment of, "Natural disasters and extreme weather conditions.[9]" By these two critical infrastructures not being in alignment as to a very critical risk, it presents a unique problem in which there could be could be a detrimental relationship.

One of the most important risks to look at is need to eat versus need consume oil and gas. If food prices rise at a similar pace as oil and gas did before reaching its heights, people will not likely cut back on food the way they would cut back on oil and gas consumption. For Oil and Gas, this is a risk that is not accounted very well by the fact that climate change has already begun to affect the way in which crops are produced. Fuel prices forced farmers to change their practices as much as possible to take advantage of lowering their operational expenses. However, should food prices become subject to the same kinds of volatility experienced during the expansion of oil exploration, the general public will ensure they will be able to eat as it is one of the five necessary needs.

Another risk of climate change that has not been accounted for by the Oil and Gas sector is that more state governments are stepping up to ensure a diverse energy portfolio. As more states adopt measures to reduce the carbon impacts of their states, oil and gas could see significant regulatory issues pop up for them. Currently, Oil and Gas only looks at, "regulatory and legislative changes—including environmental and health—as well as increased cost of compliance."[10] This is far from factoring in climate change as a true risk to the sector. States will continue to legislate based on environmental and health issues, however, more will legislate on climate issues in the future, thus affecting Oil and Gas in a way that has not necessarily been accounted. The risks will be anything from moratoriums on extraction to energy diversification that targets removal of Oil and Gas from a state's energy portfolio.

Another risk factor to the Oil and Gas sector is the expansion of alternative energy sources. While this may not seem immediately apparent, the market shift of autos to electric has had other consequences. Many users are seeing the value of having their vehicle powered by renewable energy sources as well. Because of the increased production of renewable energy sources, the price of building and supplying that source has become more accessible. It is now easier than ever to include solar cells or home wind turbines as part of the purchase of a home. The tax incentives for adding these mechanisms make it more plausible to invest in these sources that would allow them to power their electric vehicles, cutting out the need for Oil and Gas or significantly reducing their dependence on the sector. As these technologies become cheaper, it will be easier for consumers to justify these expenses for their home and vehicles as a cheaper, cleaner power source.

While it would take time for states to move away from oil and gas, a critical component has shown that Oil and Gas may not be as vital as it was once. The market has been shifting towards hybrid vehicles and now all-electric vehicles. All-electric was once considered impractical due to the inability to store enough power within a vehicle or the cumbersome batteries that were either inefficient or unsafe. As engineers have made strides to create a more appropriate battery that supplied the power necessary, automakers have moved toward a diversified line of hybrid and electric vehicles. Even heavier transport vehicles are now starting to make the shift to all-electric. BMW released their electric tractor-trailer in July of 2015.[11] While it is certainly not capable of the range that tractor-trailers have currently, it shows that there is an application for these vehicles. As battery solutions continue to develop, that range will soon be like current all-electric cars now and be comparable to their predecessors. It is also more attractive as an option due to the tax breaks companies can receive and the fact that it is cheaper to "fill the tank" on an electric car than it is to do the same with a gasoline engine. As storage or interchangeable batteries become more practical and have better distance, the limitations for the agricultural sector will begin to get smaller, and thus making all-electric power for transportation a more viable option.

The large machinery such as combines, tractors, and other heavy equipment will eventually benefit from hybrid technology. John Deere has already begun to release a line of hybrid combines that will help farmers benefit from a power source many major industries already use. While the amount of power is small compared to the power needed to operate a machine, the 224 kW powered battery will undoubtedly provide a benefit to farmers in two manners. First, there will be the reduction of fuel used during the course of harvest. Second, as more hybrid combines come available with larger, more powerful batteries, the impact that the agriculture industry has on CO_2 production will diminish so long as the engines remain entirely powered by diesel engines. Should these vehicles become plug in hybrids, there will need to be a method of power generation by alternative energy sources that would offset the need for increased energy production.

What we have to keep in mind is that the Agriculture sector only accounts for 9 percent of CO_2 emissions.[12] The other major sources of emissions would need to be trimmed from the Transportation sector and from other sources of electrical generation that use natural gas as its source. Overall, it should be the goal of the Energy sector as a whole to ensure that its mission also helps align with our country's need to continue being self-sufficient in agricultural production. As long these two sectors do not align with the science of what drives climate change, the Energy sector will do irreparable harm to the Food and Agriculture sector. This risk will ultimately drive up the cost of food and even have an effect on the Oil and Gas sector's ability to be profitable. People will make cuts in many areas; however, there will be a lot of cuts made to people's consumption of transportation. Telecommuting to work is becoming a more viable option for many people, and given the option and ability, it could end up being far more viable for those individuals seeking to make changes in order to assure their ability to eat.

Mitigation of the risks to the Oil and Gas sector is very tricky. This sector needs consumption in order to survive. However, the consumption as it stands currently is doing damage to the environment and threatening the ability of Food and Agriculture to sustain its output. Food and Agriculture needs Oil and Gas right now because it currently could not produce at the level needed. As agriculture continues to expand and diversify its power source, it will help reduce the risk to itself by using Oil and Gas. More importantly, as auto and Ag machinery makers continue to diversify their energy sources, either it will force Oil and Gas to become a more environmentally stable power source, or it will be forced out of the picture entirely. Oil and Gas would have to find a way to become a near zero-emission product. The progress that it has made to clean up the emissions created from gasoline, diesel, and natural gas has been an important first step. That work will most likely be for naught.

As solar, wind, and hydroelectric become more widely used and batteries become more powerful, the uses of brute force power will be minimized. Even in the brute force side of combustion engines, work on hydrogen combustion engines has made a remarkable leap in terms of potential. What makes hydrogen so unique is that it is a powerful combustion fuel source that would only have water and water vapor as its byproducts. The power created by this combustion fuel source could leave Oil and Gas behind as it would no longer be necessary to burn complex carbon chains that have known negative effects on the environment. It would most likely even be possible to use these engines in a hybrid capacity as well, allowing for minimal impact.

The Oil and Gas sector's CO_2 emissions will surely be shrunk as scientific advancements allow alternative energy to become the cheaper fuel source. While CO_2 is important for sustaining plant life, it is also very clear that once a certain threshold is surpassed, the yield of wheat will decrease. Couple that with the damage to the climate that is creating weather patterns that make prolonged droughts, devastating floods, and fire seasons that start earlier and last longer, Oil and Gas sector is looking at changing landscape that threatens its very existence. Now add in the fact that it has been and will continue to affect Food and Agriculture to the point where production will cap, then decrease due to CO_2 levels, weather patterns that make production more difficult, and a world population that needs to eat, Oil and Gas finds themselves in a position where their sector is doing more harm to the world populace every year, and that harm can eventually hit a tipping point that would send our planet into a tailspin.

The risks presenting in regards to the Food and Agriculture sector by the Oil and Gas sector are very real threats that are happening at this very moment. The science is sound, the risks are real, and the consequences of inaction would have long reaching effects that would make the world population choose between power and food. The alignment of the Oil and Gas to the Food and Agriculture sector is that of a chemical dependency. It is keeping an industry going while doing irreparable damage to it and at some point, that damage will be permanent and there will be no way to mitigate these risks.

---

[1] *Employment, Hours, and Earnings from the Current Employment Statistics survey (National).* Bureau of Labor and Statistics, U.S. Department of Labor. N.D. Accessed May 2016 <data.bls.gov>.

[2] "Frequently Asked Questions: How Much Carbon Dioxide Is Produced From Burning Gasoline And Diesel Fuel?" U.S. Energy Information Administration. N.D. Accessed 27 May 2016 <www.eia.gov>.

[3] Bugbee, B. et al. "CO2 Crop Growth Enhancement And Toxicity In Wheat And Rice." The National Center for Biotechnology Information. Nov. 1994. Accessed Jun. 2016 <www.ncbi.nlm.nih.gov>

[4] "Sources of Greenhouse Gas Emissions." U.S. Environmental Protection Agency. N.D. Accessed 1 Jun. 2016 <www3.epa.gov>.

[5] "Frequently Asked Questions."

[6] "Full Mauna Loa CO2 Record." Earth System Research Laboratory, Global Monitoring Division. National Oceanic and Atmospheric Administration. Accessed 1 Jun. 2016 <www.esrl.noaa.gov>

[7] Bugbee, B. et al.

[8] *Food and Agriculture – Sector Specific Plan 2015.* Food and Drug Administration; U.S. Department of Agriculture; U.S. Department of Homeland Security. Feb. 2016 Accessed 27 May 2016 <www.dhs.gov>.

[9] Ibid.

[10] Ibid.

[11] Hard, Andrew. "18 Wheels, Zero Emissions: BMW Premiers All-Electric Material Transport Truck In Germany." *Digital Trends.* 10 Jul. 2015. Accessed 1 Jun. 2016 <www.digitaltrends.com>.

[12] "Sources of Greenhouse Gas Emissions."

Paying for a Rundown U.S. Surface Transportation System

Ermenejildo "Meadow" Rodriguez, Jr.
Publication Month: March 2017

Abstract: The U.S. transportation systems sector has an incredibly huge financial issue at hand. Congress does not have a plan for how to pay for damaged or dilapidated roads, highways, bridges, and tunnels. The fund to pay for these segments of the surface transportation system is already in the red. Within the next 18 years, it is likely going to be severely underfunded, even more so that now. This paper will focus on the risks associated with the U.S. surface transportation system, and financing its improvement within the public and private realms.

The U.S. Department of Transportation (DOT) and the Department of Homeland Security (DHS) are responsible for the Transportation Systems sector, which works to move goods and people within the country and overseas securely, carefully, and swiftly.[1] This sector is made up of seven important modules, or subsectors: 1) Freight Rail, 2) Passenger Rail and Mass Transit, 3) Aviation, 4) Postal and Shipping, 5) Pipeline Systems, 6) Maritime Transportation System, and 7) Motor Carrier and Highway. The Motor Carrier and Highway mode incorporates over four million miles of road, more than 350 tunnels, and over 600,000 of bridges.[2]

Relatedly, the U.S.'s infrastructure composes of sea and airports, mass transit systems, bridges, water infrastructure, roads, highways, and tunnels. [3] As the U.S. Chamber of Commerce (COC) has recognized, this infrastructure are vital assets to the nation that propel safety, jobs, worldwide competitiveness, and growth.[4] Nevertheless, the Chamber reports that the U.S. has not been able to agree about how to finance for incredibly necessary repairs and maintenance.[5] Therefore, this issue raises not only concerns of the costs to U.S. citizens, but also the implications to their personal safety and U.S. national security.

The U.S. Government Accountability Office (GAO) has identified the funding of the country's surface transportation system as a high-risk area.[6] The GAO stated that addressing the issue is a matter that primarily entails an act of Congress; and thusly, is an operational risk attributed to people. A major source of money for the U.S. surface transportation system is from the Highway Trust Fund; however, that support has been dwindling. The provisions for that fund come from various truck-affiliated and motor fuel taxes. Since federal taxes on motor fuel have not risen since 1993, inflation has created a downward trend in the trust funds value. Given the outlook for vehicles and fuel usage, they have concluded that the downhill trend is likely to endure as the desire for gasoline goes down along with the institution of alternative fuel and more fuel-efficient automobiles. The highway trust fund balance for 2015 was projected to be negative $2 billion, and it is expected that it will be negative $157 billion by 2024. [7] So, money to help finance the U.S.'s surface transportation system will need to be increased towards the trust fund, or the country will need to find money elsewhere.

The reason that the U.S.'s surface transportation system is at such a high risk is because lack of funds means that new roads, bridges, and tunnels cannot be developed, nor can there be repairs or maintenance to them. The surface system is crucial to the nation's economy and affects most American's lives daily, as it moves both freight and people.[8] So, having a corroding transportation surface system means that repairs, maintenance, or new developments will not only be expensive, but with a potential extra cost coming from prolonged wear and tear or increased risk of catastrophic events that could take the lives of many people, or damage or destroy current subpar transportation surfaces. As the system is currently under mounting stress, the price to upgrade or repair the system, for now and the future, is assessed to cost hundreds of billions.[9]

Not only are the sources of funding worsening, but also the financing is additionally problematic due to the economic condition and financial outlook of the federal government. The U.S. cannot substitute committed federal revenue, such as with clever financing methods or loan programs, for federal transpiration.[10] So, for an upturn in the U.S.'s highway network, dependable sources of revenue need to be found. Now, to better understand the challenge to the U.S.'s surface transportation system, we can explore the issues and risks associated with it in its public and private spaces.

U.S. News and World Report noted that the American Society of Civil Engineers (ASCE) just recently graded the U.S. with a D+ for infrastructure, which includes roadways and highways.[11] The group stated that the rundown roadways and highways had "a pressing need for modernization."[12] They also determined that a portion of the $3.6 trillion needed for infrastructure will need to be distributed to those dilapidated roadways, just to elevate it to a satisfactory level by 2020. As for those roadways and highways, the ASCE gave them D rating.[13]

Furthermore, the ASCE mentioned that 42 percent of the U.S.'s main urban highways continue to stay jammed, which costs the economy approximately $101 billion in fuel and wasted time each year.[14] Additionally – and in spite of improved circumstances in the immediate period – local, state, and federal capital investments for road work have moved up to $91 billion annually; and yet, that level of financing has been inadequate.[15] That funding is still anticipated to lead to a drop in performance and conditions for the long run. As of now, the Federal Highway Administration projected that $170 billion of capital investment will be needed yearly to create a substantial improvement to performance and conditions of the highways and roads.[16]

The ASCE found that the country's roads could gain an assistance from substantial performance enhancements without having to add new highway lanes.[17] In addition, unfavorable community influences – such as highway infrastructure that has a high price by adding capacity, problems in gaining necessary right of way, and induced sprawl – suggest that all efforts need to look towards improving current roadway network management. States and cities around the U.S. are raising the use of technology to increase efficient signal timing, enhance the flow of traffic and variable speed limits, and decrease congestion. A heightened practice of telecommuting, in addition to available and convenient alternative methods of transportation, are a few instances of how added enhancement can be better overseen and how the demand for capacity rises.[18]

Also, safety remains to be a significant emphasis for investment as numbers allude that road and highway conditions result in about one-third of the U.S's entire traffic fatalities.[19] On a positive note, road fatalities have dropped annually, equating just fewer than 33,000 deaths in 2010, or a decline of around 24 percent since 2005. On the other hand, these collisions amounted to $230 billion yearly on the country's economy. The ASCE suggests improving or installing median barrier mechanisms, broadening shoulders and lanes, and decreasing exposure to obstacles offer chances to bring down collisions, deaths, and injuries.[20]

Along with roads and highways, a significant amount of risk comes from dilapidated bridges. The current state of many of these can be attributed to risk from people, systems, and external factors. As for failing bridges, Congress, and state and local governments have showed little to no significant progress towards addressing them. To state the criticality of the situation, a 2015 article by U.S. News and World Report indicated that the more time that it takes to deal with bridge needs, the costlier it will become - it can cost three to four times as much to repair a bridge with advanced degeneration than one that is moderately requires repair.[21] For example, the state of Rhode Island was obligated to pay $167 million for an entire bridge replacement since it was unsuccessful at preserving the original.[22]

A Harvard Business School article reports that 24.3 percent of the nation's bridges – 64,000 in total – had been recognized as "structurally deficient or functionally obsolete,"[23] and the ASCE has put it that one-ninth of the country's bridges are as structurally inadequate, where the average age is 42 years for the country's 607,380 bridges.[24] They also have it that of the U.S.'s 102 biggest metropolitan areas, deficient bridges are logging more than 200 million trips daily by vehicles. Right now, only $12.8 billon is sent on the nation's backlog of bridge deficiency; although, it would cost $20.5 billion yearly to get rid of the insufficiency by 2028, the Federal Highway Administration approximated. The ASCE said that the problem for local, state, and federal governments is that they need to add $8 billion each year to bridge investments so they can deal with the $76 billion needed for insufficient bridges throughout the U.S.[25]

Along with the trouble to pay for roadways, highways, and bridges, there is also a definite challenge to pay for broken-down or new tunnels. Conversely, a positive light has shined on the U.S.'s ability to utilize tunneling technologies in the face of the money crunch. Nevertheless, many metropolitan areas are addressing their growth issue by using the latest advances in tunneling.[26] So, to deal with unrelenting growth, urban areas are extending underneath their cities at an extraordinary pace. However, the drive to expand underground is not only a growth concern from above, but also because of the remarkable advances in tunneling. Recent decades have seen engineers advance automated and mechanized systems to crunch through deep muck and rock, while preventing collapse and without bothering the city above. Instead of masses of men to work on these, robotic worms – or TBMs (tunnel-boring machines) – have helped to create tunnels on budget and on time. The use of these TBMs can come with applied chemistry to get through terrain that is incredibly hard or consists loose materials, along with electronic monitors and precision guidance. Thus, allowing people to burrow through underground areas that were once considered impenetrable. Bottom line, these advancements in materials, analytical tools, and technologies have enabled tunnel design for unfavorable conditions.[27]

Yet, in spite of the remarkable accomplishments from tunneling developments, it does deliver some risks. Operational risks to create these paths can be from people, systems, and external sources. For example, the people who operate these machines need to be cognizant and skilled to operate the behemoth-sized excavators. Operational mishaps while using these machines can be quite costly to the machines if damaged, and dangerous or deadly due from concerns of collapse. Also, the various materials in the ground can create adverse digging scenarios, therefore disrupting the process. In addition, there can be issues that the TBMs that may be faulty. Notably, these concerns are quite relevant with Seattle's own venture to create a tunnel. The city's TBM, or "Bertha" as it is known, sat inactive for two years until December 2015, as the machine underwent repairs after it unexpectedly struck metal piping near the beginning of the excavation.[28] The setback was costly, in terms of money and time.

Not at the size of public roadways, private roads are another element within the U.S.'s immense surface transportation infrastructure. Where the private sector takes a stake at the nation's roadways, the public sector can step aside under certain circumstances.[29] One way that private roads can take the place of public ones is when they have established that they are a reasonable advantage against government agencies.[30] Another way is that private roads must be defined well, with unambiguous criteria for determining failure and success. Thirdly, the performance of private contractors must be grounded by constant competition, so that multiple contractors can bid to help control costs and that substandard performers can be promptly. Lastly, private road development is optimal when there is accountability of the government officials who make the decision to privatize.[31]

Therefore, while those conditions are satisfied and development of these roads is practical, these benchmarks are also applicable to the privatization of bridges and tunnels. However, there are some identified risk concerns from privatization of these surface transportation realms. One issue is that – even though privatization may propose relief transpiration budget troubles in the short-term – the public will not receive the entire benefit for toll revenues in the future. The reasoning for this is that private investors will payoff their deals early, thus not provide states the estimated revenues that were calculated in the initial deals. Secondly, the public loses jurisdiction on transportation policy, thus can lead to extra cost where the private operators can request compensation for dealing with transportation issues. Finally, there is no ensuring from public officials that private contracts will be reasonable and effective.[32]

A multitude of risks can identified as one looks at Washington State's HIVA which can also be applied to many other roads, highway, bridges, and tunnels throughout the U.S.[33] Near the upper elevations or during the winter seasons, natural hazards can adversely affect these surface transportation elements (roadways, bridges, and tunnels) by avalanches, landslides, and volcanic eruptions. A mudslide – similar or worse to the one in Oso, Washington in 2014 – can cause tremendous damage to those elements as well as loss of life. Earthquakes, floods, and tsunamis can severely damage or completely destroy these transportation elements, or inundate them with water to damage them or make access to these roads impossible.

Technological hazards, identified in the same HIVA above, can adversely affect roads, bridges, and tunnels, as well. Chemical, hazardous material, radiologic, dam failure, exploding pipeline, urban fire, and local hazard events can affect transportation surfaces by damaging their strength or structural integrity, or making them inaccessible. Civil disturbances, such as criminal activities, or terrorism/cyber-terrorism can wreak havoc on these transportation elements causing massive disruption, damage, injury, or loss of life. Lastly, transportation itself can be seen as a risk because faulty or damaged roads, highways, bridges, or tunnels can create massive financial losses to vehicles, injuries, or deaths.

In order to address the incredibly-steep and uphill trek to pay for transportation surface needs, those within the U.S. may need to dig deep within their own pockets in order to finance that shared – and necessary – component of U.S. infrastructure. As mentioned earlier, the GAO determined that the nation has failed to find common ground about how to pay for required repairs and maintenance. The Highway Trust Fund is eroding and does not appear to be gaining any financial support. This is stacked on top of the current trend of drivers who want more efficiently running vehicles that use less fuel. Without more money coming in via fuel or trucking-affiliated taxes, that single trust fund is merely an empty tank that is growing immensely. It appears that the country cannot continue to substitute already-committed federal revenue, nor use clever financial methods or loan programs. Yet, money still needs to come in to pay for it, somehow.

It has been stated by many, that Congress needs to step up and push for higher taxes, and agree on long-term plan for funding surface transportation work. However, this may be political suicide. Nevertheless, it seems that they will need to make that decision in order to get money for the needed repairs and maintenance. So, how can they do that?

In order for Congress to get a bill passed for more money to transportation surfaces, there needs to be grass roots efforts to rally support for higher taxes. This idea may sound incredibly unpalatable, but what other choice does the U.S. have? There needs to be a push for understanding that the roads are used by its citizens and must be maintained by them. Who else is going to pay for the huge bill? Privatization? The risks involved with having private operators can create setbacks towards surface transportation. Nonetheless, they can still be involved with the efforts, if the private operators and government can both perform their due diligence, so that there is a mutual agreement and neither side takes advantage of the other.

Furthermore, before Congress can get the support needed, they should consider reexamining their current programs in place. In addition, Congress should implement performance-based approaches to measure surface transportation program effectiveness. If Congress can get the support for higher taxes, they should continue with program reexamination and utilizing performance-based approaches. In addition, governments at all levels should strongly consider the "fix it first" philosophy. The attention that politicians and the media can receive from new – and more attractive – surface projects generally mean that these cost for these are more than repairing or maintaining them.[34] They should look to fix these surface elements before deciding that it is better to build. If they do choose to build, Congress should also look into using effective technologies and materials to keep develop cost to a reasonable minimum.

To conclude, many roads, highways, bridges, and tunnels are in dire need of repair, replacement, or development. To help keep the U.S. optimally functional, Congress needs to find a long-term plan for investing in the U.S. surface transportation system. Clever financing, loans, and bipartisan squabbling will not help to solve the problem. The U.S. Chamber of Commerce may have said it best that "It's time to stop thinking about infrastructure as a problem, but as an opportunity for bipartisan agreement to invest wisely and carefully in our most critical needs, while eliminating wasteful spending." [35] What is more, and aside from loss of property, at what human cost is this going to have, if we do not address this issue? How much loss of reputation, and how much injury or loss of life is it going to take before any action takes place? Thusly, Congress will need to raise taxes, but it must first rally support for that from its citizens, and create a well-developed and long-term plan. Thus, the people of the nation will need to swallow a huge and bitter pill to remedy ailments of a system that they so critically need.

[1] "Transportation Systems Sector". U.S. Department of Homeland Security. 2016. Accessed May 28, 2016. <www.dhs.gov>.

[2] Ibid.

[3] "Infrastructure." U.S. Chamber of Commerce. 2016. Accessed May 28, 2016. <www.uschamber.com>.

[4] Ibid.

[5] Ibid.

[6] "Funding the Nation's Surface Transportation System." U.S. Government Accountability Office. 2015. Accessed May 28, 2016 <www.gao.gov>.

[7] Ibid.

[8] Ibid.

[9] Ibid.

[10] "Roads: Investment and Funding." 2013 Report Card for America's Infrastructure: American Infrastructure Report Card - American Society of Civil Engineers. 2013. 2016. Accessed May 29, 2016 <www.infrastructurereportcard.org>.

[11] "Is U.S. Infrastructure Destined to Crumble?" U.S. News and World Report. 2016. Accessed May 29, 2016 <www.usnews.com>.

[12] Ibid.

[13] "Infrastructure Grades for 2013." 2013 Report Card for America's Infrastructure: American Infrastructure Report Card - American Society of Civil Engineers. 2013. 2016. Accessed May 29, 2016 <www.infrastructurereportcard.org>.

[14] "Roads." 2013 Report Card for America's Infrastructure: American Infrastructure Report Card - American Society of Civil Engineers. 2013. 2016. Accessed May 29, 2016 <www.infrastructurereportcard.org>.

[15] Ibid.

[16] Ibid.

[17] "Roads: Conditions & Capacity." 2013 Report Card for America's Infrastructure: American Infrastructure Report Card - American Society of Civil Engineers. 2013. 2016. Accessed May 29, 2016 <www.infrastructurereportcard.org>.

[18] Ibid.

[19] Ibid.

[20] Ibid.

[21] Renn, Aaron M. "Beyond Repair?" U.S. News and World Report. 2015. Accessed May 30, 2016 <www.usnews.com>.

[22] Ibid.

[23] Gerdeman, Dina. "A Road Map to Fix America's Transportation Infrastructure." Harvard Business School. 2015. Accessed May 31, 2016 <www.hbswk.hbs.edu>.

[24] "Bridges." 2013 Report Card for America's Infrastructure: American Infrastructure Report Card – American Society of Civil Engineers. 2013. 2016. Accessed May 31, 2016 <www.infrastructurereportcard.org >.

[25] Ibid.

[26] Michaels, Daniel. "The High-tech, Low-cost World of Tunnel Building." *MarketWatch*. 2016. Accessed May 31, 2016 <www.marketwatch.com>.

[27] Ibid.

[28] Ibid.

[29] Baxandall, Phineas. "Private Roads, Public Costs". *U.S. PIRG Education Fund*. 2009. 4. Accessed May 31, 2016 <www.uspirg.org>.

[30] Ibid.

[31] Ibid.

[32] Ibid.

[33] *Washington State Hazard Identification and Vulnerability Assessment*. State of Washington. April 2001. Accessed June 1, 2016 <www.okanogandem.org>.

[34] Jaffe, Eric. "America's Infrastructure Crisis Is Really a Maintenance Crisis". CityLab. Feb. 12, 2015. Accessed June 26, 2016 <www.citylab.com>.

[35] "Infrastructure." U.S. Chamber of Commerce.

Michael Callier

Can the U.S. Treasury Keep Your Money Safe?

Michael Callier
Publication Month: December 2015

Abstract: The U.S. Department of the Treasury (the "Treasury Department") is responsible for facilitating collaboration between public and private entities, in order to strengthen the security and resilience of the U.S. financial services sector (FSS), a designated critical infrastructure. The threat of cyber-attacks, amplified by the private sector's general resistance to regulated breach incident information sharing and lack of FSS third-party vendor cyber security controls, pose significant risks to FSS security and resilience. This paper analyzes the above risks and recommends appropriate risk management strategies for each.

Introduction

Critical infrastructure provides essential services, jobs, and resources that underpin life in the US. Without them, US society would arguably fall into chaos. On February 12, 2013, President Obama called for an updated national plan to enhance the security and resilience of critical infrastructure against both physical and cyber threats.[1]

In response, the Department of Homeland Security (DHS) developed the National Infrastructure Protection Plan (NIPP). NIPP's mission is to "strengthen the security and resilience of the U.S. critical infrastructure, by managing physical and cyber risks through the collaborative and integrated efforts of the critical infrastructure community."[2] Critical infrastructure community means Federal, State, regional, local, tribal, territorial, private sector, and other critical infrastructure partners and stakeholders.

NIPP identifies 16 sectors deemed critical to the U.S. infrastructure. Each critical sector has a Sector Specific Plan (SSP) and a Sector Specific Agency (SSA) responsible for implementing that SSP. The Treasury Department is the SSA for the Financial Services Sector (FSS) and is responsible for deploying the FSS SSP to ensure that NIPP's stated objectives are met in the FSS.

The Threat Environment

The risk of data breach poses a threat to all critical infrastructure sectors but the FSS in particular. Verizon's Data Breach Report (2015) indicates that only the IT sector experienced more data breach incidents than FSS – a less than comforting statistic considering FSS's dependency on IT.[3] In terms of likelihood, data breach has become less a question of "if" and more a matter of "when." Forty-three percent of U.S. organizations experienced a data breach in 2014, up 10 percent from 2013.[4] A 2014 Ponemon Institute study found the probability of an organization experiencing a material breach involving a minimum of 10,000 records to be more than 22 percent.[5] More than one billion total records were breached in 2014, an increase of 78 percent over 2013.[6]

The impact of data breach incidents is also significant. Ponemon found that the U.S. average cost of data breach in 2014 was $201 per record with U.S. average cost of data breach at $5.85 million and a 15 percent annual increase in average cost around the world.

Gemalto (2015) also found that, although 25 percent of breaches were the result of accidental loss, 55 percent percent of attacks came from malicious outsiders.[7] The Internet is a critical infrastructure for FSS and the FSS SSP indicates that the FSS's greatest vulnerabilities exist through its interdependence on telecommunications and IT.

Treasury Department Challenges

In light of the existing cyber threat and FSS's dependency on the Internet, the Treasury Department faces at least two significant challenges to achieving its objectives.

A. Resistance to Information Sharing

In December 2012, the Obama administration initiated the U.S. government information sharing strategy through the National Strategy for Information Sharing and Safeguarding.[8] The PPD-21, Executive Order 13636 and the NIPP all followed, promulgating public/private partnerships as an element of strengthening critical infrastructure resilience and security. The federal government subsequently developed three information sharing bills, which are currently circulating through Congress: the Cybersecurity Information Sharing Act (CISA), the

Protecting Cyber Networks Act (PNCA) and the National Cybersecurity Protection Advancement Act of 2015 (NCPAA). Collectively, these are the "Information Sharing Acts." In addition, both the Pentagon and DHS plan to open offices in Silicon Valley to further efforts at public/private partnership and information sharing.

According to Sorcher (2015), private industry remains wary of the government's efforts, particularly with regard to the Information Sharing Acts, due to their perceived unnecessary infringement on privacy rights.[9] According to a joint letter written by prominent security industry professionals, the threat data that security specialists use to resolve cyber incidents is far more narrow than the personal identifiable information that the bills targets as breach incident data.[10] In addition, commercial enterprises prefer to avoid disclosing data breaches for fear of litigation and loss of consumer confidence. In fact, banks are not required to report breach incidents unless the bank concludes that the breach resulted in financial loss to customers.

B. Third-Party Vendor Vulnerabilities

In May 2014, the New York State Department of Financial Services (NYSDFS) published a report highlighting the continuing challenge facing the FSS due to its dependency on third-party service providers for critical banking functions.[11] According to the report, existing third-party cyber security controls are inadequate. Fewer than half of the organizations surveyed conduct onsite due diligence of vendors: only 46 percent required initial onsite due diligence of potential vendors and only 35 percent required periodic onsite due diligence of even high-risk vendors. The report also found that, although all surveyed institutions had written vendor management policies, the policies varied greatly. For example, 79 percent of respondents required that vendors maintain information security requirements but only 36 percent of respondents extended that requirement to subcontractors. In addition, 21 percent did not reserve the right to audit their vendors, and 44 percent did not require vendors to warrant the integrity of their data or products. Further, 30 percent of surveyed institutions did not require vendor notification in the event of a data breach. Only 38 percent of respondents used encryption for data "at rest" and 30 percent did not use multifactor authentication for at least some vendors to access sensitive information. Only 63 percent of respondents carried cyber insurance, and only 47 percent of those policies explicitly cover vendor data breach incidents. Finally, only half of institutions had vendor contracts that included indemnification clauses.

Qualitative Risk Assessment and Risk Management Strategy

A1: Resistance to Information Sharing

The risk level for this threat is medium because, if the risk happens, the Treasury Department can still help to strengthen the security and resilience of the FSS infrastructure through existing channels like FBIIC and FSSCC,[5] although its public/private collaboration and integration would be less effective. Since the Edward Snowden event, the cyber security private community has distanced itself from Washington. So long as the Information Sharing Acts reach for private information beyond that necessary to address data breach incidents, the distrust is likely to continue.

A2: Recommended Risk Strategy:

Tolerate/Transfer. The Treasury Department does not have authority to compel information sharing in its role as FSS SSA. Therefore, it can only continue to tolerate lack of information sharing with the private sector and continue its efforts through the FBIIC/FSSCC partnership until Congress passes some form of the Information Sharing Acts and state regulators, like the NYFDSF, enact disclosure requirements that the Treasury Department can rely on to compel desired information sharing.

---

[5] FBIIC stands for the Financial Banking Information Infrastructure Committee. FBIIC is comprised of 17 financial sector regulatory agencies and is responsible for encouraging coordination and communication between financial regulators, promoting public-private partnerships, and enhancing overall FSS resilience. FSSCC stands for the Financial Services Coordinating Council for Infrastructure Protection and Homeland Security. FSSCC is comprised of FSS private entities and helps to identify the need for sector protective programs and resilience strategies. The FSSCC collaborates with the FBIIC to support sector resilience efforts and also deploys independent efforts when its members identify industry security needs.

B1: Third-Party Vendor Vulnerabilities

The risk level for this threat is high because of the high likelihood of breach (indicated above) and, if it happens, the impact will be to weaken security and resilience in the FSS, including consumer confidence, as did the JP Morgan breach. Still further, it is not just the cost of breach remediation that threatens FSS security and resilience but also consumer lawsuits (including class actions) and commercial disputes between companies and their third-party vendors. Target has already incurred breach costs of $162 million (a total of $252 million with insurance payout offset of $90 million) and paid $19 million in settlement funds to MasterCard. [12] Any additional litigation damages will only add to Target's already sizeable breach costs, not to mention reputational damage.[13] Financial institutions face the same threat for breach incidents caused by their third-party vendors and, conversely, harm that they may cause to their third-party vendors.

B2: Recommended Risk Strategy: Treat.

The Treasury Department should leverage FBIIC to encourage state agencies, like NYSDFS, to enact regulatory standards that require constituent FSS entities to: (1) conduct onsite due diligence for all potential third-party vendors and periodic onsite due diligence for third-party vendors (or at least for high-risk vendors); (2) require both vendors and vendor subcontractors to maintain at least NIST Framework Implementation Tier 3; (3) execute written agreements with all relevant third-party vendors and ensure that such agreements reserve the right to audit vendors, require vendors to warrant the integrity of their data or products and include indemnity provisions in favor of the bank; (4) use encryption for all data, including data at rest, and require third-party vendors to do the same; (5) require that vendors use multifactor identification protocols to access bank network and information; and (6) require banks to carry cyber insurance that explicitly covers vendor data breach incidents.

---

[1] "Presidential Policy Directive -- Critical Infrastructure Security and Resilience (PPD-21)." The White House. 12 Feb. 2013. Accessed Jun. 2015 <www.whitehouse.gov>.

Executive Order (EO) 13636 Improving Critical Infrastructure Cybersecurity. U.S. Department of Homeland Security. Mar. 2013. Accessed Jun. 2015 <www.dhs.gov>.

The Comprehensive National Cybersecurity Initiative. The White House. Mar. 2010. Accessed Jun. 2015 <www.whitehouse.gov>.

[2] *NIPP 2013: Partnering for Critical Infrastructure Security and Resilience*. U.S. Department of Homeland Security. Jan. 2014. Accessed Jun. 2015 <www.dhs.gov>.

[3] *2015 Data Breach Investigation Report*. Verizon Enterprise Solutions. May 2015. Accessed Jun. 2015 <www.verizonenterprise.com>.

[4] Weise, Elizabeth. "43 percet of Companies Had a Data Breach in the Past Year." USA Today. 24 Sep. 2014. Accessed Jun. 2015 <www.usatoday.com>.

[5] *2014 Cost of Data Breach Study: Global Analysis*. Ponemon Institute LLC. May 2014. Accessed Jun. 2015 <www.ibm.com>.

[6] Warren, Zach. "Gemalto Reports That More Than One Billion Total Records Were Breached." *Inside Counsel*. 17 Feb. 2015. Accessed Jun. 2015 <www.insidecounsel.com>.

[7] Ibid.

[8] *National Strategy for Information Sharing and Safeguarding*. The White House. Dec. 2012. Accessed Jun. 2015 <www.whitehouse.gov>.

[9] Sorcher, Sara. "At Cybersecurity Gathering, the White House Steps up Charm Offensive." *The Christian Science Monitor*. 24 Apr. 2015. Accessed Jun. 2015 <www.csmonitor.com>.

[10] Granick, Jennifer. "Technologists Oppose CISA/Information Sharing Bills." The Center for Internet and Society, Stanford Law School. 16 Apr. 2015. Accessed Jun. 2015 <www.cyberlaw.standford.edu>.

[11] *Update on Cyber Security in the Banking Sector: Third Party Service Providers*. Department of Financial Services, New York State. Apr. 2015. Accessed Jun. 2015 <www.dfs.ny.gov>.

[12] Hill, Mitzi L. "Companies Target Each Other In Data Breach Disputes." *Business Insurance*. 26 Apr. 2015. Accessed Jun. 2015 <www.businessinsurance.com>.

[13] Lunden, Ingrid, "Target Says Credit Card Data Breach Cost It $162M In 2013-14" *TechCrunch*. 25 Feb. 2015. Accessed Jun. 2015 <www.techcrunch.com>.

Chapter III
Impact of the Digital Age

The Big Bad NSA

A Risk-Based Analysis of Domestic Spying Practices

Jared Williams

Publication Month: April 2016

Abstract: This paper discusses the major risks around government domestic surveillance programs, particularly the U.S. National Security Agency (NSA). While domestic surveillance is not a new practice by governments, technological innovations have changed the game. The paper discusses the issues, both from the perspective of the risks to governments and the risks to citizens under domestic surveillance.

Part I: The State of Things and Significance

Though we often imagine domestic spying to be a new concept, governments have been keeping tabs on their people forever. In the time of Caesar, politicians had spies to keep note of rivals, and indeed Caesar himself had a network to watch for possible threats in the domestic realm.[1] As a more recent example, many of us know of the Watergate scandal, in which the Nixon administration was found to have bugged, watched and kept record of the private conversations and actions of rivals and those they found suspicious.[2] This trend of governmental leaders spying on their people has only worsened with time and the advancement of technology. With each advancement in communication technology, it becomes easier for governments to watch larger numbers of the populace, more often and with greater efficacy. With smart phones, social networks, cameras and national paranoia a government may watch every step you take. Knowing this, we can analyze the major risks and failures in domestic spying, in order to develop a strategy to treat and terminate the problems they create. By dissecting the National Security Agency (NSA) and other current governmental spying actions both within and outside the U.S., I hope to highlight the risks and errors of domestic surveillance. These issues will be examined on both the side of risk to the governments in question and the risk to citizens within and affected by these nations.

We know that a government spying on its citizens is not a new concept, nor is it exclusively an American issue. From Caesar in ancient Rome, to the Catholic Church through the fourteenth century,[3] to the United Kingdom's Government Communications Headquarters (GCHQ) today, domestic surveillance has been a standing practice for centuries. In its earlier forms, this spying was meant to either give political candidates and leaders the upper hand over their competition, or to protect them against plots against their wellbeing. In the U.S., domestic spying has been used as far back as 1861 when Pinkerton's National Detective Agency unearthed a plot against the life of Abraham Lincoln, which was then prevented.[4] By 1919, the U.S. had its first federal intelligence agency that worked during peacetime, known as the Cipher Bureau. Before this, federally sanctioned spying was a matter of war. Though those in power may have had their own spy networks (generally focused internally, on rivals), until 1919 there had never been an American peacetime spy agency. At this time the surveillance focus was on political action in other countries.[5] Not until the 1960's did domestic surveillance become a commonality. From the early 60's to today, the UK government has been building a Closed Circuit Television Network (CCTV) that watches the actions of those within cities – primarily London - to ensure safety.[6] The government-owned CCTV system in the UK marks the first large-scale domestic surveillance system, and it has been questioned and criticized by privacy advocates since its inception. But why does it matter?

From the standpoint of a government, domestic spying has great significance. Through watching people within their borders, a government can theoretically profile dangerous inhabitants and stockpile information on actions, conversations, and other communications between people. This information may help identify trends or outliers in actions that can help lead a government to preventing crises. The NSA has been known to do this with conversations and specific key words, watching the use of words over time and deducing potential threats based on this data.[7] Meanwhile European CCTV systems allow for real-time tracking of crimes - seeing everything at once means the government can know what is going on in any given moment. Ultimately, from a government's perspective, domestic spying provides a feeling of greater security.

At the same time, however, this gathered information comes with great risk. Most openly, there is huge reputational risk for the government and the agency in charge of surveillance. For them the risk is two sided; in the event that a crisis occurs, a government will be asked "why did you let this happen" and they fear losing the confidence of the people in their ability to provide security. At the same time, while a government agency works to give this security, they may take too many liberties. In this case they again see reputational risk, if the people learn of the overstepping organization they are likely to lose trust in the governments ability to provide an acceptably free environment. With the great reputational risk a government also takes on significant internal risk. The risk internally manifests in two main forms, people and process. People are a risk to the government because people are unpredictable, and within spying agencies the people are also highly skilled. All too often we ignore the human element within agencies as a risk,[8] but in cases such as these where the people are highly skilled and poorly regulated they have a large chance to create crisis. This means that when a person dislikes what the organization is doing, or decides to act maliciously, they have the skills to steal information or out the organization, as we saw with Edward Snowden. The processes are a risk to the government on a number of levels. Firstly the vast majority of spying occurs on the internet where there are dangerous actors that would like nothing more than to break into the agencies systems and tear everything down, or worse yet, steal information. This is the second danger, an agency that keeps watch of so many people has an immense amount of data, and this data is a huge target for both other nations, and individual hackers. In fact, the NSA created a map[i] that showed, over a five year period, over six hundred successful attacks on corporate, private and government systems.[9] A further risk in process, is the vetting process for agents within government surveillance organizations. It is extremely hard to ensure your employees are reliable and trust worthy, an agency must know everything about a person and measure risk on many scales. However, we saw within the American government, after Snowden, that vetting processes are far from water tight and tended to favor time and odds over data, leading the

---

[i] This is an NSA file explaining some of their visualization methods and how words are tracked.

government to sue the external organization responsible for background checking their candidates.[10] As for the significance to persons within such governments, the risks and benefits are quite similar. In terms of benefit, the obvious gain is security, as this is what the government is working to provide. However, through these security gains the citizens are losing privacy, and without the work of an inside man such as Snowden, may never know to what extent there security is lost. Further, when unacceptable are found out, the citizens are likely to feel less secure, and thus distrust their government. However, this distrust of government is not the only issue with exposure of government surveillance. In order to get a better idea of the fallout of exposure, let us compare the NSA debacle with the state of CCTV.

When Snowden released information on the NSA and its practices public opinion changed quickly, and international conversation began to focus on privacy. It became clear that the government had taken on massive surveillance projects, and was overstepping the bounds of what was acceptable, through examining phone metadata, internet usage and many other private data. Knowing this, the NSA took a large hit in reputation and the government was forced to respond. At the same time, this opened up a global conversation and inspection of surveillance in many other nations. Recently, it has been in the news that Australia's surveillance has begun to overstep bounds in metadata collection.[11] This story comes based on statements and data from Snowden, and has created a conversation about Australia across the western world. Clearly, the effect of the NSA exposure was not a confined matter, and has spread across nations. I believe this effect is only seen due to the fact that the NSA chose secrecy in their invasion of privacy. At the same time, CCTV has been gradually increasing its coverage and people have been raising questions about invasion of privacy. However, this has led to a much smaller outcry, and little international coverage. This I believe is due to the fact that the governments using CCTV, has been surprisingly open with the use and rules of the network. This may be that people have been slowly losing their privacy and simply grew accustomed to it, but it is clear that government transparency on the matter has ensured little fallout.

Part II: Summary, Solutions and Suggestions

Until recently, technology has only allowed for small scale surveillance. A government wishing to spy domestically needed a specific target with a specific danger in mind. That is to say, if Caesar wanted to protect against being murdered, he would have to hire a spy to watch the politicians he feared would overthrow him. Now, with technology like CCTV and smart phones, the game has changed. We now have the ability to spy on a vast group for a wide variety of fears. That is to say, the NSA may collect millions of people's cellphone data and check it all for everything from the word "bomb" to conversation about attacks. But why does this surveillance lead to lost privacy? Where does it break down? Before a nation begins domestic surveillance, there will be a reason, something both the government and the people fear. This fear may be violence, treason, or terrorism. Once a nation fears something, the people will look to the government for security. In response, we have seen that the government will likely give an agency, such as the NSA, an excess of power. I do not believe that, at least in the case of the NSA, this is done in an attempt to harm the people, though the loss of privacy has shown to be a direct byproduct. When an agency like this is handed too much power, and there is a poor oversight and regulation system in there processes, there is bound to be an internal failure. Be it an employee leaking information, like Snowden, or some other failure, when masses of information and poor process are involved something will eventually give. Once this happens, there is a public unrest that leads to governmental distrust and a feeling of security lost. Still, this does not have to be the case.

Disaster in domestic spying need not always follow this model. Recently, in response to the Snowden leaks and the following public response, the U.S. government has acted to reform their system. With a re-examination of the background check process, and punishment of the parties responsible[12] we can hope that new employees responsible for surveillance will be reliable and trustworthy. At the same time, the U.S has chosen to limit the expansion of the NSA, thus ensuring that increased domestic surveillance cannot occur. Not only will this help prevent further failures due to unmanageable amounts of information, but will allow for easier regulation and oversight of the organization.

With this, the government has chosen to create greater oversight systems, to ensure that everything occurring within domestic spying agencies is within the confines of the law. Finally, the American government has acted to roll back and remove programs that were unacceptable and unlawful, with policy to make court orders necessary in order to retrieve private metadata.[13] This focus on a warrant based system means that when an agency sees a place where invasion of privacy may have a genuine value, they must first prove that there is valid reasoning. This ensures that all surveillance done is clear and the reputation of the agency is no longer based on secrets that may be lost but rather on a system of checks and balances. These actions have great potential to prevent further loss of privacy and represent steps all governments working toward a sustainable and acceptable domestic surveillance policy should consider. Alongside this, the American people have taken steps to ensure their own security. In general, conversation has erupted nationwide. With people questioning in place policy and voicing what they desire on the fronts of security and privacy, the government has been given a clear indication of what must be done. This is perhaps one of the most important results of the American domestic surveillance issue. From the massive surprise came a massive voice, and the people were able to force change. This is not the case in Europe, where surveillance has been a slow burn, and in kind the conversation about privacy has been far from loud. All together, the changes made in the U.S. policy, are a significant step in the right direction, but they have not created a foolproof system, and may still allow for continued breakdown.

In order to prevent failure and overstepping of domestic surveillance systems around the world, governments should prevent the over-expansion of spying agencies, introduce significant oversight, limit agency power, remove unlawful programs, and introduce warrant dependent systems. Additionally, they should also act in a number of other ways as well. First and foremost, a government spying agency should build, or in the case of the NSA rebuild, a culture against the use of widespread domestic spying. It should not be the default of the organization to surveil people within their borders. This means an agency should not only prevent mass surveillance whenever possible, but also work to increase the privacy of citizens. Prior to the events of

9/11 the NSA had worked to ensure widespread domestic spying did not occur, in fact, before these events, policy was passed on multiple occasions to prevent domestic spying.[14] With this, when a government finds a true need for domestic spying, the spying should be specific and targeted. Surveillance should not be of a large group or population. In order to spy domestically a government agency should have evidence against a specific person or cell and should act only on these persons. At the same time, the agency should have a specified surveillance plan built for these targets, ensuring that any spying done is efficient and within the confines of both the law and the power of the agency.

Furthermore, agencies should significantly reform vetting processes for new agents. It should never be the case that money or time out prioritizes real data and trustworthiness when placing highly skilled people in charge of the privacy and security of citizens. Agencies should not only carry out background checks with one party, but should indeed receive checks from multiple reliable agencies. These agencies should also have some form of government oversight to ensure the checking process is proper. This change in vetting will ensure that hired agents are reliable and will prevent situations where the failure is with internal employees. With these reforms to vetting, it should also be that contractors are avoided whenever possible. Not only is it much harder for contractors to be vetted, but if a contractor finds a failure somewhere within the agency, it is much harder for them to get this fixed or to whistleblow. Knowing this, there should also be a much more robust whistleblower policy within the government. As was seen in the wake of Snowden, the government saw whistleblowers as "villains who compromised what the government classifies as some of its most secret, crucial and successful initiatives."[15] It was seen that when employees tried to follow the proper channels to prevent unlawful spying, they were shut down. The government should change this culture, and ensure that when a whistleblower surfaces, they are given routes to inform those in power of what they have found. This needs to be a matter handled outside the surveillance agency, by a government bureau or agency that has reliance or relation with it. This will help ensure that matters are looked at with an unbiased eye and may be handled accordingly. With all of these recommendations taken into account, a government can be far more confident in the fact that its handling of domestic spying will be lawful, watched, safe internally and externally, and when something does go wrong, the proper process will be in place to bring the failure to light.

Understanding the history, reasoning, and process of domestic surveillance is the key to creating a system in which a government can assure security for their citizens while also allowing privacy to remain in society. From the age of Caesar domestic surveillance has existed and evolved with the world and what technology allowed; recently this evolution led to failure in systems and distrust of government in citizens. With agencies given excessive power with little oversight, and spying practices being hidden from citizens, it became a guarantee that the system would eventually fail on some level. This, however, need not remain the case; through examination of major risks, and treatment or termination thereof, national spying agencies can create a sustainable system. Through a culture against invading privacy and a tightening of regulation and process within organizations, crisis within and caused by domestic spying agencies will be removed. That is not to say that the suggestions presented in this paper will ensure a secure and private society forever. Indeed, as this issue continues to develop, and as our system becomes more adequate, new risks will arise that must be met with equal thought. Still, by examining domestic spying through the eyes of risk and on both the side of security and privacy, we will be capable of working toward a more perfect system. The process will take time; however, through determination on both the side of the people and that of the government we can create strong regulation and build a secure, private society.

---

1 Zucher, Anthony. "Roman Empire to the NSA: A World History of Government Spying." BBC News. 1 Nov. 2013. Accessed Dec. 2015 <www.bbc.com>.

2 Woodward, Bob. "FBI Finds Nixon Aides Sabotaged Democrats." The Washington Post. 10 Oct. 1972. Accessed Nov. 2015 <www.washingtonpost.com>.

[3] Zucher.

4 Prince, Sam. "A History of Domestic Espionage in the United States." Heavy.com. 10 June 2013. Accessed Nov. 2015 <www.heavy.com>.

5 "The Evolution of the U.S. Intelligence Community-An Historical Overview." Federation of American Scientists. 23 Feb. 1996. Accessed Dec. 2015 <www.fas.org>.

6 "The History Of CCTV In The UK by Camtrak Ltd." SRMTi. 12 Apr. 2012. Accessed Nov. 2015 <www.srmti.com>.

7 "An Information Visualization Primer and Field Trip." The Next Wave: Vol. 17 No. 2 2008. The National Security Agency. Accessed Nov. 2015 <www.nsa.gov>.

8 Fischhoff, Baruch, and John David Kadvany. Risk a Very Short Introduction. Oxford: OUP Oxford, 2011.

9 Windrem, Robert. "Exclusive: Secret NSA Map Shows China Cyber Attacks on U.S. Targets." NBC News.30 July 2015. Accessed Dec. 2015 <www.nbcnews.com>.

10 Schneider, Joe. "Security Firm Sued by U.S. Over Bad Background Checks." Bloomberg. 24 Jan. 2014. Accessed Dec. 2015 <www.bloomberg.com>.

11 Milman, Oliver. "Edward Snowden Says Australia's New Data Retention Laws Are 'Dangerous'" The Guardian. 8 May 2015. Accessed Dec. 2015 <www.theguardian.com>.

12 Schneider.

13 Strohm, Chris. Talev, Margaret. "Obama Unveiling NSA Changes in Response to Snowden Leaks." *Bloomberg*, 16 Jan. 2014. Accessed Dec. 2015 <www.bloomberg.com>.

14 "Timeline of NSA Domestic Spying." Electronic Frontier Foundation. 30 Nov. 2012. Accesssed Dec. 2015. <www.eff.org>.

15 Peter, Eisler. Page, Susan. "3 NSA Veterans Speak out on Whistle-blower: We Told You so." *USA Today*. 16 June 2013. Accessed Dec. 2015 <www.usatoday.com>.

Artificial Intelligence as a Weapon

Jorge Borunda

Publication Month: October 2015

Abstract: This paper examines some of the concerns that are on the horizon around the development, implementation, and regulation of autonomous weapon systems. The U.S. Infrastructure Plan employs the Defense Industrial Base Plan, and while the Plan serves as a good resource to address risk and mitigate potential threats, but there is something the DIB does not cover, particularly the development of new technologies as weapons, such as artificial intelligence. When it comes to military artificial intelligence, Lethal Autonomous Weapons Systems (LAWS) select and engage targets without human intervention; they become lethal when those targets include humans. The International Committee of the Red Cross (ICRC) has raised concern on lethal autonomous weapon systems since 2011, arguing that there are no regulations to assess potential risks around how these new technologies will be used, as well as a lack of standards and methodologies.

Every day, the world is in a constant and imminent threat of war, whether it is a nuclear war, a terrorist attack, a political coup, or simply a social uprising due to differences of opinions. Each country, within their laws and regulations, can defend their people from internal and external attacks. A key component for a defense plan is complex but efficient risk assessing and resiliency programs that will allow countries' armed forces to analyze and tolerate possible war or attack threats. To gain an edge in terms of war and attacks, technology has played such an important role – but it can also be considered as a wild card. Armed forces around the world are developing very sophisticated military technology and for the past few years, artificial intelligence has been the front-runner as the new modern warfare technology.

The U.S. Infrastructure Plan employs the Defense Industrial Base Plan (DIB), a unique plan that sets the U.S. apart from other countries in terms of developing a weapon system. The U.S. Department of Defense (DoD) uses the DIB as medium for its Risk Assessment Program, which it is very comprehensive yet it does not have regulatory requirements for companies to implement the risk assessment program into their operations. This seems very inconsistent because as the U.S. is trying to assess possible risks and threats, the DoD is ignoring potential threats from within. The start of security and defense starts internally, then it can be rolled out to assess and mitigate outside threats.

Sector-specific agencies are required to focus on four important consequences: public health & safety, economic, psychological, and the impact on mission assurance. As stated in the DIB, "the last category is most relevant for the DIB as it relates to the impact on DoD's ability to execute its roles, responsibilities, and mission under the Constitution and as assigned in statute and Executive Orders, policy, and national and defense strategies."[1] However, the DIB or DoD should not solely focus on the impact on mission assurance, since these four consequences are interrelated and one leads to another. At the very least, they can affect each other at any given time, and the DoD should not shy away from the other three consequences. Therefore, they should adapt the DIB to better address these consequences as a whole. Diving deeper into how the DIB assesses consequences, vulnerabilities and risks, the DIB focuses on implementing its plan on a business, economic and technology level. It appears to be a well thought out process, but war and defense against possible threats are very sensitive subject matters, and the DIB needs to take into consideration the inclusion of ethical matters into its plan. Making or adding ethical changes to a plan, specifically to a government protection plan could become a very elaborate and difficult process but in order to achieve such result, Moeller says "as part of building an effective ethical culture in an enterprise, the 'tone of the top' messages of senior executives to others in the enterprise are very important."[2] Unfortunately, with the constant battles in the White House, the finger pointing among this country's representatives and the frizz between Republicans and Democrats, an ethical shift at this level could be very lengthy and a messy one.

Aside from government's structure and organization - and the political battles - the DIB does an amazing job at outlining its levels of defense. The DIB states five levels of defense starting with the First Level of Protection where asset owners are responsible for the risk. The Second Level is entitled to the local civilian law enforcement authorities, and as risk escalates, the Third Level is managed by the State and Federal law enforcement authorities. The Fourth Level is handle by the State Governor, and the final Fifth Level of protection escalates to the President. Although these are not similar to what Girling suggests with the first line of defense being the business line where "business owns operational risk should be managing it as it arises,"[3] the DIB expanded Girling's first line of defense into a more structural approach to have a better and more efficient chain of command system. Girling's second line of defense is at the corporate level, for the DIB case, its Second Level of defense depends on its partnerships with DoD contractors. The Third Level of defense, an internal audit, the DIB employs a Sector Performance Measurement System in the form of scorecards that allow for review of sector performance.

Overall, the DIB - like the rest of the Department of Homeland Security - is a good resource to address risk and mitigate potential threats, but there is something the DIB does not cover. This is the creation or development of new technologies, in terms of weapons. Every country wants to have a competitive advantage, and wants to get ahead to be well prepared when it comes to protecting its people from a potential attack, whether it is internally or from a foreign country. Currently, the debate of the use of nuclear power for military purposes from North Korea and Iran has been a very heated topic. The United Nations and countries around the world have voiced concerns about the potential next "Third World War," whether in the form of a nuclear war or just the fight against extremists such as the ISIL (Islamic State in Iraq and the Levant). But there is something that has not been talked about, because it is an emerging technology with implications that have not been thought out yet: the use of artificial intelligence to produce weapons and be fully autonomous weapons.

Now, the use of robots in military settings has been researched for quite awhile, as countries want to reduce soldier casualties. But with the newest advancements in technology, artificial intelligence can be a game changer for better or for worse. This is a very thin line between trying to prove what the advantage or disadvantages of using robots are; the problem is how the armed forces will deploy them. Firstly, it is important to clarify a term that has been problematic and misused.

When it comes to military artificial intelligence, "Lethal Autonomous Weapons Systems (LAWS) select and engage targets without human intervention; they become lethal when those targets include humans. LAWS might include, for example, armed quad-copters that can search for and eliminate enemy combatants in a city, but do not include cruise missiles or remotely piloted drones for which humans make all targeting decisions."[4] Remote-controlled systems such drones or guided missiles are not considered LAWS as humans operate them.

LAWS are what the world needs to pay attention to, because the current research has raised the following fundamental ethical and principle questions:

- Can the decision over death and life be left to a machine?
- Can fully autonomous weapons function in an ethically "correct" manner?
- Are machines capable of acting in accordance to international humanitarian law (IHL) or international human rights law (IHRL)?
- Are these weapon systems able to differentiate between combatants on the one side and defenseless and/or uninvolved persons (noncombatants)?
- Can such systems evaluate the proportionality of attacks?
- Who can be held accountable?[5]

But instead of answering each question, countries interested in implementing or developing LAWS into Defense plans should considered if they are acting in accordance with international humanitarian law. The International Committee of the Red Cross (ICRC) has raised concern on lethal autonomous weapon systems since 2011, arguing that there are no regulations to assess potential risks around how these new technologies will be used, as well as a lack of standards and methodologies. In 2014, the ICRC facilitated a discussion among 21 countries and only two - the U.S. and the United Kingdom - have implemented national policies on lethal autonomous weapon systems. The U.S. policy states "autonomous and semi-autonomous weapon systems shall be designed to allow commanders and operators to exercise appropriate levels of human judgment over the use of force,"[6] and the UK policy states that autonomous weapons will not be permitted and should be under human supervision. Even though these are only two countries, there is still agreement on how to deploy autonomous weapons. Yet, the ICRC does not have a clear definition for LAWS, so this author is assuming that the disagreement amongst other countries is due in part to the lack of clarification on terminology.

The ICRC has raised several talking points on which countries should think about when they implement autonomous weapon systems and the talking points are as follow:

- Civilian robotics and developments in autonomous systems
- Military robotics and drivers for development of autonomous weapon systems
- Autonomy in existing weapon systems
- Research and development of new autonomous weapon systems
- Military utility of autonomous weapon systems in armed conflict
- Current policy on autonomous weapon systems
- Autonomous weapon systems under international humanitarian law
- Accountability for use of autonomous weapon systems
- Ethical issues raised by autonomous weapon systems

These are great points to start a discussion but if the ICRC or any international governing body does not enforce any of them, then autonomous weapons systems will be developed without the accordance of IHL and these systems will become unlawful and illegal.

In conclusion, ethical problems can lead to endless discussions but they should not be left unattended. If ethical problems are being considered, the outcomes of discussions can be closer to resolving social problems. At this time, the ethical questions identified by the research community and the concerns of the ICRC are very valid. However, these kinds of weapon and defense systems are an extension of the armed forces and they should still funded, but they must monitored very closely to adhere to international humanitarian laws. The U.S., as a military power house and as one the leading researching countries, should lead the way for a more regulated implementation and development of programs of lethal autonomous weapons. While every country wants to earn the edge in terms of military power, this kind of technology can lead to another kind of war.

---

[1] *Defense Industrial Base Sector-Specific Plan: An Annex to the National Infrastructure Protection Plan.* Department of Homeland Security, U.S. Department of Defense. May 2010. Accessed 1 Jun. 2015 <www.dhs.gov>.

[2] Moeller, Robert R. *COSO Enterprise Risk Management: Establishing Effective Governance, Risk, and Compliance (CRC) Processes.* Hoboken, New Jersey: John Wiley & Sons. 2011.

[3] Girling, P. (2013). Operational Risk Management A complete Guide to a Successful Operational Risk Framework. Hoboken, New Jersey: Wiley & Sons.

[4] Russell, Stuart. "Ethics of Artificial Intelligence." *Nature.* 27 May 2015. Accessed Jun. 2015 <www.nature.com>.

[5] Acheson, Ray and Beatrice Fihn. *Fully Autonomous Weapons.* Jul. 2013. Accessed Jun. 2015 <www.reachingcriticalwill.org>.

[6] "Report of The ICRC Expert Meeting On 'Autonomous Weapon Systems: Technical, Military, Legal And Humanitarian Aspects.'" International Committee of the Red Cross. 9 May 2014. Accessed Jun. 2015 <www.icrc.org>.

Hypervigilance and the Digital Age

Matthew Welden

Publication Month: September 2016

Abstract: This paper discusses the development of a hypervigilant culture within the U.S., with attention-grabbing low-frequency incidents overshadowing the far deadlier but less sensational every day risks. While we now live in a modern world where people are living longer, free-er, and richer than ever before, more of us have become captives of fear. The author defines the condition of hypervigilance, illustrates the condition with historical examples, and then offers some solutions to the condition and ethical arguments for their consideration.

Introduction

In his 1933 inaugural address, U.S. president Franklin Roosevelt spoke the prescient words that forewarned of a coming century of hypervigilance when he declared that, "...the only thing we have to fear is fear itself—nameless, unreasoning, unjustified terror which paralyzes..." This "unreasoning" fear began with Emperor Hirohito, transitioned to the Third Reich, and continued on through the Soviet threat, China, Iran, and today manifests as a pantheon of boogeymen that threaten to destroy the collective 'us' at every turn. While there is a documented psychological need for allies and enemies,[1] there are also sound ethical and legal arguments against fear-mongering and stoking public unrest. In the 21st century, the western world is absent of clear and definable enemies, and entire industries have sprung to define the 'unseeable' threats to our modern way of life. Although the current leading fear is undeniably that of aggressive stateless bodies, or 'terrorists', the more amorphous threat driving citizens to hypervigilance is that of cybersecurity. The minority that Westin[2] terms privacy fundamentalists stoke the fear that technological advances will lead to a dystopian future and despotism.

Hypervigilance is often closely related to post-traumatic stress disorder (PTSD)[3] but is applicable to a host of psychological states. This paper examines the post-World War 2, post-911, and post-Snowden hypervigilance within the western world related to data terrorism, and the ethical problems of the industries reliant on the perseverance of the condition. First, we define the condition of hypervigilance, and then outlines differences between hypervigilance in the third world versus that of those that live within the safety of the first world economies. We will illustrate the condition with historical examples of anti-technology manias and the modern celebrity cases that fuel the condition today, and finally examine the role of the military-industrial complex and its impact on the public psyche. After defining these conditions through illustrations, we will explore the impacts upon citizens, and then the ethical conundrums facing organizations, industry, and government related to hypervigilance in the digital age. Finally, we will offer some solutions to the condition and ethical arguments for their consideration. This paper argues that the condition of hypervigilance is ethically untenable, and has yielded diminishing returns since before Roosevelt warned of the condition. In short, the paper tigers of fear are truly the greatest risk to society and the public health here at the threshold of the twenty-first century. We are, in Roosevelt's terms, captives of fear in a world where people are living longer, free-er, and richer than at any time in the history of man.

What is Hypervigilance?

The National Institute for Health (NIH) defines hypervigilance as, "a cognitive, physiological, and behavioral pattern in which an individual responds to ambiguous stimuli as if they were threatening."[4] The condition is closely linked with Post Traumatic Stress Disorder (PTSD), and manifests in a condition wherein the subject is hyper-alert to threats real or imagined. The NIH goes on to say that the condition leads to, "significant functional impairment." In war-torn countries, the rate of PTSD and hypervigilance is as much as 5 times higher than in the U.S.[56] In these countries, life expectancy is as much at 40 percent lower than in the U.S.,[7] and the odds of being killed by something other than your diet (read: violent) are as much as twenty-two times more likely.[8] In the Honduras, a man has approximately a one in six hundred chance of being murdered, and in Syria, a citizen's odds of dying unnaturally are as high as one in a hundred.[9] For these people hypervigilance is undoubtedly rooted in a fear of actual direct threats to their life. In the U.S. clinical PTSD and the related condition of hypervigilance affects approximately 7 percent of the population.[10] This is induced through trauma, either physical or mental.

Although traditionally assigned to survivors of trauma such as war and assault, a mild form of this serious condition is prevalent throughout much of western society and has been termed, "living under condition yellow"[11] in reference to the American security coding system promoted by the Department of Homeland Security (DHS). This mild form sells newspapers, props up industries, and can drive politician in to or out of office. The only party that does not prosper is the general citizenry. Hypervigilance is a mania. We are in what Castro and McQuinn[12] term the rising panic portion of the privacy panic cycle. Unfortunately, the cycle is quickly churning as new technologies emerge, and fear of mature technologies yield to new nascent fears. (Figure 1)

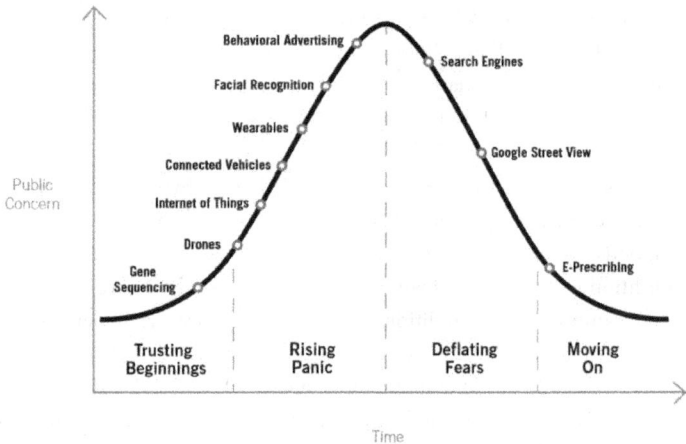

Figure 1: Technology on Castro and McQuinn's panic cycle[13]

Who or What do we Fear?

According to a 2015 study of fear in America, three of the top five fears for Americans are related to technology, and the other two are closely related to the technology fears.[14] Some 44.8 percent of Americans fear

Cyberterrorism, 44.6 percent fear corporate tracking of personal information, and 41.4 percent fear government tracking of person information. The top spot was held by the fear of corruption of government officials, which aligns with the fear of government tracking of personal information, and the fourth spot is held by general terrorism. People are less afraid of a violent terrorist attack than that of a cyber-attack. Seventh on the list is identity theft, with credit card fraud coming in 10th with 36.9 percent of Americans afraid of this eventuality. Let us take a quick look at the facts behind these fears that keep American's awake at night.

Cyberterrorism is defined by the Federal Bureau of Investigation (FBI) as "the premeditated, politically motivated attack against information, computer systems, computer programs, and data which result in violence against noncombatant targets by sub-national groups or clandestine agents."[15] The possibility of an attack against the U.S. information systems resulting in violence or harm is the second largest fear for Americans. Yet, there has yet to be a single documented incidence of a cyber-terrorism attack on the U.S.[16] Certainly, there have been documented cases of cyber-espionage, and outright cyber-theft, but there has not been a single case of an attack that meets the definition as defined by the FBI. Meanwhile, Americans continue to get in their cars every day – a place where the National Highway Traffic Safety Administration reports that over 30,000 Americans die every year[17]. We are afraid of an idea, while we buy our sixteen-year old children documented killing machines. Which is a greater threat to American lives?

The third greatest fear Americans currently live with is the fear of corporations tracking our every move and using our data for nefarious purposes. This is a fact-based fear. Corporations do in fact make every effort to collect data on customers and potential customers for profit and to improve their services. Data breaches of customer data have led to financial consequences for customers, but of course that is more in line with the seventh (identity theft) and 10th (credit card fraud) biggest fears for Americans. This fear is purely a fear of the loss of privacy. Similar fears have captured the public attention in history, when the portable camera was first introduced by Eastman Kodak a wave of fear crossed the country about the threat to privacy. In 1897, the Chicago Tribune warned readers of this "fearful craze," and the New York Times railed against, "the Kodak fiend," who would take photos our private moments.[18] In Castro and McQuinn's model, this fear falls into in the rising panic stage with little end in sight.

Finally, we land at the fifth greatest fear for Americans today, the fear of government tracking of personal information. As with corporate information collection, this action is well documented. Leaks by insiders and government disclosure confirm that our government is continuing the practice of collecting information on citizens. Government data collection is first documented as far back as 4000 BC.[19] The threat of harm due to this for everyday Americans is based upon the 'slippery slope' theory. In the slippery slope theory, "actions seem to lead inevitably from one action or result to another with unintended consequences."[20] For those afraid of government tracking, the act of tracking leads to some dystopian future where Americans are held hostage by the government via their own data. Of course, as was demonstrated during the "red-scare" of the 1950's, the government can just as easily fabricate information on Americans for this end. Although the practice of data collection is as old as civilization, this fear has peaked in the digital age and reached a fevered pitch with the release of National Security Agency (NSA) files by former analyst Edward Snowden.

Each of these fears is real, but upon examination pose only hypothetical risk to the lives and safety of most Americans. The biggest direct threats to American lives are heart disease (611,105 killed in 2014); cancer (584,881 killed in 2014); respiratory disease (149,205 killed in 2014); and accidents (130,557 killed in 2014).[21] In short, butter, asbestos, cigarettes, and slippery floors are what we should fear the most. Instead of being afraid of the wolf at the door, we overwhelmingly fear these technological paper tigers. In the following section, we will explore historical illustrations of the technology panics of the past.

Historical Precedent and the Panic Cycle

Although difficult to confirm, Plato is believed to have said, "writing is a step backwards for truth," and allegedly believed that the invention of writing would lead to a weakening of the mind and a step backwards for mankind.[22] Fortunately, someone wrote down his words and we have managed to not slide back into the muck from whence we came. Fear of new technologies has a long and colorful history. Some are simply amusing, while others led to manias that moved law itself.

In 1877, the *New York Times* attacked the new technology of the telephone as an "atrocious" and "nefarious instrument" and called for the "death of the inventors and manufacturers of the telephone." The newspaper went on to describe how no man or woman was safe to speak even near this invention for fear others would overhear their conversations. They warned residents that if the telephone wires were strung across the city, "there will be an immediate end of all privacy."[23] While early party lines did allow others to listen in on conversations of their neighbors, society managed to survive, and privacy did not vanish from the face of the earth. In fact, the telephone has allowed for far greater privacy than had existed before. Two people are able to speak to each other without fear of being seen together, or without leaving a written trace to be absently picked up by a spouse or an employer. Yet, the phone is still today at the center of the privacy debate and privacy fundamentalist use a host of tactics to hide their tracks on this device.

In 1888, (technologies were invented at a quick clip in the 19th century as well), George Eastman introduced his newest invention, the portable Kodak camera. The camera was portable unlike previous photography equipment, and allowed users to take "snapshots" or quick pictures of others without the need for them to hold a pose for 60 to 90 seconds as was previously necessary. The first camera came preloaded with film for 100 photos. The technology was relatively affordable, and was a popular product. Newspapers quickly proclaimed this device to be an assault on privacy and pressed for a "revolt against these photographic machines."[24] For a time these nefarious machines were even banned from the grounds of the Washington Monument by law.[25] Again, the world seemed to make it through this crisis, privacy was not erased from the planet, and ironically, the photographic camera and telephone have now been combined into a single device that is ubiquitous as shoes and more common than hats.

More recently, the introduction of the radio-frequency identification tag (RFID) at first seemed to be a welcome way to track inventory for retailers, but soon privacy advocates began assailing the passive trackers as a gateway to a dystopian future. In 2003, the privacy advocate group CASPIAN called it "the most invasive consumer technology ever," and called for manufacturers to provide "kill codes" so these tags could be disabled after purchasing a product.[26] Just over a decade later, few consumers even think about these inventory management tags, and have moved on to new and more exciting things to fear. In 2015, industry experts estimated that as many as 40 million Americans carry RFID on their person every day.[27] Unfortunately, for the alarmists at CASPIAN and other privacy groups, RFID tags have not yet succeeded in turning our world into a police state.

As demonstrated in these examples, fear of technology and its risk of destroying our very way of life are a common theme though history. Everyone from Plato to Time magazine have outlined the threats, and yet we have somehow survived over the millennia to create new fearsome technologies. In 2005, CNN released a report warning us "email hurts our IQ more than pot."[28] I am not sure if this is an endorsement of cannabis consumption or a crazy run at email. Fear mongering and driving our fellow man into a state of hypervigilance seems to be an ongoing phenomenon. In the next section, we will examine the cases that have recently seized the public attention and driven them to build their biggest fears of cyberterrorism, "big-brother" privacy invasions, and large corporations.

Celebrity Inciters

Great and irrational fears require demonstration of the aggressor. The current fear of how technology will or has stripped our privacy and threatens to enslave us in some dystopian gulag has many bandleaders, but three stand out as relevant to our conversation. A CIA analyst who made the public worry their naked photos were being ogled by analysts at the NSA; a supposed attack on a film studio by a country with limited internet access; and a fight between the FBI and a phone manufacturer over access to a mobile phone that had what one law enforcement official calls, "no information we don't already have."[29] These three celebrity cases have captured the public's imagination, and turned the small fringe of privacy fundamentalists into a growing group of fear-mongering talking heads on the nightly news.

In June of 2013, Edward Snowden - a technologist for the NSA - leaked thousands of classified documents to journalists outlining foreign and domestic electronic surveillance conducted by the U.S. government.[30] The 'revelation' that the government was collecting information on both its own citizens and foreign allies set off an explosion of paranoia amongst the American public. The sensationalism was enough to spur the production of two biopics, one produced by the prince of paranoid biopics, Oliver Stone. Seemingly capturing another great fear, Snowden revealed that the "spy agency sometimes shared sexually explicit photos they intercepted."[31] At the very heart of American privacy is the fear that someone will see us naked, and the evidence showed that the government was doing just that. This captures the American imagination much more that the abstract thought of the collecting of phonecall meta-data, or the British tapping into fiber-optic cables. Although the violations of domestic and international law raised by Snowden are serious, the fears of having a nude photo seen or illicit phone call overheard by some 25 year old analyst are what the average American most fears. Just like when journalists railed against the portable camera because people could supposedly take illicit photos of women in their swimsuits,[32] the media has pressed these worthless stories as the primary reason Americans should worry about their privacy. Meanwhile the world seems to be unchanged from three years ago. No black helicopters and detainment camps have yet sprung up in my neighborhood.

In November 2014 the sixth largest film studio in America, Sony Pictures, was reportedly hacked into by the isolated country of North Korea[33]. This was supposedly done in retaliation for the spoof comedy "The Interview" which portrays two bumbling operatives and their attempt to assassinate the supreme leader of North Korea. The story captured the imagination of the American public. Although in the end most sources debunked the idea that the hack was carried out by North Korea, the insinuation that America was somehow attacked by a country with fewer computers that an average U.S. university evoked the fear of cyberterrorism. In the end no theatres were bombed for screening "The Interview" (although those who paid $15 for a ticket may have considered it). The nameless terror that may very well have just been a misconceived publicity stunt was successful in seizing the American imagination, and even prompting the president to speak directly about the case.

Following a mass shooting in San Bernardino, California by a husband and wife duo, the FBI requested a court to compel Apple to unlock one of the suspect's work phone. If this couple had been Caucasian this may not have made a high-ratings news story, but the couple were both Muslim and racially Arab. The median portrayed the FBI as using terrorism as a door to forcing a technology firm into opening up the secrets encrypted into the phone. In truth, the phone was a work issued phone, and investigators already had all of the meta-data including to whom calls had been made, when they were made, and how long they lasted. Not surprisingly, the calls were all work related. The fight between the FBI and Apple, however, rages on with one side declaring that the safety of the American people is at stake, and the other side declaring that this is another government assault on privacy. Both sides beat their chests; Americans stand by transfixed; and the world continues to stand as the free-est it has ever been in the history of mankind. Surely, the government will be able to catch bad guys without access to their Snapchat accounts, and surely our very existence as a free world is not imminently threatened by hacking into a boring work phone. Perhaps they will find the last lunch order in the memory. The sensationalism of the event has captured the attention of politicians, technophiles, and average citizens across the world.

Admittedly, these cases have some interesting facets that will influence back room policy creation and may even spawn a subsection in future legislation. Yet, the point of this paper is to show that these threats are paper tigers and that although the sensation sells newspapers and increased link clicks, it unnecessarily flames the irrational fears of an already dopey public. Even if there was a NSA analyst assigned to listen to every phone call ever made in the U.S., it is highly unlikely we would stop dying from heart disease in droves, or demonstrating some of our other hard earned freedoms. Journalists and security 'experts' are not the only parties to blame in fanning these hysterias; we can also blame the government industry. The military-industrial complex seeking to grow budgets and politicians looking to drive voters to the polls are made up of people who do, after all, want to make a living.

Politics as an Industry

On the list of highest defense budgets, the U.S. spends more money on defense than the next 12 countries combined.[34] The U.S. spends an average of $596 billion per year on defense. An estimated $13.3 billion piece of this pie is dedicated to cybersecurity.[35] This is an industry. To increase this spending, the industry needs the public to have a healthy fear of the impeding threat to their lives. I mean, Honduras spends almost nothing on cybersecurity and people are murdered there all the time. Although that particular claim has not likely been made by an industry expert on CNN, these have: "we are at risk of a digital pearl harbor"[36]; "we are already engaged in a cyber-war"[37]; and "we will be facing an Armageddon-type cyber-attack...a cyber 9/11."[38] According to these individuals, whose jobs rely on the perceived ongoing threat to the American way, we face another world war, are already in this war, and are on the brink of an end-of-the-world event. Of course, they may be overstating the situation to illustrate their point, but not every American may get this subtlety.

In addition to those that rely on defense spending for their paychecks, there is also an industry of people who rely on scaring people out of their Barcaloungers. Politicians are famous for telling the public that the world stands on the edge of a new era or is at the verge of a new threat to their world. Even if we guessed at a fifty-fifty split, half the time they use the new threat to motivate the public to rouse themselves and head to the polls. It is unlikely that the candidate that tells voters, "Everything is fine. Tomorrow will be the same as yesterday," would motivate a single voter to complete a ballot. Instead, politicians are happy to debate wildly unlikely scenarios for our entertainment, like when Reagan scared us about the imminent threat of furloughed murderers in 1988.[39] If that got us to go vote, surely the threat of a cyber-Armageddon should have us running to the voting booth.

Each of these examples demonstrates that fanning the flames of mania serves to both entertain us, motivated us, and bilk us. In fact, we are always at the threshold of tomorrow. That is the function of the present; it is always in front of the future. We are always threatened with death. That is a function of being alive, and is why we consume poly-unsaturated-fats and lay in tanning beds. We are happy to be bilked out of our money or we would not pay 99 cents for an app that allows us to throw birds at pigs. The unfortunate part is that the public does not seem to see the humor in the 'threats' to America.

Hypothesis

The illustrations provided to this point have shown that the public seems to desire sensational distractions. Our hypothesis is that in a world of unprecedented peace, prosperity, and health, society has a need to create proxies for the natural drivers of survival. In the U.S., we currently enjoy an average lifespan 68 percent longer than we did in 1900[40] and 2.6 times longer than people did in the 1800's. According to the IRS, we are earning 21 percent more than we did fifty years ago.[41] In just the last fifty years, the rate of poverty has fallen by over half.[42] Finally, since 1945 the true threats to peace in America have degraded from that of a failed state (USSR) to uncoordinated bands of nomads in rural areas of the world. Overall, it would appear to an outside observer that Americans actually have less to fear than at any time in the history of their existence.

Psychologists describe the phenomenon of needing enemies and allies to be a "profound aspect of human psychology."[43] Perhaps we should not blame the fear mongers, but rather our own psychology, and our own prosperity. In a world with ever diminishing threats to our lives, perhaps it is hard to be afraid of a cheeseburger, the sun, or wet floors. Perhaps instead we have a deep-seated need to create an enemy that is truly frightening. The fact that butter contributes to the death of over 600,000 Americans every year does not motivate us, but the specter of cyber-terrorism that has killed exactly zero Americans is the kind of boogeyman that can really motivate the human psychology. This is our hypothesis; that fear of a dystopian future keeps us warm at night and is a necessary mechanism for a prosperous society.

Risks

Perhaps the fear of being watched, or of having some unknown enemy shut down the Internet is a necessity of our psyche, but it is also an unhealthy distraction. Studies show that fear and irrationality make people engage in "suboptimal decision making."[44] This distraction causes our brains to ignore pressing threats, and instead utilize mental energies to fight these paper tigers. This is similar to worrying about the safety of an airplane while eating cheeseburgers and drinking beer. The immediate threat that is faced is ignored, while the imagined threat we have no ability to influence absorbs our mental capacity. The other risk we face is not cognitive, but social. Citizens, corporations, and governments comprise of individual human beings. Citizens fear corporations and governments when they are convinced to disassociate these bodies from the individual parts. This is analogous to damning entire religions because of the actions of a few, or entire races because of the actions of a few. When people fear these 'bodies' they have become irrational animals, and regress from their earned humanity. This irrationality may manifest in a dangerous mania. The Oklahoma City bombers were caught in the throes of this type of mania. History is littered with examples of citizens caught up in their irrational fears. From John Wilkes Booth to Randy Weaver we have seen how manias can destroy both men and communities.

Conclusion

The world is full of risks. It always has been, and always will be. There are certainly new threats presented by new technology, but these threats are not the ones that the media and government heads seem to want us to focus on. Instead, we are distracted into fearing the same encroachments upon our privacy that were above the fold a century and a half ago. We fear someone sneaking a peak at our bare backsides, and the possibility of someone overhearing our scintillating conversation with our friend about fantasy football. If we believe what we have been told, the government spends almost $14 billion a year to read our forwarded memes, and corporations are using similar funds to diabolically figure out what type of diaper to stock in their stores. Privacy fundamentalism has taken hold of the American imagination and stoked our fears. The road to a dystopian autocratic blade-runner type future is apparently presaged by ridiculously low unemployment and an average life expectancy bordering on 80 years. Surely, the future is not so bleak.

Over the course of human history, society has proven itself to both be ignorant of imminent threats and fearful of progress. This paper has illustrated that the current condition of hypervigilance is not unique, but prolonged. With a 24-hour news cycle and an annual election cycle, the need to stoke fear has become an industry. The situation calls for cooler heads, and a moderation of sensationalism. Leaders should be cautious with 'slippery-slope' arguments. These are almost never supportable. These intense arguments by individuals on both extreme sides of the privacy and data security spectrum have ignored the moderate voice. We need to harken back to the time when Franklin Roosevelt spoke to citizens from his fireside and treated us as adults. In summary, the fears that we face are shadows cast upon the wall by paper tigers. Paper tigers that are based in fact, but blown up into monsters that threaten to distract us from both the imminent dangers and the progress we have made.

[1] Volkan, Vamik (1989), *The Need to Have Enemies and Allies: From Clinical Practice to International Relationships, Political Psychology Vol. 10, No. 2 (Jun., 1989), pp. 351-353, retrieved from* http://www.jstor.org/stable/3791655

[2] Westin,Alan (2003), *Social and Political Dimensions of Privacy*, Journal of Social Issues, Vol. 59, No 2, 2003, retrieved from
http://www.privacysummersymposium.com/reading/westin.pdf

[3] Kimble, M. O., Fleming, K., & Bennion, K. A. (2013). Contributors to Hypervigilance in a Military and Civilian Sample. Journal of Interpersonal Violence, 28(8), 1672–1692. http://doi.org/10.1177/0886260512468319

[4] ibid

[5] Neria, Y., Bravova, M. & Halper, J. (2010) Trauma and PTSD among Civilians in the Middle East, PTSD Research Quarterly, 28(8), retrieved from http://www.ptsd.va.gov/professional/newsletters/research-quarterly/v21n4.pdf

[6] Gradus,Jaimie (2016) How Common is PTSD?,U.S.Department of Veterans Affairs, National Center for PTSD website, retrieved from http://www.ptsd.va.gov/public/PTSD-overview/basics/how-common-is-ptsd.asp

[7] Central Intelligence Agency (2015), Life Expectancy, The World Fact Book, retrieved from https://www.cia.gov/library/publications/the-world-factbook/rankorder/2102rank.html

[8] The Economist (2014), Dicing with Death, *The Economist*, retrieved from http://media.economist.com/sites/default/files/media/2014InfoG/databank/IR2a.pdf

[9] CNN (2015) Syrian War Fast Facts, CNN.com, retrieved from http://www.cnn.com/2013/08/27/world/meast/syria-civil-war-fast-facts/index.html

[10] Gradus, Jaimie (ibid)

[11] Schneier, Bruce (2015) Living in a Code Yellow World, Schneier on Security, retrieved from
https://www.schneier.com/blog/archives/2015/09/living_in_a_cod.html

[12] Castro,D. & McQuinn, A. (2015) The Privacy Panic Cycle: A guide to Public Fears About New Technologies, Information Technology and Innovation Foundation, retrieved from http://www2.itif.org/2015-privacy-panic.pdf

[13] ibid

[14] Ledbetter, Sheri (2015) Chapman University Survey of American Fears, retrieved from https://blogs.chapman.edu/wilkinson/category/fear-index/

[15] Tafoya, William (2016) Cyber Terror, Federal Bureau of Investigation, Law Enforcement Bulletin, retrieved from
https://leb.fbi.gov/2011/november/cyber-terror

[16] Lachow, Irving (2014) CyberTerrorism: Menace or Myth, CyberPower and National Security, Patomac Books, retrieved from
http://ctnsp.dodlive.mil/files/2014/03/Cyberpower-I-Chap-19.pdf

[17] National Highway Traffic Safety Administration (2013) NHTSA Data Confirms Traffic Fatalities Increased In 2012, retrieved from http://www.nhtsa.gov/

[18] Bilton, Nick (2013) Disruptions: At Odds Over Privacy Challenges of Wearable Computing, New York Times, May 26, 2013, http://bits.blogs.nytimes.com/2013/05/26/disruptions-at-odds-over-privacy-challengesof-wearable-computing/

[19] Office of National Statistics (2016) Census taking in the Ancient World, The National Archives, retrieved from
http://webarchive.nationalarchives.gov.uk/20160105160709/http:/www.ons.gov.uk/ons/guide-method/census/2011/how-our-census-works/about-censuses/census-history/census-taking-in-the-ancient-world/index.html

[20] Merriam Webster (2016) Slippery Slope, retrieved from http://www.merriam-webster.com/dictionary/slippery%20slope

[21] National Center for Health Statistics (2014) Leading Causes of Death, retrieved from http://www.cdc.gov/nchs/fastats/leading-causes-of-death.htm

[22] Burger, Ronna. Plato's Phaedrus: A Defense of a Philosophic Art of Writing. Tuscaloosa, AL: U of Alabama P, 1980

[23] The New York Times (1877) The Telephone Unmasked, retrieved from NYTime archives at http://query.nytimes.com/mem/archive-free/pdf?res=9B0CE1DB103FE63BBC4B52DFB667838C669FDE

[24] Bilton, Nick (2013) Disruptions: At Odds Over Privacy Challenges of Wearable Computing, *New York Times*, retrieved from http://bits.blogs.nytimes.com/2013/05/26/disruptions-at-odds-over-privacy-challenges-of-wearable-computing/?_r=1

[25] ilid.

[26] Booth-Thomas,C. (2003)The See it All Chip, Time Magazine, retrieved from http://content.time.com/time/magazine/article/0,9171,485764-1,00.html

[27] Foley,Mary (2015) RFID Chips and your Privacy, Norton.com, retrieved from http://us.norton.com/yoursecurityresource/detail.jsp?aid=rfid

[28] CNN(2005) Emails 'hurt IQ more than pot', retrieved from CNN at http://www.cnn.com/2005/WORLD/europe/04/22/text.iq/

[29] Masnick, Mike (2016) No, The FBI Does Not 'Need' The Info On Farook's iPhone; This Is Entirely About The Precedent, Techdirt, retrieved from https://www.techdirt.com/articles/20160220/22412933661/no-fbi-does-not-need-info-farooks-iphone-this-is-entirely-about-precedent.shtml

[30] Bamford, James (2014) The Most Wanted Man in the World, Wired Magazine, retrieved from http://www.wired.com/2014/08/edward-snowden/

[31] Schmidt, Michael (2014) Racy Photos Were Often Shared at NSA, Snowden Says, The New York Times, retrieved from http://www.nytimes.com/2014/07/21/us/politics/edward-snowden-at-nsa-sexually-explicit-photos-often-shared.html?_r=0

[32] Bilton.

[33] Box Office Mojo (2015) Studio Market Share, retrieved from http://www.boxofficemojo.com/studio/

[34] International Institute for Strategic Studies (11 February 2015). The Military Balance 2015. London: Routledge. ISBN 1857437667.

[35] Security Week (03 December 2010). Federal Cyber Security Spending Expected to Reach $13.3 Billion by 2015. Security Week, retrieved from http://www.securityweek.com/federal-cyber-security-spending-expected-reach-133-billion-2015

[36] CBS News (2000) Digitial Pearl Harbor Warning, retrieved from http://www.cbsnews.com/news/digital-pearl-harbor-warning/

[37] Levin, Adam (2013) Top Five Ways to Prepare for the Coming Cyber War, ABC News, retrieved from http://abcnews.go.com/Business/top-ways-prepare-coming-cyber-war/story?id=18570685

[38] Whitehouse,Kaja (2015) Regulator Warns of 'Armageddon' Cyber Attack on Banks, USA Today, retrieved from http://www.usatoday.com/story/money/business/2015/02/25/lawsky-goldman-sachs-banks

[39] Toner,Robin (1988) Prison Furloughs in Massachusetts Threaten Dukakis Record on Crime, *The New York Times*, retrieved from http://www.nytimes.com/1988/07/05/us/prison-furloughs-in-massachusetts-threaten-dukakis-record-on-crime.html

[40] Centers for Disease Control, National Vital Statistics Reports, Vol. 50, No.6. Life Expectancy at Birth, by Race and Sex, Selected Years 1929-98

[41] DeNavass, C.,Proctor, B. & Smith, J. (2013) Income Poverty and Health Insurance in the United States, United States Census Bureau, retrieved from http://www.census.gov/prod/2013pubs/p60-245.pdf

[42] Ibid

[43] Volkan, Vamik (1989), *The Need to Have Enemies and Allies: From Clinical Practice to International Relationships, Political Psychology (see footnote 1)*

[44] Simon H (1957) A Behavioral Model of Rational Choice in Models of Man. London, UK: Taylor & Francis

An Analysis and Review of the Ethical Frameworks

Adam Lewis

Publication Month: July 2016

Abstract: This paper reviews the actions of major Internet communications companies in China and identifies the ethical framework each has applied while operating in the Chinese market. Specifically, the ethical framework that is outlined by Michael Quinn in the publication "Ethics for the Information Age."

Introduction

I lived in China for two years from 2003 to 2005 and returned a handful of times for extensive visits. After China, I remained living in Asia for the next five years before returning to the U.S. During my years in Asia I became intrigued by the challenge China presented to the world's status quo and to my American values. China joining the World Trade Organization in 2001 began an explosion of change, opportunity, and crisis—within China and in its relationships with other countries. The years between 2001 and 2010 represent the formative years in China's re-emergence on the world stage, climaxing in the 2008 Beijing Olympics. Now, by 2016, the ramifications of China's re-emergence are clearer, and non-Chinese Internet companies in particular have been seasoned by their experiences in China. In 2010, two distinct visions of the Internet were formally defined, one by the U.S. and one by China. The fundamental question for the future of Internet governance worldwide became:

Is cyberspace entirely made up of domestic spheres, each under a different country's sovereign rule, or is the Internet as a whole subject to international rule in the name of "universal values"?[1]

Ethical Frameworks

In this paper I will review the actions of major Internet communications companies in China and identify the ethical framework each applied when operating in the Chinese market. To do so, I will use the ethical frameworks as outlined in our reading from *Ethics for the Information*

Age by Michael Quinn.[2] Specifically, I will examine the decisions of Yahoo!, Microsoft, Skype, and Google, focusing on the period from 1999 when Yahoo! became the first Internet company to enter the Chinese market, to 2010 when Google decided to exit the Chinese market.

We will see the American Internet firm Yahoo! employ an ethical framework of *Cultural Relativism*—operating by one set of values in the U.S., and a contradictory set of values in China. By implication, this contradiction demonstrates that Yahoo! operated by no universal value of right or wrong, and that, from Yahoo!'s perspective, these definitions change from culture to culture. Additionally, we will see the fallout when this contradiction is brought to light, especially in Yahoo!'s culture of origin, the U.S. By employing cultural relativism, Yahoo! had no way to reconcile its actions in the U.S. and China and chose to turn operations over to a Chinese company, essentially exiting the Chinese market. The European online communication company Skype also initially employed a cultural relativist approach in its partnership with Chinese telecommunications company TOM, which lead to similar disastrous results.

In Microsoft we will see and evolution in the ethical framework employed by the American company operating in China. Microsoft's approach most closely resembled that of *Ethical Egoism*. Microsoft believed it was in their best interest financially to operate in China and sublimated its American values to do so, favoring instead to the company's own best interests. Microsoft willingly engaged in censorship, claiming that some access to information is better for Chinese citizens than none. This may seem to be a *Utilitarian* approach, however, Microsoft's censorship went beyond what was obligated by the Chinese government by deleting blogs outside of China and censoring searches in simplified Chinese worldwide. It chose to appease and ingratiate itself with the Chinese government instead of serve in the best interests of the rest of the world—especially the Chinese diaspora outside mainland China. In this sense, Microsoft put its own interests ahead of its American values and also its benefits to the Chinese people. To its credit, Microsoft's does act by certain uncompromisable core values. Unlike Yahoo!, Microsoft is not willing to aid the Chinese government in jailing dissidents, an approach seen most clearly in the changes at Skype once Microsoft bought it in 2013.

Next we will examine Google's ethical framework when operating in China. Google's cautious and thoroughly considered approach stemmed not only from the lessons learned from Yahoo!, Skype, and Microsoft, but also from the importance of the company's clearly stated core set of values. An uneasy relationship between Google and Chinese authorities ended when Google detected a serious hacking intrusion it all but directly blamed on the Chinese government. In response Google exited the mainland and stopped filtering search results.

In its approach to China, Google employed a *Kantian* ethical framework. The company has clearly stated moral imperatives and endeavors to operate by these principles universally. While Google's initial foray into China contradicted these values, their core values remained the touchstone of the decision making process. A blog post announcing the Google.cn launch stated, "For several years, we've debated whether entering the Chinese market at this point in history could be consistent with our mission and values."[3] Eventually, the company concluded that its categorical imperative, reflected in the company's then slogan of "Don't Be Evil" and goal "to organize the world's information and make it universally accessible and useful,"[4] could not be compromised and could not be enacted successfully in China. By leaving China and refusing to censor information, Google lost access to the lucrative Chinese market, proving that Google doesn't see Chinese consumers simply as a means to make money, but as ends in themselves, potential beneficiaries of Google's moral imperative and universal values.

Finally, we will return to the question stated in the introduction—the two divergent visions of Internet governance that developed between 2000-2010, now explicitly stated by the U.S. and China—and how American information companies are operating in China currently.

Yahoo! Approach 1999 - 2005

Yahoo! entered the Chinese market ahead of the curve, launching its Chinese service Yahoo! China on **September 24, 1999**. Shortly thereafter an America-China trade deal finalized on November 15, 1999, paving the way for China to join the World Trade Organization (WTO) in 2001. It was an optimistic and exciting time for businesses contemplating an untapped consumer market of over a billion Chinese people. To put it bluntly, "Foreign telecommunications companies are in awe of the prospect of access to the Chinese market."[5] Yahoo! China operated in China, with Chinese employees and equipment storing user information located within the mainland. This was a mistake on the part of Yahoo! and served as an important lesson to Internet companies following Yahoo! into the mainland Chinese market, as we shall see.

In **September 2005**, an investigation by Reporters Without Borders revealed that **in 2004** Yahoo! China's Beijing office had given Chinese authorities detailed account holder information—including email contents—at the request of the Beijing state security bureau. Based on that information, Chinese journalist Shi Tao was arrested and found guilty of "providing state secrets to foreign entities" and sentenced to 10 years in prison.[6]

What had Tao done to receive such a serious charge and lengthy sentence? He took notes from a meeting where a senior Chinese newspaper editor relayed to his staff government censorship instructions, detailing what could and could not be published in the weeks leading up to the June 4 Tiananmen Square massacre anniversary. Tao then logged into his Yahoo! China email account and emailed those notes to a New York-based editor. This simple act of relaying notes about newspaper censorship instructions was enough to warrant a ten year sentence in the eyes of the Chinese government.

Soon thereafter, Reporters Without Borders demonstrated that Yahoo! China complied with Chinese authorities in other similar cases, resulting in an eight year sentence for Li Zhi for "inciting subversion," and a ten year sentences for Wang Xiaoning for "incitement to subvert state power."[7]

The news that an American company colluded with Chinese suppression of free speech was not received well in the U.S. and worldwide. In congressional hearings held **February 15, 2006,**

Congressman Tom Lantos told Yahoo! executives, "morally you are pygmies." Congressman Chris Smith compared Yahoo! to companies that cooperated with the Nazis during World War II[8], and stated, "Your abhorrent activities in China are a disgrace."[9]

Disgraced, defeated, and looking for a way out, Yahoo! entered into a partnership with up-and-coming Chinese ecommerce company Alibaba, turning over control and operation of Yahoo! China to Alibaba in **October 2005.** In response, Lucie Morillon of Reporters Without Borders remarked that Yahoo! is, "trying, more or less, to hide behind Alibaba."[10]

The Chinese owned Alibaba did not have the same ethical conflict and external pressures as Yahoo!. In response to a question about free speech, Alibaba CEO Jack Ma responded, "We are a business! Shareholders want to make money. Shareholders want us to make the customer happy. Meanwhile, we do not have any responsibilities saying we should do this or that political thing. Forget about it!"[11]

The damage to the Yahoo! brand was severe, not only on the world stage, but also to Chinese citizens who felt betrayed by the American tech giant. Well known and influential Chinese blogger Zhao Jing, known by his pen name, Michael Anti, remarked, "A company such as Yahoo! which gives up information is unforgivable. It would be for the good of the Chinese netizens if such a company could be shut down or get out of China forever,"[12] and "Yahoo is a sellout. Chinese people hate Yahoo."[13]

In **August 2013**, Alibaba shut down Yahoo! China.

Microsoft Approach 2005

Michael Anti & MSN

In **May 2005**, Microsoft launched the Chinese version of its Microsoft Network (MSN), an Internet portal to news, blog hosting, and email. Initial testing showed that the blogging service was subject to strict censorship.[14]

The aforementioned popular Chinese blogger Zhao Jing used MSN to publish his blog under the pseudonym Michael Anti. In **December 2005**, Chinese officials unofficially requested the Michael Anti blog be shut down after he posted behind the scenes details of a Beijing News staff protest. Microsoft complied with the request.[15]

According to the New York Times, "What was most remarkable about this was that Microsoft's blogging service has no servers located in China; the company effectively allowed China's censors to reach across the ocean and erase data stored on American territory."[16] The move led even notable Microsoft supporter and blogger Robert Scoble to point out, "It's one thing to pull a list of words out of blogs using an algorithm. It's another thing to become an agent of a government and censor an entire blogger's work."[17]

It is also important to note that Microsoft removed the blog "without even receiving a formal legal request from the Chinese government."[18] Without an official request, there is no way to confirm or track such requests, creating an arbitrary, opaque, and undefined regulatory environment.

Skype Approach 2005 – 2008

TOM-Skype

Skype is a popular free online voice, text, and video-call software that advertises secure end-to-end encryption.[19] In **September 2005,** Skype distributed a custom Skype client in the Chinese market through a joint venture with Chinese mobile Internet company TOM. Chinese users wanting to download Skype were redirected to the TOM site and had no choice but to download TOM's Skype client.

In **2008**, security researchers revealed that the TOM version of Skype had been not only censoring conversations through a keyword filter, but also saving personally identifiable information including full text of conversations when particularly politically sensitive words appeared. This included communication within China, and internationally, as well. The study's lead researcher, Nart Villeneuve, wrote in his 2008 report *Breaching Trust*, "the underlying purpose of such widespread and systematic surveillance seems obvious. Dissidents and ordinary citizens are being systematically monitored and tracked."[20]

Publically, Skype denied the accusations, but the evidence Villeneuve compiled demonstrated these denials to be false. Eventually, Skype's Jaanus Kase explained, "As part of the joint venture, TOM provides guidance to Skype about how to cooperate with local laws and regulations in China. In every country we operate in, we always work with local authorities to follow local laws and best practice."[21] Best practice in this case apparently included not informing users that a program is secretly downloaded onto their computer and their communications possibly stored for Chinese authorities.

Later, Niklas Zennström, the chief executive of Skype, said that TOM "had implemented a text filter, which is what everyone else in that market is doing. Those are the regulations." He also stated, "One thing that's certain is that those things are in no way jeopardizing the privacy or the security of any of the users."[22] Again, Villeneuve's evidence proved this to be false. This incident and Skype's response should as Rebecca MacKinnon states, "raise[s] questions about how trustworthy Skype as a company really is."[23]

Microsoft bought the online communication service Skype in **2011** US$8.5 billion. We will return to Microsoft-Skype later.

Bing 2009

Microsoft launched the Chinese version of its Bing search engine on **June 1, 2009**. By June 24, New York Times journalist Nicholas Kristof wrote that searches conducted in simplified Chinese (the type of Chinese used in mainland China) are censored *worldwide*.[24] At first Microsoft denied that Bing censored simplified Chinese results, claiming that any unusual results were the result of a bug in the newly launched service.[25] However, by November the company announced that results—especially images—were indeed censored to comply with Chinese law. Kristof notes, "Now Microsoft is sacrificing the integrity of Bing searches so as to cozy up to State Security in Beijing. In effect, it has chosen become part of the Communist Party's propaganda apparatus."[26]

Google Approach 2006 – 2010

In 2000, Google began a Chinese language version of its main Google.com search. The service was set up outside China to serve the vast numbers of Chinese speakers worldwide, outside of mainland China. Users inside China could access Google's search engine and view unfiltered, uncensored results. As a result, the Chinese government regularly blocked or significantly slowed Google.com and all Google related services, such as Gmail.

By January 27, 2006, Google decided to enter the Chinese market officially in an attempt to better serve Chinese users attempting to access Google's search, which was routinely blocked. Google seemed to have carefully considered how it would approach the Chinese market and its censorship requirements weighed against its corporate motto, "Don't Be Evil," and mission to make the world's information universally accessible.[27] According to a senior Google executive, "While removing search results is inconsistent with Google's mission, providing no information [or a heavily degraded user experience that amounts to no information] is more inconsistent with our mission." [28]

Google's approach to the Chinese market was carefully considered in an attempt to maintain its core values and also comply with Chinese government censorship requirements. To walk this thin line, Google took the following steps:

- The Chinese mainland search engine (Google.cn) would exist alongside Google's uncensored Chinese language search (Google.com's simplified Chinese version). Users had the option to use either search and even compare results, when Google.com was not being blocked. This is in contrast to Yahoo! China and Bing.cn which each only offered one simplified Chinese language search service.
- Google.cn *notified users* when their results were being filtered in accordance with Chinese law, making the censorship more explicit and transparent to users—in contrast to the secretive and opaque approaches by Skype-TOM and Bing.

- While Google.cn's servers resided within mainland China for better speed and accessibility, servers storing personal or confidential user information like Gmail and Blogger would remain outside of China's borders—out of reach of Chinese authorities. This would ensure Google couldn't be forced to endanger people as Yahoo! China did in the Shi Tao case.
- The Chinese government never publishes exactly what websites are forbidden. The censorship system relies heavily on companies self-censoring based on what they suspect *should* be censored. Often, companies will over-censor to remain in good standing with the government, avoid fines, and keep their Internet business license.[29] In order to avoid this Kafka-esque game of censorship Google established servers inside mainland China programmed to test websites against the Chinese firewall. Any websites that were blocked were added to Google's list blacklist.

Despite its best efforts to justify its decision to launch Google.cn, Google was heavily criticized for betraying its values and accused of colluding with the repressive Chinese government. By **January 2007,** Google admitted that its decision to censor its Chinese site had damaged the company. Google founder, Sergey Brin, said "On a business level, that decision to censor was a net negative."[30]

Google Hacking Incident 2010

In **January 2010**, in a post on its official blog Google's Chief Legal Officer David Drummond announced Google had discovered a sophisticated and targeted attack on its servers that resulted in the theft of Google source code. The attack emanated from China, was focused on the email accounts of Chinese activists, and also involved at least twenty other large companies ranging from finance to the chemical industry.

As a result of these attacks, Google's already uncomfortable relationship with Chinese censorship came to a swift end. Google decided to stop censoring results on Google.cn—redirecting Google.cn traffic to Google's Hong Kong service, Google.hk. Hong Kong's special administrative status in China means that companies are not required to censor as they are on the mainland.

In that same blog post, Drummond stated that the seriousness of the incident finally ended an uneasy relationship and highlighted its broader implications. "We have taken the unusual step of sharing information about these attacks with a broad audience not just because of the security and human rights implications of what we have unearthed, but also because this information goes to the heart of a much bigger global debate about freedom of speech."[31]

For the first time an American Internet company had decided that its free speech values were more important than complying with China's censorship requirement in exchange for access to its huge market. Along these lines Drummond said that Google's business in China will certainly suffer in the short-term, but "over time, Google would benefit from taking a principled stand in China and elsewhere. It is good for our business to push for free expression."[32]

Internet Freedom Speech 2010

The dramatic exchange between China and Google and the hacking revelations prompted Secretary of State, Hillary Clinton to address Internet Freedom in her remarks on **January 21, 2010.** Clinton explicitly stated the U.S.' position of a *single, connected, international Internet.* "On their own, new technologies do not take sides in the struggle for freedom and progress, but the U.S. does. We stand for a single internet where all of humanity has equal access to knowledge and ideas."[33] She continued:

...ultimately, this issue isn't just about information freedom; it is about what kind of world we want and what kind of world we will inhabit. It's about whether we live on a planet with one Internet, one global community, and a common body of knowledge that benefits and unites us all, or a fragmented planet in which access to information and opportunity is dependent on where you live and the whims of censors.

She compared the virtual walls that are appearing on the Internet to the physical walls that separated countries during the Cold War, saying "a new information curtain is descending across much of the world. And beyond this partition, viral videos and blog posts are becoming the samizdat of our day."[34] In her speech, she highlighted the *freedom to connect*—the ability of people to connect with others without government interference, noting the contrast between some governments' efforts to restrict citizen participation and America's rush to embrace connectedness for political gain as seen in the 2008 presidential campaign.

Finally, she emphasized that a distorted, asymmetrical flow of information can lead to further misunderstanding and potentially to conflict, and that countries that restrict the freedom to connect stultify development and innovation, saying "countries that restrict free access to information or violate the basic rights of internet users risk walling themselves off from the progress of the next century. "[35]

Chinese Internet Sovereignty Whitepaper 2010

Six months after Clinton's speech on Internet Freedom, the Chinese government responded by releasing *The Internet in China*, a white paper outlining China's global vision of the Internet.[36] In sharp contrast to America's concept of a single Internet that all have freedom to connect to, China emphasized the concept of Internet Sovereignty. Much like its physical borders, China says, "Within Chinese territory the Internet is under the jurisdiction of Chinese sovereignty."[37] These information borders, in China's vision, should not apply just to China, but should be the international legal order, arguing that "each country has a right to strengthen control over its own domestic Internet, and that such actions will help safeguard order and stability on the global Internet system."[38] The Chinese version recognizes that even though cyberspace is commonly considered borderless, the Internet does manifest itself physically in a specific regulated infrastructure. For example, there are eight "gates" where China's Internet connects to the rest of the world. As China's Minister of Posts and Telecommunications said, "If you go through customs, you have to show your passport. It's the same with management of information."[39] Accordingly, each country will censor and regulate the Internet according to each county's government policy, meaning the Internet experience would vary from country to country.

Current Approach

In the roughly ten years between Yahoo! China's initial foray into China to Google's exit, American Internet companies have faced intense ethical challenges that forced them to define core values and reflect on their behavior when faced with the temptation of market access to over a billion potential customers. Despite the rhetoric of free speech and human rights, Internet companies' early advances into China failed ethically. In a rush to access the potential gold mine of the Chinese market, Internet companies helped jail dissidents, delete writings posted in another country without warning, censored and recorded text conversations without notifying users—and then lied about it, and censored search results—and then lied about that, too. Shameful behavior for companies whose businesses are based on creating and sharing information and facilitating communication, all ostensibly within the context of Universal Human Values.

It is interesting, looking back, to watch these companies travel up a learning curve in an effort to remain ethical within the requirements of a repressive information regime with such large potential riches at stake.

After the early ethical failures and public drubbing at the 2006 congressional hearing on Global Online Freedom, Yahoo, Google, and Microsoft formed a coalition with academics, human rights advocates, and IT leaders, known as the Global Network Initiative (GNI) in **October, 2008**. The goal of the GNI is "protecting and advancing the rights to privacy and freedom of expression,"[40] by providing a framework and pooling learning resources. For example, the GNI requires "governments to put information requests in writing and [that companies] interpret those requests as narrowly as possible."[41] Since its formation, the GNI has added Facebook and LinkedIn to its list of members.

When Yahoo! entered Vietnam in 2009 in a government context similar to China's, it located servers with confidential user information in Singapore, inaccessible to Vietnamese authorities.[42] Microsoft bought

Skype in 2011. In 2013 Microsoft ended Skype's relationship with TOM, and began encrypting messages.[43] In recognition of the difficult regulatory and business environment foreign companies face in China, Microsoft has made Chinese search company Baidu, not Bing, the default search for Chinese versions of Windows 10.[44]

Another approach that some American companies are taking is launching Chinese services that are similar but completely separated from their international offerings. LinkedIn, Evernote, and Uber are thriving within China based on stand-alone, isolated, Chinese only versions of their services. While this is congruent with China's Internet Sovereignty approach, repressive governments representing smaller markets are unlikely to receive this level of differentiated service in a viable way.

As part of China's push promote its Internet Sovereignty concept, it recently established its own World Internet Conference. Widely derided and a subject of amusement to Chinese citizens, one scheduled conference speaker, James A. Lewis, had this to say, "China's on the losing side of history in this one...The Russians agree with them that free speech is a bad idea, but the Indians don't, the Brazilians don't, most of the world doesn't." It is worth noting that participants at the World Internet Conference—which included Russia, Pakistan, Kazakhstan, and Kyrgyzstan—were given special access to an uncensored version of the Internet.[45] Also, it must be noted that China needs services like Google, especially for scientific and economic development. As Internet Freedom advocate Rebecca MacKinnon notes, "The government cannot afford to sever links between the domestic Chinese Internet and the international Internet without disrupting the international business, trade, and finance upon which its economy now depends."[46] On the other hand, the Edward Snowden revelations show that the U.S. concept of freedom to connect may need to be amended to freedom to connect under surveillance.

Ultimately, China's closed system of heavy monitoring, censorship, and active information manipulation is unlikely to succeed as the chosen standard of world Internet governance. The only reason for the existence of such an expensive, inefficient policy is to ensure the continuation of the Chinese Communist party in power. This, however, doesn't mean the U.S. model of one universal Internet will succeed by default. Behind Hillary Clinton's flowery language are the machinations of the NSA and other monitoring agencies. Additionally, private companies are continually expanding control over Internet access, be it services such as Facebook or Google, or telecommunication companies such as Comcast. Between all of these great powers are the individuals who must continually push to defend their rights and privileges.

---

[1] Tiezzi, Shannon. "China's 'Sovereign Internet'" The Diplomat. N.p., 24 June 2014. Web. 11 Mar. 2016.

[2] Quinn, M. (2011). Chapter 2: Introduction to Ethics. Ethics for the Information Age. 4th ed. Pearson. pp 53-99.

[3] McLaughlin, Andrew. "Google in China." Official Google Blog. N.p., 27 Jan. 2006. Web. 11 Mar. 2016.

[4] "Company – Google." Company – Google. N.p., n.d. Web. 11 Mar. 2016.

[5] Hankins, Michelle. "Telecommunications Companies Poised to Enter Chinese Market." SIGNAL Magazine. N.p., Feb. 2000. Web. 11 Mar. 2016.

[6] "Information Supplied by Yahoo! Helped Journalist Shi Tao Get 10 Years in Prison - Reporters Without Borders." Information Supplied by Yahoo! Helped Journalist Shi Tao Get 10 Years in Prison - Reporters Without Borders. N.p., 6 Sept. 2005. Web. 11 Mar. 2016.

[7] "Race to the bottom": Corporate complicity in Chinese Internet censorship. (2006). New York: Human Rights Watch. Pp. 32.

[8] Hickey, Matt. "Yahoo In China: An Unfair Attack." TechCrunch. N.p., 8 Nov. 2007. Web. 11 Mar. 2016.

[9] MacKinnon, Rebecca. "In China, Bing's Turn to Show Some Spine." CNN. Cable News Network, 24 Mar. 2010. Web. 11 Mar. 2016.

[10] Gunther, Marc. "Yahoo's China Problem." CNNMoney. Cable News Network, 22 Feb. 2006. Web. 11 Mar. 2016.

[11] Thompson, Clive. "Google's China Problem (and China's Google Problem)." The New York Times. The New York Times, 22 Apr. 2006. Web. 11 Mar. 2016.

[12] Zhao Jing, "The Freedom of Chinese Netizens Is Not Up To The Americans," blog, original Chinese at http://anti.blog-city.com/1634657.htm; English translation by Roland Soong at EastSouthWestNorth, http://www.zonaeuropa.com/20060217_1.htm (retrieved July 12, 2006).

[13] Thompson, Clive. "Google's China Problem (and China's Google Problem)." The New York Times. 22 Apr. 2006. Web. 11 Mar. 2016.

[14] MacKinnon, Rebecca. "Screenshots of Censorship." Global Voices. N.p., 17 June 2005. Web. 11 Mar. 2016.

[15] Barboza, David, and Tom Zeller. "Microsoft Shuts Blog's Site After Complaints by Beijing." *The New York Times.* 05 Jan. 2006. Web. 11 Mar. 2016.

[16] Thompson, Clive. "Google's China Problem (and China's Google Problem)." *The New York Times.* 22 Apr. 2006. Web. 11 Mar. 2016.

[17] Barboza, David, and Tom Zeller. "Microsoft Shuts Blog's Site After Complaints by Beijing." *The New York Times.* 05 Jan. 2006. Web. 11 Mar. 2016.

[18] Thompson, Clive. "Google's China Problem (and China's Google Problem)." *The New York Times.* 22 Apr. 2006. Web. 11 Mar. 2016.

[19] "Breaching Trust": An analysis of surveillance and security practices on China's TOM-Skype platform. (2008). Toronto: Information Warfare Monitor ONI Asia. Pp. 3.

[20] ibid

[21] MacKinnon, Rebecca. "Skype and China Censorship." 'RConversation' N.p., 20 Apr. 2006. Web. 11 Mar. 2016.

[22] Maitland, Alison. "Skype Says Texts Are Censored by China - FT.com." Financial Times. N.p., 18 Apr. 2006. Web. 11 Mar. 2016.

[23] MacKinnon, Rebecca. "Skype Messes Up, Badly." 'RConversation' N.p., 2 Oct. 2008. Web. 11 Mar. 2016.

[24] Kristof, Nicholas. "Microsoft and Chinese Censorship." Nytimes. New York Times, 24 June 2009. Web. 11 Mar. 2016.

[25] Ibid

[26] Kristof, Nicholas. "Boycott Microsoft Bing." Nytimes. New York Times, 20 Nov. 2009. Web. 11 Mar. 2016.

[27] "Company – Google." Company – Google. N.p., n.d. Web. 11 Mar. 2016.

[28] Dickie, Mure. "Google to Launch Censored China Service." Financial Times. N.p., 25 Jan. 2006. Web. 11 Mar. 2016.

[29] Thompson, Clive. "Google's China Problem (and China's Google Problem)." The New York Times. The New York Times, 22 Apr. 2006. Web. 11 Mar. 2016.

[30] "Google's Turbulent Five Years in China: A Timeline." The Telegraph. Telegraph Media Group, 13 Jan. 2010. Web. 11 Mar. 2016.

[31] Drummond, David. "A New Approach to China." Official Google Blog. N.p., 12 Jan. 2010. Web. 11 Mar. 2016.

[32] Helft, Miguel, and Michael Wines. "Google Faces Fallout as China Reacts to Site Shift." The New York Times. The New York Times, 23 Mar. 2010. Web. 11 Mar. 2016.

[33] Clinton, Hillary. "Remarks on Internet Freedom." U.S. Department of State. U.S. Department of State, 21 Jan. 2010. Web. 11 Mar. 2016.

[34] Ibid

[35] Ibid

[36] "The Internet in China." The Internet in China - China.org.cn. Information Office of the State Council of the People's Republic of China, 8 June 2010. Web. 11 Mar. 2016.

[37] Jiang, M. (2012). Authoritarian informationalism: China's approach to Internet sovereignty. Jiang, M.(2012). "Authoritarian Informationalism: China's Approach to Internet Sovereignty." Essential Readings of Comparative Politics (4th Ed.), New York: WW Norton & Company.

[38] Tiezzi, Shannon. "China's 'Sovereign Internet'" The Diplomat. N.p., 24 June 2014. Web. 11 Mar. 2016.

[39] Quoted in Jack Goldsmith & Tim Wu, Who Controls the Internet? Illusions of a Borderless World (New York, NY: Oxford University Press, 2006), 467.

[40] "About Us." Global Network Initiative. N.p., n.d. Web. 11 Mar. 2016

[41] Jones, K.C. "Google, Microsoft, and Yahoo Unveil Human Rights Guidelines - InformationWeek." InformationWeek. N.p., 28 Oct. 2008. Web. 11 Mar. 2016.

[42] MacMillan, Douglas. "Google, Yahoo Criticized Over Foreign Censorship." Bloomberg.com. Bloomberg, 12 Mar. 2009. Web. 11 Mar. 2016

[43] Carsten, Paul. "Microsoft Blocks Censorship of Skype in China: Advocacy Group." Reuters. Thomson Reuters, 27 Nov. 2013. Web. 11 Mar. 2016.

[44] Parkhurst, Emily. "No Bing in China: Microsoft Picks Baidu for Windows 10 on Chinese Browsers - Puget Sound Business Journal." Puget Sound Business Journal. N.p., 24 Sept. 2015. Web. 11 Mar. 2016.

[45] Tiezzi, Shannon. "The Internet with Chinese Characteristics." The Diplomat. N.p., 20 Nov. 2014. Web. 11 Mar. 2016.

[46] MacKinnon, R. (2012). Consent of the networked: The world-wide struggle for Internet freedom. New York: Basic Books. Pp. 47.

Cell Site Location Information and Fourth Amendment Protection

Brian Stanley
Publication Month: May 2017

Abstract: This timely paper delves into an in-depth look at implications of government access to and use of cell site location information (CSLI), and the implication for citizens' fourth amendment protection. In 2017, the U.S. Supreme Court will review of Carpenter vs. United States, that argues that CSLI should be protected under the Fourth Amendment.

> "The right of the people to be secure in their persons, houses, papers, and effects, against unreasonable searches and seizures, shall not be violated, and no warrants shall issue, but upon probable cause, supported by oath or affirmation, and particularly describing the place to be searched, and the persons or things to be seized."

> - "The Constitution of the United States," Amendment 4

Over the past three decades, a period during which wireless telecommunications technology frequently outpaced (and outpaces) Fourth Amendment-based legislation, lower federal and state courts rendered conflicting decisions in the interpretation and application of its protections involving personal wireless cell site location information.

Regarding government's access to and use of non-content communications information, in 2017, U.S. citizens remain uniformly unprotected. Specifically, the Fourth Amendment provides no protection for the majority of U.S. citizens who possess wireless telecommunications devices (cellphones) with respect to their cell site location information (CSLI). Citizens of six U.S. states, based on lower court rulings, have Fourth Amendment protections involving CSLI. Citizens of the remaining forty-four states, based on lower court rulings or no such rulings, have no Fourth Amendment CSLI protections.

In 2017, based on appeal of a Sixth Circuit Court's decision, the U.S. Supreme Court will review Petitioner Timothy Ivory Carpenter's argument (represented by Nathan Freed Wessler) proposing CSLI should be protected under the Fourth Amendment. Ironically, in 2010, the Sixth Circuit Court proclaimed under appeal from the U.S. District Court for the Southern District of Ohio at Cincinnati "...the Fourth Amendment must keep pace with the inexorable march of technological progress, or its guarantees will wither and perish."[1]

From a technological standpoint, it is material to the 2017 *Carpenter vs. United States* case, that in 2012 the Justices ruled "the Government's attachment of the GPS device to the vehicle, and its use of that device to monitor the vehicle's movements, constitutes a search (requiring a warrant) under the Fourth Amendment."[2]

Currently, Americans have no uniform protection of their CSLI that is generated by devices, typically, carried on their person twenty-four hours per day. The near-permanence of these personal devices is especially significant given much less time, on average, is spent inside a personal vehicle (for the subset of Americans who possess or use one). While CSLI's accuracy rate is, currently, slightly inferior to that recorded by GPS tracking devices, future FCC mandates must be adopted by U.S. wireless carriers which will result in eventual closure of this (accuracy) difference.

Advances in wireless telecommunications technology, combined with the patchwork of state and lower federal court rulings involving CSLI, necessitates a ruling in favor of U.S. Supreme Court Petitioner Timothy Carpenter's appeal. Rejection of his appeal, in the words of the Sixth Circuit Court unfortunately places the Fourth Amendment at continued risk of obsolescence.

Fourth Amendment

The Fourth Amendment to the U.S. Constitution protects the people's right "to be secure in their persons, houses, papers, and effects, against unreasonable searches and seizures."

Third-Party Doctrine

This doctrine holds "that knowingly revealing information to a third party relinquishes Fourth Amendment protection of said information." While probable cause and a search warrant are required to search one's home, under the third-party doctrine only a subpoena and prior notice (a much lower hurdle than probable cause) are needed to subject, for example, an Internet Service Provider (ISP) to disclose the contents of a customer's email.

In Katz v. United States (1967), the United States Supreme Court "established its reasonable expectation of privacy test." In 1976 (United States v. Miller) and 1979 (Smith v. Maryland), the Court affirmed "a person has no legitimate expectation of privacy in information he voluntarily turns over to third parties."[3]

In Smith v. Maryland (1979), the Court addressed "the question whether the [government's] installation and use of a pen register constitutes a 'search' within the meaning of the Fourth Amendment." The Court distinguished the use of a pen register from a listening device because pen registers "do not acquire the contents of communications"; they merely acquire the numbers dialed. The Court used this determination to characterize the defendant's argument as a "claim that he had a 'legitimate expectation of privacy' regarding the numbers he dialed on his phone."[4]

Stored Communications Act (SCA)

Enacted as Title II of the Electronic Communications Privacy Act (ECPA) of 1986, the "Stored Communications Act (SCA) is a law that addresses voluntary and compelled disclosure of "stored wire and electronic communications and transactional records" held by third-party ISPs.

The SCA regulates access to stored wire and electronic communications information and transactional records and describes the procedures available to law enforcement agencies to obtain this information under two mutually exclusive categories: "information which contains the contents of communications" or "information which does not contain the contents of communications".[5]

Under the "non-content" communications category, the ECPA mandates a subpoena is sufficient in cases where the (non-content) data contains "specific articulable facts" related to an investigation. In contrast, under the "content" communications category, issuance of a warrant is required once "probable cause" is approved by a court.

While the Fourth Amendment does not define "probable cause", courts over time have established its defining factors: "information sufficient to warrant a prudent person's belief that the wanted individual had committed a crime (for an arrest warrant) or that evidence of a crime or contraband would be found in a search (for a search warrant)".[6]

U.S. Public Commercial Wireless Telecommunications Services

Just three years before the SCA's passing, implementation of the first commercial analogue cellular systems (named Advanced Mobile Phone System, AMPS) was successfully completed in the U.S. in select major metropolitan areas, e.g. Chicago.

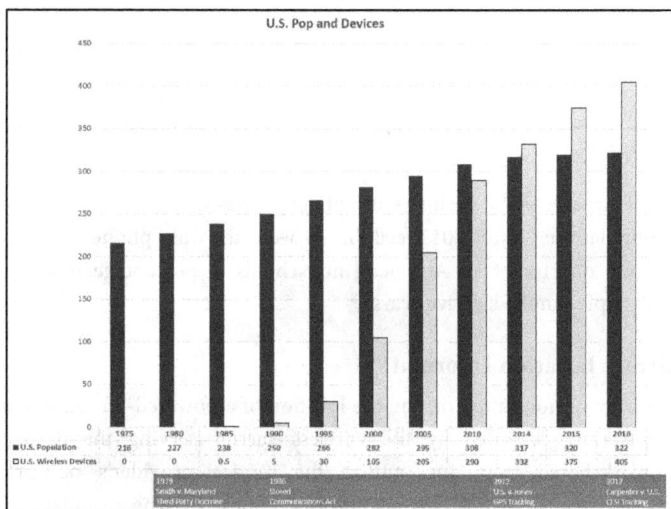

Figure 1

At its inception, due to the high cost of equipment and service and the lack of ubiquitous coverage, the SCA's ruling affected an infinitesimally small number of Americans. In the three decades since its passage, as shown in Figure 1, the number of Americans possessing cellphones has increased dramatically.

While Figure 1 (gray vertical bars) shows the number of U.S. Wireless devices (inequivalent to the number of Americans who own wireless devices), a 2017 Pew survey indicates, "95 percent of Americans own a cellphone" (Figure 2).[7]

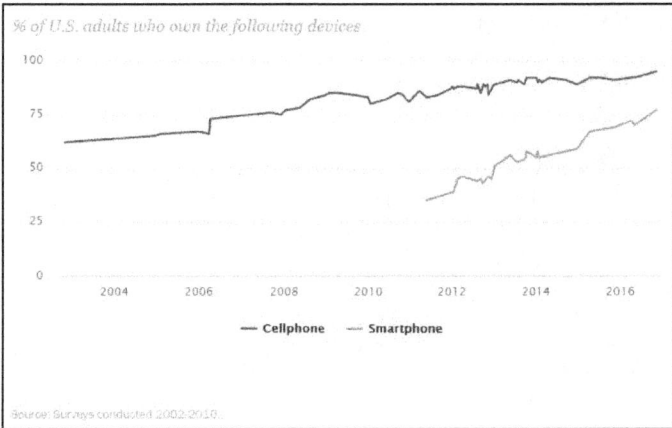

Figure 2

Equally notable is the exclusive use of cellphones by a large segment of the population: "As of 2012, cellphones were the only phones used in over one quarter of all American households, a percentage that has nearly tripled in the last five years."[8]

Cell Site Location Information

Stationary or not, in use or not, the location of a powered-on cellphone is constantly recorded by the wireless carrier serving the device. "Network-based techniques utilize the service provider's network infrastructure to identify the location of the handset. The advantage of network-based techniques (from a mobile operator's point of view) is that they can be implemented non-intrusively, without affecting the handsets. The accuracy of network-based techniques varies, with cell identification as the least accurate and triangulation as moderately accurate, and newer "Forward Link" timing methods as the most accurate. The accuracy of network-based techniques is both dependent on the concentration of base station cells, with urban environments achieving the highest possible accuracy, and the implementation of the most current timing methods."[9]

There are three different means by which a law enforcement agency may compel a wireless carrier to disclose a subscriber's (current and/or historical) CSLI: the agency may "obtain a warrant or obtain a court order for such disclosure... or get the consent of the subscriber or customer to such disclosure."

Specifically, a "court order for disclosure . . . shall issue only if the governmental entity offers specific articulable facts showing that there are reasonable grounds to believe that . . . the records or other information sought are relevant and material to an ongoing criminal investigation."

Therefore, a law enforcement agency's showing of reasonable suspicion is sufficient for a court to grant a governmental entity's order request. The government "is not statutorily required to show probable cause in order to obtain a court order compelling a CSP to disclose a subscriber's records."[10]

First State Ruling Protecting CSLI

In 2005, Magistrate Judge Orenstein in the Eastern District of New York was the first judge to deny a government request for CSLI based on his determination it lacked proof of probable cause. In doing so, Judge Orenstein "revealed that the Justice Department had routinely been using a baseless legal argument to get secret authorizations from a number of courts, probably for many years. Many more public denials followed from other judges, sharply rebuking the government and characterizing its legal argument as "contrived," "unsupported," "misleading," "perverse," and even a "Hail Mary" play. Unfortunately, the government succeeds in its reliance of their argument in nearly all other lower federal and state courts."[11]

State-By-State CSLI Rulings

As shown in Figure 3, Fourth Amendment protection of CSLI is dependent not on where you reside – it is dependent upon your current and past locations. For example, a Washington State resident, within their home state's border, have zero Fourth Amendment protection – law enforcement may request attainment of CSLI sans warrant.

In contrast, the same Washington State resident traveling in Montana and California (and four other states) is protected under the Fourth Amendment – a warrant is necessary to obtain their CSLI.

In Illinois and Indiana, a warrant is required for real-time CSLI tracking whereas a court order is sufficient to obtain historical CSLI.[12]

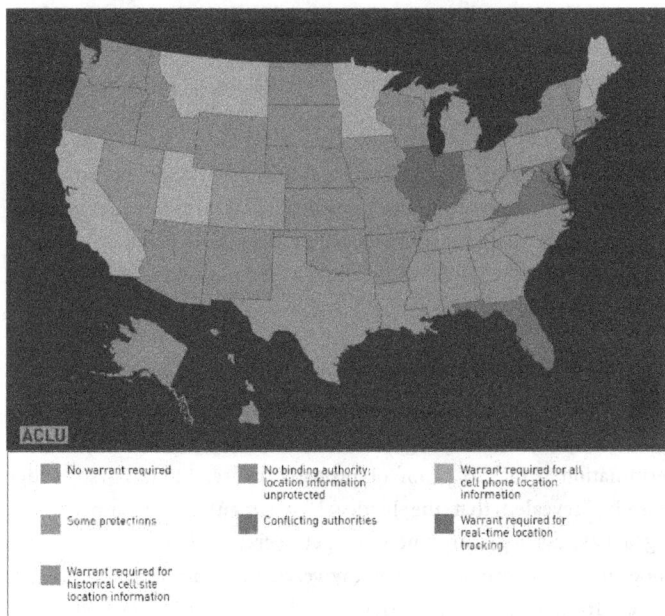

Figure 3

U.S. Wireless Carriers CSLI Information Policies

The four largest U.S. wireless carriers (AT&T, Sprint, T-Mobile, Verizon), which combined serve ninety-nine percent of all U.S. wireless devices,[13] require a warrant when served a CSLI request. This CSLI information policy is documented in each of their "Transparency Reports" which are published (publicly online) semi-annually. Among other metrics, the reports detail the number of CSLI requests submitted, by government and law enforcement agencies, and processed by each wireless carrier.

In 2014, the first-ever "Transparency Report" was published by a wireless carrier. "San Francisco-based CREDO is a progressive organization that supports causes like marriage equality and environmental activism… its wireless service arm is a small part of that, with around 125,000 subscribers."[14]

Transparency Reports were, initially, published by a small number of non-telecom companies including Apple, Facebook, Google, Microsoft, Twitter, and Yahoo. The publications were in response to concerns customers' information was being shared with government agencies without regard to Fourth Amendment protections. In one of the most recent egregious cases of illegal surveillance, beginning in 2001, AT&T conspired with the National Security Agency (NSA) to allow interception of "phone calls and Internet communications." and "receiving wholesale copies of American's telephone and other communications records." (NSA Spying on Americans, 2015)

In 2014, Verizon became the first major wireless carrier to publish Transparency reports detailing CSLI requests. Within the past three years, AT&T, Sprint, and T-Mobile joined Verizon in publishing biannual Transparency Reports. Each carrier, except T-Mobile, provides the specific number of CSLI requests received and processed. Figure 4 shows the total number of CSLI requests annually by carrier. T-Mobile's Transparency Report provides only the total number of warrants received and processed – a superset of requests which include CSLI. For this reason, their data is excluded from Figure 4.

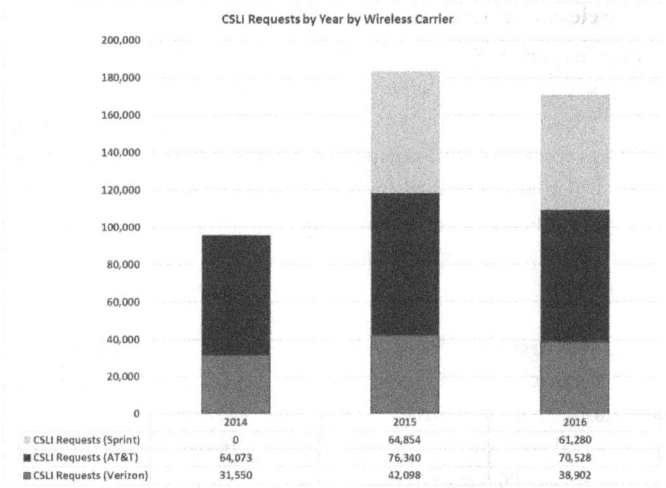

Figure 4

2012 U.S. Supreme Court Rules Vehicle GPS Tracking is protected under the Fourth Amendment

In this case, the government obtained a search warrant permitting it to install a Global-Positioning-System (GPS) tracking device on a vehicle registered to a spouse of Jones who was a suspected Washington D.C. narcotics dealer.

The warrant authorized installation of the device only within Washington D.C. and no later than 10 days after its issuance. On the 11th day after issuance of the warrant, law enforcement agents installed the device while the vehicle was parked in the state of Maryland.

Over the subsequent 28 days, the government tracked the vehicle's movements. Following the investigation, an indictment was secured (and, later, a conviction) against Jones (and others) on drug trafficking conspiracy charges. Under the indictment, however, the District Court suppressed the GPS data that was obtained while the vehicle was parked at Jones' residence. Data, recorded while the vehicle was on public streets, was ruled admissible because Jones had no reasonable expectation of privacy under such conditions.

Ultimately, the D. C. Circuit reversed Jones' conviction, concluding that admission of the evidence obtained by warrantless use of the GPS device violated the Fourth Amendment – due to its installation occurring after the warrant's deadline and outside its jurisdiction.

Under appeal, in United States v. Jones, 2012, the U.S. Supreme Court ruled "The Government's attachment of the GPS device to the vehicle, and its use of that device to monitor the vehicle's movements, constitutes a search (requiring a warrant) under the Fourth Amendment."[15]

Ubiquity of Wireless Coverage and Wireless Device Use and CSLI Accuracy

This five-year-old ruling is remarkable given that citizens, currently, have no uniform protection of CSLI that is generated by devices most Americans carry on their person nearly twenty-four hours per day. Time that, on average, is significantly greater than that spent traveling in a personal vehicle (for those who own or use a personal vehicle).

One may argue that CSLI is far less accurate than GPS tracking devices and is therefore unworthy of Fourth Amendment protection. This position, in years past when legacy wireless technology was less sophisticated, was not entirely baseless. Future technological advances and government mandates, however, render the argument groundless.

In 2015, the Federal Communications Commission (FCC) issued its Fourth Report and Order requiring upgrades to its Wireless E911 Location Accuracy Requirements. Specifically, all wireless carriers must provide "(911) dispatchable location or x/y (coordinates) location within 50 meters (164 feet) for the following percentages of wireless 911 calls within the listed timeframes":[16]

- By end of 2017: 40 percent of all wireless 911 calls
- By end of 2018: 50 percent of all wireless 911 calls
- By end of 2020: 70 percent of all wireless 911 calls
- By end of 2021: 80 percent of all wireless 911 calls

Currently, by utilizing sophisticated measurements taken at the time of transmission, CSLI may be determined within 200 feet – a capability which is a five-fold improvement on the FCC's standing requirement that "wireless carriers have the ability to locate ninety-five percent of calls made to or from cellphones accurately within 300 meters (984 feet) or less."

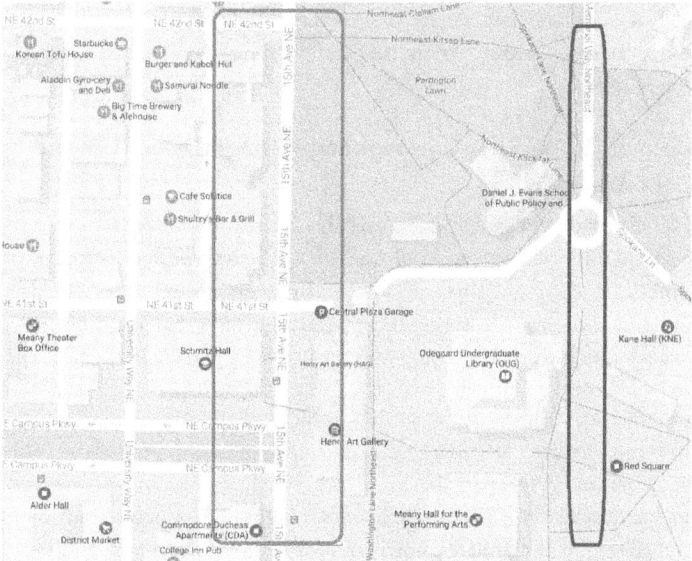

Figure 5

In contrast, "cellphones equipped with GPS can be pinpointed within fifty feet.[17] Figure 5 shows a simplistic example of the differences, on the University of Washington campus, between a 50-foot width (GPS) space (purple rectangular) and a 200-foot width (CSLI) space (blue rectangle). The 200-foot space equals, approximately, one city block whereas the 50-foot space is one-quarter of one city block. In both cases, tracking an individual is relatively non-complex in an urban environment offering standard wireless coverage.

In 2008, seven years prior to the FCC's 2015 mandate, Magistrate Judge Lisa Pupo Lenihan of the Western District of Pennsylvania wrote a lengthy denial of an application to compel a cellphone service provider to disclose historical CSLI without a warrant: "As technology now stands... CSLI enables a covert observer to know our physical movements/locations within 50 feet; and our cellphones... broadcast this information continuously. It is, therefore, extremely difficult to see how a cellphone is not now precisely an electronic... device which permits the tracking of the movement of a person or object. As other courts have observed, tracking device and cellphone technologies have converged."[18]

Conclusion

In April 2016, the Sixth Circuit Court of Appeals held, in *Carpenter vs. United States*, that "we lack any privacy interest in the location information generated by our cellphones... a complete disregard for the sensitive and revealing nature of cell site location information and a misguided response to the differences between the analog technologies addressed in old cases and the data-rich technologies of today."[19]

In four separate opinions, eight courts of appeals judges have explained their conclusion that "there is a reasonable expectation of privacy in historical CSLI and that the third-party doctrine does not apply."[20]

The 2012 *United States v. Jones* ruling, combined with the large volume of law enforcement requests for CSLI, conflicting patchwork of laws, significant advances in wireless technology, use of cellphone devices by most American adults, near ubiquitous coverage of wireless services, and future FCC mandates, ought to compel the U.S. Supreme Court to favor Petitioner Timothy Ivory Carpenter's 2017 argument thereby extending Fourth Amendment protection to both historical and real-time CSLI.

---

[1] *United States Court of Appeals for the Sixth Circuit. U.S. v Steven Warshak.* Electronic Frontier Foundation. 14 Dec. 2010. Accessed Mar. 2017 <www.eff.org>.

[2] *United States vs. Jones.* Legal Information Institute, Cornell University Law School. Jan. 23 2012. Accessed Mar. 2017 <www.law.cornell.edu>.

[3] "What You Need To Know About the Third-Party Doctrine." *The Atlantic.* Dec. 2013. Accessed Mar. 2017 <www.theatlantic.com>.

[4] Fox, Christopher. "Checking In: Historic Cell Site Location Information and the Stored Communications Act." *Seton Hall Law Review,* Seton Hall University. 14 May 2012. Accessed Mar. 2017 <www.scholarship.shu.edu>.

[5] Ibid.

[6] "Search and Seizure." The Oxford Index. N.D. Accessed Mar. 2017 <www.oxfordreference.com>.

[7] "Mobile Fact Sheet." Pew Research Center. 12 Jan. 2017. Accessed Mar. 2017 <www.pewinternet.org>.

[8] Fox.

[9] "Cell Phone Tracking." The STADIUM Project, the European Commission. Oct. 2012. Accessed Mar. 2017 <www.largeevents.eu>.

[10] Fox.

[11] "USA v. Pen Register (Cellphone Tracking Cases)." Electronic Freedom Foundation. N.D. Accessed Mar. 2017 <www.eff.org>.

[12] "Cell Phone Location Tracking Laws By State." American Civil Liberties Union. N.D. Accessed Mar. 2017 <www.aclu.org>.

[13] "How Wireless Carriers Stack-Up in Q3 2016." 11 Nov. 2016. Fierce Wireless. Accessed Mar. 2017 <www.fiercewireless.com>.

[14] Fung, Brian. "The First Phone Company to Publish A Transparency Report Isn't AT&T Or Verizon." *The Washington Post.* 9 Jan. 2014. Accessed Mar. 2017 <www.washingtonpost.com>.

[15] *United States vs. Jones.*

[16] "Wireless E911 Location Accuracy Requirements - Fourth Report and Order." Federal Communications Commission. 29 Jan. 2015. Accessed Mar. 2017 <www.fcc.gov>.

[17] Malone, Kyle. "The Fourth Amendment and the Stored Communications Act: Why the Warrantless Gathering of Historical Cell Site Location Information Poses No Threat to Privacy." *Pepperdine Law Review.* 15 Apr. 2012. Accessed Mar. 2017 <www.digitalcommons.pepperdine.edu>.

[18] Lenihan, Lisa Pupo. "Opinion and Memorandum Order: In the Matter of the Application of the U.S.A. for an Order directing a Provider to disclose records to the Government." U.S. District Court for the Western District of Pennsylvania. 19. Feb. 2008. Electronic Freedom Foundation. Accessed Mar. 2017 <www.eff.org>.

[19] Lynch, Jennifer. "Sixth Circuit Disregards Privacy in New Cell Site Location Information Decision." Electronic Freedom Foundation.13 Apr. 2016. Accessed Mar. 2017 <www.eff.org>.

[20] "Reply in Brief in Opposition – *Carpenter vs. United States.*" American Civil Liberties Union. Feb. 2017. Accessed Mar. 2017 <www.aclu.org>.

Chapter IV
Global Risks

The Digital Divide

Kristine Nelson
Publication Month: September 2015

Abstract: Despite efforts to close the digital divide, there is no question that in the U.S. a gap persists. When the term was coined, the digital divide was largely defined and measured in terms of physical access to the Internet. Progress has been made, but certain populations and organizations are still lagging including many of our public schools. Moreover, the conversation has matured, and the digital divide is recognized as a more nuanced phenomenon. Many more individuals have physical access to the Internet and related technologies today but lack the motivation, skill, or guidance necessary to use these technologies productively. This new divide – a problem that most certainly perpetuates economic and societal inequalities - particularly impacts public schools and their students. Policies and programs are working to address this new digital divide but have much work to do.

> "Like electricity a century ago, broadband is a foundation for economic growth, job creation, global competitiveness and a better way of life. It is enabling entire new industries and unlocking vast new possibilities for existing ones. It is changing how we educate children, deliver health care, manage energy, ensure public safety, engage government, and access, organize and disseminate knowledge.[1]"
>
> -- From the FCC's National Broadband Plan Executive Summary

The term "digital divide" – much like the problem itself - has evolved. At its introduction in the mid 1990s, it meant, simply, the gap between those that do and those that do not have access to the Internet and related technologies. It could be measured in a straightforward manner: for example, by counting the number of households who reported owning a computer and/or those who reported having access to the Internet. Advocates of digital access equality understood that it would become table stakes for full participation in society – much like the telephone nearly a century ago. Government policies and private sector programs have been working for more than twenty years to close the access gap, and though much progress has been made, these efforts addressed only the first level problem -- what we might term the digital divide 1.0.

Today the digital divide represents a broader, more nuanced set of inequalities. It is not just physical access that separates the technology-haves and have-nots but a variety of issues including motivation to adopt technology and possession of relevant technology skills. We might call this the digital divide 2.0. The new digital divide must be measured not just by whether a person uses the internet but how often and for what purpose. Researchers and advocates began to describe this new, multi-dimensional digital divide more than a decade ago. Many discussed not only the need for physical access but also the development of motivation and skills -- with the goal being empowerment, not just entertainment. Professor of sociology and communication science Jan van Dijk is one such proponent, and he describes the divide as getting worse, not better.

"The digital divide is deepening where it has stopped widening. In places where people are motivated to gain access and physical access is spreading, differences in skill and usage come forward. The more information and communication technology is immersed in society and pervades everyday life the more it becomes attached to all existing social divisions."[2]

The skill set needed for digital productivity and empowerment has also been referred to as technological or digital literacy. Literacy is in fact a useful term for defining the problem of digital divide 2.0. At its narrowest definition, literacy simply means to read and to write, but it also encompasses education more broadly, and a literate person is assumed to have the ability to understand and communicate ideas and to participate in her or her community. A literate citizenry is the bedrock of a democracy and a prerequisite for the accumulation and advancement of knowledge. As van Dijk suggested, a lack of digital literacy will exacerbate social inequality in a digital society. Individuals who cannot acquire knowledge – whether via analog or digital means –

for personal improvement or empowerment will not maintain their socioeconomic status. Therefore, we must not only take stock of our progress on digital access, we must measure and promote digital literacy.

In the U.S., policies and programs on the national level have been largely designed to address the former but are gradually evolving to focus on the latter. Current federal government action is rooted in the Communications Act of 1934, which codified the concept of Universal Service, the principal that all Americans should have access to communications services. At its origination, Universal Service covered simply to telephone and telegraph access. The American Telephone & Telegraph Company (AT&T) was granted monopoly status, but in return, it agreed to federal regulations that required it provide service to rural, hard-to-reach, and poor communities. The Telecommunications Act of 1996 updated the 1934 Act and expanded the goal to include advanced telecommunications services and high-speed Internet – "for all consumers at just, reasonable and affordable rates." The 1996 Act delineates five major goals including to "advance the availability of such services to all consumers, including those in low income, rural, insular, and high cost areas, at rates that are reasonably comparable to those charged in urban areas" and "increase access to telecommunications and advanced services in schools, libraries and rural health care facilities."[3] To accomplish these aims, the Universal Service Fund (USF) was created. It is supported by charging telecommunications companies a quarterly fee that is often passed on to customers as a separate, billable item. The funds are then provided to entities or programs serving certain populations such as qualifying telephone companies that serve high-cost areas or to low-income customers who receive assistance in paying for monthly telephone charges. Another result of the 1996 Act is the "E-Rate" program, which provides telecommunication services, Internet access, and internal connections to eligible schools and libraries. The E-Rate program has also been a recipient of the USF.

These federal efforts are ongoing but have been adjusted to meet changing needs. The Federal Communications Commission (FCC) has administered the programs under the 1996 Act and evolved its approach and its aims under the direction of Congress and with guidance from the White House. For example, in 2010 the FCC released the National Broadband Plan that reformed certain universal service mechanisms to specifically support deployment of broadband to essential entities (first responders, hospitals, etc.) and to disadvantaged regions and populations.[4] Additionally, the FCC is not the only federal regulatory body promoting broadband adoption. The National Telecommunications & Information Administration (NTIA) is an executive branch agency within the U.S. Department of Commerce that is focused on expanding broadband Internet access and adoption in America and ensuring that the Internet remains an engine for continued innovation and economic growth.[5] The NTIA administers the $4 billion Broadband Technology Opportunities Program (BTOP), which provides matching grants for projects that use technology to solve social problems and improve community access to modern telecommunications.

Numerous innovative programs, too many to mention, have been initiated at the state and local levels as well. As only one recent and innovative example, New York City announced the LinkNYC initiative. Up to 10,000 legacy telephone booths will be converted into kiosks offering free Wi-Fi. Each hotspot will serve up to 250 devices with speeds up to 100mpbs, and the program will be funded via advertising shown on the kiosks' digital displays. The mayor's office has framed this as a fight against inequality since low-income citizens, particularly minorities, rely disproportionately on cellphone browsing to get online, and wireless data charges can add up.[6]

Moreover, corporate entities have brought resources to bear, often in public/private partnerships. For example, in 2011 Comcast announced its Internet Essentials program that offered a combination of discounted broadband service, low-cost computers, and free training programs to teach people how to use the technology. The program is targeted at families eligible for national free lunch programs.[7] Comcast and the Internet Essentials program works in partnership with EveryoneOn, a national non-profit entity "working to eliminate the digital divide by making high-speed, low-cost Internet service and computers, and free digital literacy courses accessible to all unconnected Americans."[8]

EveryoneOn partners broadly with several leading cable companies including Cox, Bright House Networks, MediaCom, and Suddenlink.

Twenty years of federal, local, corporate, and non-profit efforts have had an effect. Recent measures of technology adoption in the United States demonstrate great progress on closing the digital divide 1.0. In 1990 only 22 percent of households in the United States owned a computer.[9] Similarly, in 1995 a Pew Center survey suggested that only 14 percent of adults were using the Internet. But, updated figures demonstrate the decline of the digital access divide. In 2013, the then acting-commissioner of the FCC noted that broadband adoption by households had increased to 70 percent. Moreover, in 2014, the Pew Research Center documented the incredible spread of the Internet, reporting that usage among adults had risen to 87 percent of the population while ownership of cell phones has risen to 90 percent of all adults, and ownership of smartphones has risen to 58 percent.[10]

However, while these gains are both meaningful and encouraging, we must recognize that adoption remains disappointingly unequal. The inequalities remain most evident along income and racial lines. Internet adoption among households earning more than $75,000 per year is 99 percent -- notably higher than that of the general populace. Similarly, adoption is 97 percent for those with a college degree -- implying that those without higher education are accessing the Internet at a much lower rate. Moreover, as recently as 2011, the broadband penetration in low-income areas was determined to be as low as fifteen percent[11] versus 70 percent for the population at large. In 2013, acting chairwoman of the FCC Mignon Clyburn noted that households without internet access at home still accounted for roughly 100 million people or one-third of the population. Certain disadvantaged populations have disproportionately low Internet access including 50 percent of rural Americans, 65 percent of the elderly, 58 percent of people living with disabilities, 41 percent of African-Americans, and 51 percent of Latinos.[12]

Moreover, figures on access address only the first level issue, digital divide 1.0. Less clear is how well policies and programs are addressing the divide 2.0, meaning digital literacy and the spread of skills required for participation in a digital society. There are signs that the gap is, in fact, widening, and it is evident among a population which is actually highly motivated to use technology: children and young adults. A *New York Times* article called "Wasting Time Is New Divide in Digital Era" suggests that children in poorer families spend more time consuming media on a variety of devices leading to a "time-wasting gap." It cites a study published in 2010 by the Kaiser Family Foundation which found that while consumption of media has increased for all children, children and teenagers whose parents do not have a college degree spent 90 minutes more per day exposed to media, compared to children from higher socioeconomic families. In fact, the gap has widened over time -- in 1999, the difference was just 16 minutes. The *Times* article quoted parents saying they did not know how to monitor and limit their children's use technology, and research supports those anecdotes. In effect, the digital divide experienced by parents, trickles down to their children.

Moreover, many of our public schools remain on the wrong side of the divides, both 1.0 and 2.0. Indeed, in 2013, the White House estimated that fewer than 30 percent of America's schools have the broadband they need to teach using today's technology, and the average American public school has about the same connectivity as the average American home while serving 200 times as many users. This is particularly problematic for a society that values equality. If we want a digitally literate population, we must certainly begin by educating our youth.

In fairness, there have been programmatic efforts directed specifically to schools. For example, the FCC's E-rate program was created specifically to ensure that schools and libraries had access to affordable Internet -- but it has received much criticism since inception. Specifically, a 2012 article by *ProPublica* revealed that AT&T charged some schools up to 325 percent more than others in the same region were charged for essentially the same services, and Verizon charged a New York school district more than twice as much as it charged government and other school customers in that state.[13] Some claim the FCC provided too little guidance and oversight to the telecommunications companies required to provide the low-cost service to schools. To revise the E-rate program and address the digital divide in schools, in 2013 the White House unveiled its "ConnectED" initiative. The program's goal are three-part: provide high-speed digital access to 99 percent of America's students by 2017, provide training and digital education tools to teachers, and enlist private company partners to create price-competitive, feature-rich educational devices and software. The White House charged the FCC with developing programs that accomplish this goal, and earmarked $2 billion in funds to be combined with $2 billion in commitments from at least nine private-sector companies including AT&T, Apple, Microsoft, and Verizon.[14] The FCC has also publicly discussed building its own "digital literacy corps" using some of the financial support from Connect2Compete, a partnership between it and EveryoneOn. The proposed funding for this program is $200 million[15] – roughly 5 percent of total ConnectED commitments – but it is a step in the right direction.

There have also been multiple well-publicized programs designed to get technology devices into the hands of students. This kind of progress is easy to announce and easy to measure – but surprisingly hard to enact. For example, in 2013, the Los Angeles United School District (LAUSD) rolled out iPads to 47 schools as an initial test, but quickly ran into problems. Distribution of the devices quickly fell behind schedule; the district recalled devices at several schools; students deleted security filters so they could freely browse the Internet; and the educational materials on license were incomplete during the first year.[16] The district made changes to the program that give schools more choice over the types of devices available, but there has been controversy over the bidding process, and the program is currently on hold.[17] Still struggling with providing access, the LAUSD has not even begun to address the question of curriculum and the nature of technology instruction. Unfortunately, this is not an unusual situation in California. In 2012, the San Jose Mercury News estimated that 56 percent of California public high schools did not offer a single course in computer science or programming. It was not a priority because computer science did not count toward the admission requirements in math or science for admission to the University of California. Moreover, California has no computer science certification to insure that teachers have the appropriate content knowledge.[18]

In fact, 25 of 50 states do not allow computer science courses to count toward high school math and science graduation requirements. A 2013 survey by the Computer Science Teachers Association revealed several challenges including a lack of support or interest from school staff (cited by 40 percent of teachers), a lack of student interest or enrollment (cited by 35 percent), rapidly changing technology (30.5 percent) and a lack of curriculum resources (23.5 percent). Despite these headwinds, here again, progress has been made. At the start of 2013, just nine states had a policy that allowed computer science to count toward graduation, but lobbying efforts by the Association and Microsoft brought that number up to the current twenty-five.[19]

Despite that progress, the state of technology instruction in California's secondary schools suggests we have only just begun to solve the digital literacy gap. A study conducted by researchers from the University of Florida provides further evidence of the divide. They gave the nearly 6,000 Florida students an "information and communication technology (ICT) literacy" test, and the results showed "a digital divide between low and high SES [socio economic status], white and non-white, and female and male students on all measures of the [test]. Specifically, high-SES, white, and female students outperformed their counterparts."

Unfortunately, these findings are not surprising. Many have written that technology has the potential to both cure and exacerbate societal ills. In 2003, Professor Mark Warschauer wrote an article in *Scientific American* with the subtitle "Handing out computers and Internet access is the wrong way to raise technological literacy" and warned that it could actually worsen inequalities by failing to address how the computers were used.[20] Other research has suggested that low income schools were more likely to offer computer activities that simply reinforced existing pedagogical practices like drills or memorization while higher income schools invested in software that promoted creativity. These approaches might serve to exacerbate the learning disparities.[21]

Of course, not every school district is struggling, and there are digital success stories. For example, Chicago Public Schools are in the process of rolling out a K-12 computer science program. In the next three years, every high school in the city will offer a foundational computer science course, and in the next five years, at least half will offer an Advanced Placement computer science course.[22] When introducing ConnectED, President Obama praised Mooresville, NC, a small district that rolled out a laptop program for students in the fourth grade and above beginning in 2009. The district has reported a climbing graduation rate, from 73 percent to 90 percent since 2007, and an increase in academic performance, with students proficient at their grade level increasing from 73 percent to 89 percent. However, Mooresville's superintendent has said improvements were not a result of the laptops, but rather thanks to the instructional changes they enabled.[23] In other words, Mooresville's success did not result simply from access but from broader educational efforts including methods and curriculum. And, there are innovative programs that allow students to be part of the solution. For example, the Net Literacy Corporation is a non-profit begun in 2004 by a middle school student who volunteered to teach computer and Internet skills to senior citizens. It operates in several states and includes multiples program that utilize student volunteers to build computer labs and teach skills like Internet safety and online financial literacy[24].

This sampling of policies and programs from a broad set of organizations indicates what is in place and represent some part of what is needed. But, given that the problems and challenges of the digital divide were identified ten and twenty years ago, these efforts also feel much delayed. In fact, progress on closing digital divide 2.0 seems much harder to achieve than that of divide 1.0. Perhaps this, too, was to be expected for it is certainly more difficult to define and measure digital literacy than it is to tally and track digital access. But, we can also see that the stakes are higher in the era of 2.0 because giving our citizens, and particularly our students, the tools of technology without the requisite guidance can have the opposite effect of what is hoped for. That being the case, it seems time to double our efforts across all channels before the digital divide becomes a breach we cannot repair.

---

[1] *The National Broadband Plan.* Federal Communications Commission. 17 Mar. 2010. Accessed Nov. 2014 <www.transition.fcc.gov>.

[2] Dijk, Jan Van. *The Deepening Divide: Inequality in the Information Society.* 2010.

[3] "Universal Service." Federal Communications Commission. N.D. Accessed Nov. 2014 <www.fcc.gov>.

[4] *The National Broadband Plan.*

[5] "About NTIA." National Telecommunications & Information Administration, U.S. Department of Commerce. N.D. Accessed Nov. 2014 <www.ntia.doc.gov>.

[6] Flegenheimer, Matt. "Pay Phones in New York City Will Become Free Wi-Fi Hot Spots." *The New York Times.* 17 Nov. 2014. Accessed Nov. 2014 <www.nytimes.com>.

[7] Reardon, Marguerite. "Comcast Offers Cheap Broadband to Poor Families." *CNET.* 20 Sep. 2011. Accessed Nov. 2014 <www.cnet.com>.

[8] "About Us." EveryoneOn. N.D. Accessed Nov. 2014 <www.everoneon.org>.

[9] Baase, Sara. *A Gift of Fire: Social, Legal, and Ethical Issues for Computers and the Internet, 4th Edition.* Aug. 2012.

[10] Fox, Susannah and Lee Rainie. "The Web at 25 in the U.S." Pew Research Center. Accessed Nov. 2014 <www.pewinternet.org>.

[11] Reardon, M.

[12] Clyburn, Mignon. "Crossing the Digital Divide." Federal Communications Commission. 7 Jun. 2013. Accessed Nov. 2014 <www.fcc.gov>.

[13] Gerth, Jeff. "AT&T, Feds Neglect Low-Price Mandate Designed to Help Schools." *ProPublica.* 1 May 2012. Accessed Nov. 2014 <www.propublica.org>.

[14] "ConnectED Initiative." White House. N.D. Accessed Nov. 2013 <www.whitehouse.gov>.

[15] Richtel, Matt. "Wasting Time is New Divide in Digital Era." *The New York Times.* 29 May 2012. Accessed Nov. 2014 <www.nytimes.com>.

[16] Blume, Howard. "LAUSD Shifts Gears on Technology for Students." *Los Angeles Times.* 29 Jun. 2014. Accessed Nov. 2014 <www.latimes.com>.

[17] Blume, Howard. "2 Firms That Won LAUSD's Tech Program Most Active in Seeking Meetings". *Los Angeles Times.* 1 Nov. 2014. Accessed Nov. 2014 <www.latimes.com>.

[18] Lewis, Dan. "Computer Science: It's Where the Jobs Are but Schools Don't Teach It". *San Jose Mercury News.* 12 Sep. 2014. Accessed Nov. 2014 <www.mercurynews.com>.

[19] Bidwell, Allie. "Making it Count: Computer Science Spreads as Graduation Requirement". *US News & World Report.* 25 Nov. 2014. Accessed Nov. 2014 <www.usnews.com>.

[20] Warschauer, Mark. "Demystifying the Digital Divide." *Scientific American.* Aug. 2003. Accessed Nov. 2014 <www.scientificamerican.com>.

[21] Natriello, Gary. "Bridging The Second Digital Divide: What Can Sociologists Of Education Contribute?" *Sociology of Education.* Jul. 2001.

[22] Bidwell, Allie.

[23] Resmovits, Joy. "Obama ConnectED Initiative Aims To Get Classrooms Online". *The Huffington Post.* 6 Jun. 2013. Accessed Nov. 2014 <www.huffingtonpost.com>.

[24] "About Net Literacy." *Digital Literacy Corps.* N.D. Accessed Nov. 2014 <www.digitalliteracycorps.org>.

Desperate Times Call for the Birth of the ICC

Ayush Soni

Publication Month: February 2016

Abstract: This paper dives into the historical background of the creation of the International Criminal Court, and then evaluates the political impact, if any, that the ICC has on U.S. domestic law. Because citizens look to a judiciary body to implement and interpret rulings, this paper also includes details from court cases that have been adjudicated at the ICC.

Widely recognized norms have significantly affected states and individuals in both beneficial and detrimental ways. A more detrimental attribute of these norms is how many human rights abuses have gone unpunished in light of the creation of an international criminal court. Even with bold international prohibitions against mass atrocities in place, it is evident that states fail to enforce these norms on a domestic level. The creation of the International Criminal Court (ICC) allows for the enforcement of domestic laws and laws banning genocide, war crimes, and crimes against humanity, which then focus on accountability mechanisms that aid in prosecuting individual actors or entities guilty of committing egregious crimes.

The young ICC has transnationally prosecuted human rights perpetrators like Laurent Gbagbo and Thomas Lubanga Dyilo, and it has adopted international treaties because they are 'self-executing.' Treaties like these augment the ICC because they are enforceable without formal incorporation of its standards into domestic law. Powerful political influence engrained within sovereign nations like the United States (U.S.) undermines the dire need of ending impunity for international criminals. Countries that have not signed onto the Rome Statute are misconceived that benefits of incorporating ICC policies into domestic laws have less tangible benefits than the concrete costs.[1] This paper, however, contends a degree of discretionary power is critical in most administrative contexts in foreign judiciaries, which then impels a position for soft law to bridge law and policy without becoming as rigid as prescriptive legislative provisions. Consequently, the ICC has dealt a reasonable compromise between competing demands of a rule-based government and flexible decision making that accord with basic notions of international justice.

This paper dives into the historical background of the creation of the ICC. After the adoption of the Rome Statute and the Geneva Convention, the paper mentions how judges are appointed with specifications to their length of terms, and how their appointment and powers are defined in the Rome Statute. The differences and similarities between the ICC and domestic courts in compliance of the Rome Statute are signified to convey characteristics of both types of institutions. Information on who/what can formally file a complaint before the ICC is provided, but then the paper progresses to evaluate political impact, if any, that the ICC has on domestic law. Because citizens look to a judiciary body to implement and interpret rulings, this paper also includes details from court cases that have been adjudicated at the ICC.

Part One

History

A peace conference was held in The Hague in 1899, which involved twenty-six countries declaring independent sovereignty.[2] After one hundred years had passed since the 1899 conference, representatives of 160 countries met in Rome to negotiate a treaty that would establish a permanent ICC.[3] The delegates struggled to define the parameters of an institution whose purpose was to respond to the atrocities that had occurred throughout the twentieth century. After five weeks of grueling negotiations, the Diplomatic Conference adopted a statute for the court with twenty-one countries abstaining.[4] It soon became a global phenomenon that the establishment of an international criminal justice system is to prevent and to punish pathological breaches of the international criminal justice system even if multiple obstacles hindered its full adoption among varying states.

Stemming from World War II (WWII) atrocities of the mass genocide of Jewish citizens in Germany rose the first major precedents exhumed from international criminal trials. The International Military Tribunal (IMT) was an integral component at Nuremberg when the four Allied powers in WWII signed an international agreement known as the London Accord, which criminally prosecuted "War criminals whose offenses have no particular geographical location whether they be accused individually or in their capacity as members of organizations or groups in both capacities."[5] In the Nuremberg trials, IMT stated that heads of state and those individuals acting under orders could be criminally liable under international law. The IMT affirmed the primacy of international law over national law in which representatives stated that the "Very essence of the Charter [of the IMT] is that individuals have international duties which transcend the national obligations of obedience imposed by the individual State."[6] The IMT established that individuals may be liable for initiating war itself and the wrongfulness of aggression in which war as well as the offenses against the laws of war were criminalized.[7] However, the IMT's judgment was not binding on either municipal or international courts.

After the Cold War ended in the 1990s, the International Criminal Tribunal for the former Yugoslavia's (ICTY) statute suggested that a permanent court was needed alongside the support of a rule-based government. Shortly thereafter, the creation of the International Criminal Tribunal for Rwanda (ICTR) undermined the establishment of an international institution that could combat serious violations of international humanitarian law since enforcement was not binding, but both the ICTY and the ICTR served to mitigate the atrocities stemming from renegade regimes.[8] Nonetheless, the difficulties of ad hoc tribunals in delivering timely justice were imminent and required further legitimization.

The Genocide Convention was formulated and adopted for the establishment of a permanent international criminal court. The newly established International Law Commission (ILC) received an invitation from the U.N. General Assembly to "Study the desirability and possibility of establishing an international judicial organ for the trial of persons charged with genocide or other crimes over which jurisdiction will be conferred upon that organ by international conventions.[9] The ILC subsequently voted at its second session in 1950 to support the desirability and feasibility of creating an ICC.[10]

The Committee on International Criminal Jurisdiction met in Geneva, Switzerland on August 1951. The committee decided that a multilateral convention would be the best initiation for the ICC's establishment of jurisprudence, which was ultimately adopted at Rome.[11] The ILC provisionally adopted a Draft Code of Crimes in 1991 and in its forty-fourth session in 1992, created a 'working group' on an international criminal court.[12] The group produced an extensive report outlining the ICC's authority and jurisdiction. With the exception of the Court's jurisdiction, which expanded in the 1994 Draft Statute, these proposals were substantially adopted in the 1994 Draft Statute issued by the ILC, and many of them became a significant component to the Rome Statute as well.

Structure and Relative Autonomy (power) of the Court

ICC ethos like the principle of complementarity embodied in the Rome Statute contend that the court must defer to state sovereignty and should only act when states have failed to administer justice.[13] ICC jurisdiction extends to the most heinous international crimes and has developed safeguard proceedings that protect state prerogatives. In examining the structure of the ICC, it is vital to consider the implications of the Rome Statute of the ICC. On July 17, 1998, almost one hundred years after the First Peace Conference in The Hague was held, the ICC Statute was signed in Rome; however, it did not enter into full force until July 1, 2002.[14] The Rome Statute is a treaty that extends the ICC's jurisdiction over domestic legal enforcement and "three core crimes of genocide, crimes against humanity, and a carefully negotiated (and thereby limited) list of the most serious war crimes."[15] It was established that a two-thirds majority of Member States is required to define and to establish ICC jurisdiction over the crime of aggression.[16]

Articles 5 through 8 include the prohibition of crimes within the jurisdiction of the ICC. The U.N. General Assembly adopted the Genocide Convention's text in 1948 for the purpose of satisfying rule-based governmental structures based in and around The Hague.[17] The text conveyed a new international consensus condemning and defining genocide as a form of mistreatment "committed with intent to destroy, in whole or in part, a national, ethnical, racial, or religious group, as such" (UN General Assembly). As well-intentioned these provisions are, many scholars perceive the principle of complementarity as creating barriers for national criminal proceedings to advance to the ICC.

Judges

The ICC consists of eighteen full-time judges divided into separate chambers dealing with trials, pre-trial matters, and appeals whose number and status may be adjusted later according to the caseload.[18] The Rome Statute establishes an Assembly of States Parties as the overseer of the other organs of the ICC, members of the States Parties decide the financial budget to fund the ICC's creation and development, and they also decide the number of ICC judges that preside over the cases brought forth.[19]

The Assembly of States Parties then elect the judges and a ballot election requires a two-thirds majority of present States Parties to vote. The judges who pass these necessary hurdles in order to preside over cases in the ICC serve a single nine-year term.[20] A president responsible for the overall administration of the ICC and two vice presidents are then elected by these selected judges, five of whom are assigned to the Appeals Division (including the President). The Trial and Pre-Trial Divisions are comprised of six judges each; they are expected to refrain from any activity that will affect their deliverance of a fair judgment.[21] The other organs of the ICC's composite are the Offices of the Prosecutor and Registrar.[22] The provisions concerning the composition and administration of the court, as well as the removal from office are specified in Part IV of the Rome Statute in Articles 34 through 46.[23] Judges can be removed from office for serious misconduct or for a serious breach of his/her duties under the Rome Statute, which is proclaimed in Article 41.[24] It requires a two-thirds vote of the Assembly of States Parties and a recommendation of a two-thirds majority vote of the other judges to remove an ICC judge.[25]

Separation of Powers

The ICC was created to complement the criminal jurisdiction of states. The ICC acts as a jurisdictional 'safety net' when domestic remedies are exhausted and no alternative forum is presented to prosecute those liable for international crimes.[26] The Rome Statute limits ICC jurisdiction to those cases where a Member State with jurisdiction has not investigated or prosecuted an alleged crime.[27] Even though the ICC abides by the complementarity principle of the Rome Statute, any state with jurisdiction can assert a more superior right to deal with a case by prosecuting; however, there is the exception in which a case in a particular state has not been prosecuted, and then it is therefore handed over to the ICC.[28]

The powers of judges in the ICC are limited in that they do not have judicial review powers. Judges are expected to rigorously apply the law as it is written in the Rome Statute. Powerful non-party nationals are often unwilling to surrender a portion of their sovereignty to the ICC. The domestic institutions have a centralized authority with a monopolized enforcement mechanism to punish criminals; conversely, there is no international authority that enforces laws and provisions on a global scale. Because of these characteristics of international treaties, it becomes viable how difficult it is for soft law and policy to strengthen governmental entities. In contrast to international law's lack of a real enforcement body, highly developed domestic systems are considered to be 'fully legalized' due to "[their]…obligations with some dome degree of precision that are in turn delegated to a third party to implement, interpret and apply the rule" (2000: 401-419). Rules have merit only when there is some realistic application of them to situations that take place in communities, which is better examined through the scope of each States' enforcement mechanism. Subsequently, domestic law is more binding to States and individuals than self-executing treaties.[29] For international law to have the authority of enforceability, domestic courts must incorporate international obligations into national legislation so that international cooperation over transnational borders can serve to maintain social control.

Access

A country that has signed the Rome Statute and/or the United Nations Security Council can refer a situation to the prosecutor of the ICC in which crimes within the ICC's jurisdiction have been committed. The ICC prosecutor him/herself may initiate an investigation proprio motu (on their own authority) if they have determined that a violation of the Rome Statute exists on the basis of information presented in court. The ICC prosecutor may inquire international organizations, states, and non-governmental organizations for additional information; however, the investigations initiated by the prosecutor are subject to authorization approval by the Pre-Trial division. Authorization is granted if the investigational elements of the alleged crime are appropriate and if three judges vote in consensus that there is a reasonable basis to proceed and that the alleged crime falls within the ICC's jurisdiction.[30] Victims of atrocious crimes are to be represented in this ignition of investigations/prosecution process by allowing individuals to submit their views and information to the prosecutor and/or judges presiding in the Pre-Trial Chamber.[31]

Part II

When the probability of detrimental loss occurring is extremely low, it is expected that individuals will take advantage of the opportunity presented in front of them. In applying this to Member States of the ICC, delegates of the countries that have ratified the ICC have weighed the costs versus the benefits of surrendering their national sovereignties and can now be held accountable for atrocious human rights violations that take place in their respective jurisdictions. The decision-making model that is referred to in this case is known as prospect theory. This theory contends that people weigh outcomes that are merely probable in comparison with outcomes that are more certain to occur; value is assigned to gains and losses rather than to final assets.[32] Risk and loss aversion is typically highlighted to assess potential gains in a rational deliberation. By weighing the loss of their complete national sovereignty (costs), these Member States, unlike the U.S., have recognized that there must be accountability mechanisms in place to restore international justice (gains).

However, the principle of complementarity mentioned earlier allows for cases to be addressed in domestic settings first and to use the ICC as a court of last resort to ensure that individuals guilty of committing human rights atrocities enlisted in the Rome Statute have been prosecuted. This principle constrains the ICC from playing an active role in judicial review and policy-making in an effort to prevent political backlash. On the other hand, prospect theory is what empowers the ICC politically as Member States relinquish their limited jurisdictional powers to an ICC. Therefore, Part II reinforces the notion that the ICC negotiates between the competing demands of various Member States and the binding powers illustrated in the Rome Statute that embodies the principle of complementarity.

The establishment of the ICC raises hopes that the lines between international law and world order are being blurred and that normative structures being created by international law might influence or even restrain the Hobbesian order established by the politics of states in which states' relations are guided by interests.[33] It was deliberated that the ICC would be different from the ICJ (International Court of Justice), which can only decide disputes between states.[34] The ICC's political impact is exemplified in the applicability of domestic laws to serve as a check in ensuring that the laws do not hamper the rights of an individual or the duties of a state as a sovereign entity. It is arguable that the ICC does not do more than what each state is expected to do; therefore, the ICC is an extension of national criminal jurisdiction and it is noted that this is the reason behind why the ICC does not infringe on national sovereignty.[35] Paradoxically, ratifying the Rome Statute was an exercise of national authority, so the ICC owes its existence to the state sovereignty that it seeks to complement.

The ICC has jurisdiction over nationals of non-party states when a crime is committed in a Member State's jurisdiction.[36] The ICC has also impacted domestic power through its use of extradition powers that domestic institutions are unable to implement transnationally. Member States demonstrate their acceptance that the ICC may exercise some of their sovereign powers in that instance. This does not, however, mean that non-party states of the ICC have had their control limited or undermined in any way. Although most scholars have the preconceived notion that the principle of complementarity limits the power of the ICC, complementarity can be used as a tool to extend state sovereignty through international measures. Robert Jennings, an expert in international legal studies, contended that what "...Is most urgently needed is not a surrender of sovereignty but a transformation and augmentation of it into new directions by harnessing it, through proper legal devices, to the making of collective decisions, and the taking of effective collective action, over international political problems."[37] States can now use the ICC to their advantage by establishing legitimacy and implementing the ICC's jurisdictional powers in areas outside of domestic courts' supremacy.

The Prosecutor v. Thomas Lubanga Dyilo and The Prosecutor v. Thomas Lubanga Dyilo are landmark cases for the ICC's assertion of international justice. Lubanga, commander-in-chief of the Forces Patriotiques pour la Liberation du Congo (FPLC), was arrested and brought to The Hague on March 20, 2006. He was accused of enlisting children under the age of fifteen, conscripting them, and using children to participate actively in hostile operations.[38] The trial proceeded January 26, 2009, and he was found guilty of all of the crimes he was accused of on March 14, 2012. On July 10 of the same year, judges in the Trial Chamber sentenced Thomas Lubanga Dyilo to fourteen years of imprisonment in the Detention Centre in The Hague. The Lubanga case proves the progression of the ICC in enforcing domestic policies that the Democratic Republic of the Congo was unable to enforce. Since this was the first case conducted in the ICC, judges will look to the Lubanga case as precedent in guiding them in future decisions.

Laurent Gbagbo, Ivorian national and former President of Cote d'IVoire, was accused of four charges of crimes against humanity at the ICC: murder, rape, and other inhuman acts, all of which are prohibited under international/domestic institutions.[39] The Pre-Trial Chamber issued the warrant of arrest in November the same year; however, the last milestone in prosecuting Gbagbo was issued on June 3, 2013 when ICC judges delayed the decision on whether or not they should officially send the case to trial, emphasizing the need for more substantive evidence from the prosecutor.[40] Following the ICC's failed attempts to bring President Omar al-Bashir of Sudan and Libya's Muammar Gadaffi to justice for the alleged crimes they committed, this case demonstrates how the ICC is playing its part to convey that even those at the highest levels of political power are unable to escape justice when they commit grave crimes.

Several countries, namely the U.S., are resistant in compromising their political interests with ICC supervisory that may hold them accountable for several violations of war crimes and crimes against humanity.

Because the U.S. was the major strategic and financial contributor of the ICYT and ICTR, it is a perplexing matter to discuss why the U.S. objects to abiding by the Rome Statute when the U.S. clearly demurred the events that initiated the Nuremberg trials.[41] Nonetheless, the U.S. issued mainly five justifications as to why it refused to sign onto the conditions binding them to the conditions of an International Criminal Court. Because there is ICC jurisdiction to prosecute Member States citizens in nationals of non-parties, the ICC essentially binds non-signatory nations like the U.S. to its discretion. If an individual or an official from the U.S. is accused of violating a domestic law or an international provision in the Rome Statute, the U.S. is concerned that the ICC could be used by hostile countries as a vehicle for challenging U.S. foreign policies to bring unsupported charges against American citizens. The accused U.S. citizens may have greater exposure to such charges than citizen of other nations; the U.S. realizes that due to the prominent role it plays in the realm of world affairs, the ICC is subject to politicized prosecution.[42]

Other objections of signing onto the statute is that the ICC prosecutor has unchecked discretion to initiate cases, which one could argue condemns the prosecutor to be unaccountable. U.S. delegates have also realized that the Rome Statute gives the ICC authority to define and punish the crime of "aggression." The definition serves as a prerogative of the Security Council of the United Nations under the U.N. Charter and can interpret the term 'aggression' in a discretionary fashion to achieve its aims.

Finally, one difference manifested between the ICC's statute and the U.S. Constitution is the lack of due process guarantees in the Rome Statute. The ICC will not offer foreigners like Americans due process rights they consider truly viable, such as the right to a jury trial[43]; therefore, Americans prosecuted in the ICC will presume that they have suffered unfair treatment in a court of international law like the ICC. Complementarity also proves deficient in providing American service-members any absolute protection against being brought to trial before the ICC. Sustaining legitimacy is consistent with how soft law constructs rely on states' political ideals, but the ICC must also avoid losing the ability to inspire the protection of human rights in treaties among nation-states.

Recently developed administrations such as the ICC and judges' imperative use of discretion connects soft law constructs like the Rome Statute to domestic law/policy to preserve global sanctities. In the cases against Gbagbo and Lubanga, it is portrayed how the ICC has difficulties in achieving its aim when it has to satisfy Member States while remaining impartial. Critics of ICC mechanisms often reflect a realist view that contends how the ICC was a cheap and deceitful way of demonstrating a façade that international crimes are being dealt with effectively. For example, Professor Kevin Ward claims that "Such trials are anticlimactic, as evil is banal, and [f]lashy show trials of certain individuals…allow the rest of us to pretend that we are not ourselves in some way responsible."[44] Though this contention means that trials at the ICC allow people to feel emotionally satisfied under the pretext that violations against humanity are being dealt with, it must be noted that a force of consensual solidarity among countries in international relations makes every nation-state equally responsible for crimes committed in their presence.

Creating an effective, but limited ICC per the Rome Statute has enabled necessary confrontations and adjudications to persist in The Hague. Throughout this paper, it was discussed how judges are appointed, their length of terms, and how their authority is defined in the ICC's statute. Analyzing the comparisons and similarities between the ICC and countries party to the Rome Statute are designed to reveal flaws and strengths of each adjudicative venue. Part one of this paper informs readers of who is able to bring forth a complaint before the ICC. The second part of this paper evaluates that the ICC has played a critical role in affecting domestic law. Through case law, it is demonstrated that desperate measures truly do call for the birth of an ICC in galvanizing international efforts to secure human rights in both internal and external legal institutions.

---

[1] Sewall, Sarah B., & Carl Kaysen. *The United States and the International Criminal*

Court: National Security and International Law. Rowman & Littlefield
    Publishers, Inc. 1992. 21, November 2015.

[2] Ibid.

[3] Ibid.

[4] Bassiouni, M. Cherif. *The Statute of the ICC: A Documentary History*.
    Transnational. 1998. Accessed Nov. 2015.

[5] Sewall.

[6] Ibid.

[7] Ibid.

[8] Ibid.

[9] Djonovich, Dusan J. *United Nations Resolutions, Series 1: Resolutions of the
    General Assembly*. Oceana Publications. 1957. Accessed Nov. 2015.

[10] Sewall.

[11] Ibid.

[12] Ibid.

[13] Ibid.

[14] International Criminal Court. "Structure of the Court." International Criminal
    Court. 2013. Accessed Nov. 2015 <www.icccpi.int>.

[15] UN General Assembly. "Rome Statute of the International Criminal Court."
    UN General Assembly. 2010. Accessed Nov. 2015 <www.refworld.org>.

[16] Sewall.

[17] Ibid.

[18] Ibid.

[19] Ibid.

[20] Ibid.

[21] Ibid.

[22] ICC.

[23] UN General Assembly.

[24] Ibid.

[25] Sewall.

[26] Ibid.

[27] ICC.

[28] Sewall.

[29] Lorenz, Frederick M. "Humanitarian Law and the Law of War: Text and
    Materials." *Exploration Seminar*. 2010. Accessed Nov. 2015.

[30] Sewall.

[31] UN General Assembly.

[32] Kahneman, Daniel, & Amos Tversky. "Prospect Theory: An Analysis of
    Decision Under Risk." *Econometrica*. 1979. Accessed Nov. 2015.

[33] Bassiouni, M. Cherif. "Perspectives on International Criminal Justice," *Virginia
    Journal of International Law*. 2010.

---

[34] Sewall.

[35] Bassiouni, 2010.

[36] Cryer, Robert. "International Criminal Law vs State Sovereignty: Another Round?" *European*

Journal of International Law. 2005.

[37] Ibid.

[38] ICC.

[39] ICC.

[40] Sewall.

[41] Sewall.

[42] Sewall.

[43] Lorenz.

[44] Cryer.

Development and Technology

How Does the Right to Information and the Spread of ICT Affect Global Society?

Keith Snodgrass

Publication Month: January 2017

Abstract: This paper discusses how the framing of the United Nation's eight Millennium Development Goal, particularly within the context of information and communications technology. The author examines some potential shortcomings of some of these approaches, and how pursuit of these development goals fits within wider efforts to achieve economic development in the poorer parts of the world.

Introduction

After the United National Development Group established the Millennium Development Goals,[1] many individuals, governments, non-governmental organizations (NGOs), and businesses started projects that attempted to use information and communications technology (ICT) to further the eight identified goals.

"The widespread hope within the international development community that ICTs could be a powerful tool of development and poverty reduction, and of achieving the Millennium Development Goals, led to a proliferation of donor-funded ICT-for-development pilot projects in several sectors in a wide range of countries in the past decade. Yet, by the time the international community was preparing to convene in Geneva in November 2003 for the first phase of the World Summit on the Information Society (WSIS), there was a growing uneasiness about the lack of detailed information on the implementation of these projects, and rigorous evaluation of their impact."[2]

Many ICT extension projects focus on providing technology and connectivity to underserved communities around the world, which are essential to reaching any of the goals their backers espouse. What these projects address less directly, or not at all, is providing access to the information needed to make best use of these technologies. Moreover, in the developing information economy, we see that information and data are the currency on which economics, education, entertainment, conflict resolution, and more are all based. What are some ways of analyzing this issue?

Alistair S. Duff utilized the philosophies of John Rawls and R.H. Tawney to argue, "once certain categories of information are accorded the status of 'primary goods,' their distribution must then comply with principles of justice as articulated by those major 20th century exponents of ethical social democracy." Duff further argues that Rawls and Tawney's theories inevitably lead, in the information society, to the following conclusion:

"The Rawls-Tawney theorem is also firm about the main referent of distributive justice in postindustrial society: it is *information*, not ICTs, nor new media, nor the information infrastructure. The latter are not unimportant, but they are *politically* significant only insofar as they impinge on the social distribution of information itself—information *qua* facts, data, the basic building-blocks of knowledge and participation."[3]

This approach also addresses several of the points articulated in the UNESCO Code of Ethics (more on that below).

This paper will not attempt to ascertain how well any of these goals were met but will rather discuss how goals are framed, what might be the shortcomings of some of these approaches, and how pursuit of these goals fits within wider efforts at economic development in the poorer parts of the globe.

History

For centuries, technology has been suggested as a remedy for societies that are perceived as, or perceive themselves as, less developed than other parts of the world. As early as the middle of the 19th century, dislocating encounters with European political, economic and military powers, led individuals in countries such as Turkey and India to debate whether it was possible to adapt the technologies of the conquering powers without also adopting the social mores. Many quickly adopted military technologies such as automatic weapons, heavy cannonry and the like, yet there was great caution around adopting other technologies such as telegraphy and rail travel. Military technology could be immediately useful in both opposing the European powers and in fending off internal and external threats to an existing political power in these countries. The apparently uncontrollable nature of wired communications and long distance travel by rail caused more concern in such societies than the progress of military prowess. Each of these new technologies made the control of subject populations appear to be more challenging.

Through the early 20th century, existing political powers in the developing world and the various political movements which sprung up to reform or resist these powers, began to adapt communications and travel technologies to their own uses. These were sometimes in support of, and sometimes in opposition to, the very idea of economic development as a public good. On one hand Japanese companies moved into manufacturing of items such as automobiles and military technology, yet one of the main leaders of India's independence movement, Mohandas (Mahatma) Gandhi, advocated that all Indians reject not only British manufactured goods but also manufactured goods made in India, in favor of village industries, particularly homespun cloth. This was in reaction to the economic damage done to India by British colonization. This idea was so powerful and popular that the home-based spinning wheel (the *charkha*) was at the center of the flag representing India's independence movement.

After World War II and the establishment of the World Bank, technological progress was on offer to the developing world in the form of heavy machinery for farming and construction. This was particularly true in the form of dams, which were widely perceived by both people from more developed economies and leaders of less developed economies as an important marker and maker of development around the world. Dams demonstrated the ability of governments to complete major projects that could help to control natural forces that were heretofore considered uncontrollable. Dams brought development, in the form of irrigation and electrification, to rural areas previously largely untouched by state-lead development efforts.

Many national governments, after gaining independence from European powers in the 1940's to the 1970's instituted large educational efforts to increase the pool of technical experts available in their countries, with an eye toward further economic development based on rapid improvement in agricultural production, engineering and manufacturing, communications and travel technology. One of the earliest of these efforts was the establishment of the Indian Institutes of Technology (IIT). The idea of such an institute was mooted even before India became independent, and the first IIT was established in Karagpur in 1950, only three years after India achieved independence.[4]

These IIT's produced many highly qualified graduates, who went on to lead major development efforts, government programs, and private businesses, in India and in other countries. Many of these people have played key roles in not only leading specific efforts at development, but also in formulating larger ideas which guide many development efforts around the world.

Many of the ideas promoted by such technologically trained individuals offered technology as a neutral power which could provide a means to develop an economy without causing disruption to existing social and political relationships. This might be considered a feature of such development efforts – they could also be presented as non-threatening to existing governments and power structures. Even so, those offering these types of models knew that part of the point of development efforts is to change the power dynamics of at least part of a society. For instance, building dams often means that some people must be displaced from their homes to make way for the reservoir that fills behind the dam, while others benefit from the electricity and irrigation provided by such projects.

Current Policy Issues

With this idea in mind, let us examine possible avenues for addressing some of these issues. One is the *Code of Ethics for the Information Society Proposed by the Intergovernmental Council of the Information for*

All Programme (IFAP), from UNESCO, published in 2011. It proposes 18 rules by which governments and other organizations should operate in order to ensure safety and equity for all in the use of ICT's.[5]

While this document contains many useful instructions, such as that everyone has a right to access the Internet, it leaves as many questions unanswered as it addresses. For instance, in regards to the issues of privacy, it states:

12. Everyone has a right to the protection of personal data and private life on the Internet and other ICTs. Users should be protected against the unlawful storage, abuse or unauthorized disclosure of personal data, and against the intrusion of their privacy.

13. All stakeholders shall work together to prevent against abusive uses of ICTs, protection of private data and privacy and violation of human rights on the Internet and other ICTs by combination of legislative measures, user education, including use of media and information literacy skills, self-regulation and co-regulation measures and technical solutions without disrupting the free flow of information. [6]

Particularly in relation to point 12, alluding to laws evades the question of which laws and who gets to make them. Repressive and democratic governments have enacted laws that restrict access to the Internet, yet these acts are still in conformity with the suggested guidelines in this UNESCO document, since they conform to local laws.

Then there is the issue of private companies attempting to expand the general customer base (and hence their own customer base) by starting projects such as Facebook's Free Basics program in India. Facebook's executives thought they had identified the major problem with expanding Internet access in countries such as India, which was that access to data was too expensive. Hence, they attempted to build a "walled garden" wherein users would get unlimited access to a limited number of curated sites. Yet this created two problems: internet users in India (and all over the world) expect to be able to access any public site, exactly as people do in the developed world: and Facebook ignored the fact that India has hundreds of different languages, thus making the task of curating all these sites extremely unlikely to be successful.

A further challenge is that India's cell phone system has many providers, and at the same time, more limited bandwidth than many countries with many fewer providers. For this reason, India's many telecom providers have access to only a small sliver of spectrum, which makes providing reliable service to customers a challenge. Wider use of unlicensed use spectrum, as is done in the U.S. and many other countries, is essential to providing service to rural areas. There is also great demand on the Indian phone networks, because broadband is not available in huge swathes of the country. It is not likely to become available either, since running cable the last mile is the most expensive portion, and almost all of the "last miles" in India are in very far-flung villages with low (relative to urban areas) population densities, making it uneconomical for telecom companies to run cable there. Hence, most of these people will be using phone systems for Internet access for the foreseeable future.[7]

These access issues are among those I contend will seriously hamper the effectiveness of technological efforts to bring development and alleviate poverty in significant portions of the world.

Privacy is a major issue when expanding ICT into new areas and populations. Many apps and programs are based around collecting information from individuals. This information may include where they have traveled, with whom they have met, what web sites and electronic books they have read, with whom they have communicated, financial and health records, and more. As we have seen in the developed world, it is easy to imagine that app developers use this information for purposes the user does not even suspect when agreeing to whatever terms (if any) associated with using the app, and unknowingly allow this information to be harvested. Will these be safe for use in societies with underdeveloped democratic and privacy rights? [8]

Aside from such information gathering, there is the issue of surveillance, whether by private or public agencies. The success of financial apps such as M-Pesa demonstrates that, so far at least, it is possible to have such interactivity without compromising security. When these types of activities are expanded to include more personal interactions and the utility of apps is based more on their ability to collect and use personal information, more problems may arise.

Take the example offered by Jeffrey Rosen in "The Deciders: Facebook, Google and the Future of Privacy and Free Speech."[9] While Rosen's article focuses on the U.S., these issues are extremely relevant around the world, and particularly so in developing countries with a less robustly developed online experiences for its citizens. The types of information sharing Rosen posits, such as Open Planet [a Facebook app which shows live video of users at any time] might find great favor not only with citizens and with consumers in developing countries, but also with businesses and governments in those countries as well. Such an open repository of information about private citizens could be an irresistible attraction for an unethical business of reporting on citizen actions or monitoring for the government. In addition, and more dangerously, given the extensive details people are willing to share on social platforms, individuals are apparently quite willing and eager to share information. Once these types of systems are established, it would be difficult to shut them down.

The issues with each of these problems extend into the opening gambit about free and equal access to information being a key feature of any successful effort to bridge the digital divide. They also highlight the challenges inherent in such an approach. Access to information is often now provided as a quid pro quo for surrendering information. "We'll show you stock quotes if you tell us where you like to shop," or "provide weather forecasts if you tell us what crops you grow", or "read our celebrity gossip if you tell us what movies you like." It all seems fine and innocent, until it becomes clear that this information, once surrendered to the app developer, cannot be recalled, and can be shared in any way the developer pleases. While we may hope that in the U.S. we can be protected from such a fate by legal systems and possibly by provisions in an End User License Agreement (EULA), it is less clear how universal these protections may be in other countries. Even in the U.S., we've seen that EULAs are used much more to protect the app developer from the user than for the reverse. There is no reason this will not be the case when similar situations arise in developing economies. This risk may be particularly acute in areas where there are extreme divisions of wealth and poverty, thus making not only access to information but also access to legal redress another factor exacerbating such divisions.

These issues will require negotiation among governments, NGOs, and private companies to establish policies and laws which will allow for the extremely important activity of extending the digital economy into areas previously not served or extremely underserved by digital technology. Just as important as extending the technology, such as devices and apps, is extending the knowledge and capability of accessing and using that information to populations which will be newly integrated into the digital world that is still in its early stages.

If policies to ensure rights and abilities to access information are not strong and equitable, the extension of ICT into previously underdeveloped parts of the world economy will only exacerbate the already sharp divisions between the haves and the have-nots. This growing divide may lead to severe social unrest and conflicts, the consequences of which are difficult to predict, but ultimately are likely to be unpleasant.

---

[1] "What They Are." Millennium Project, United Nations Development Program. N.D. Accessed Mar. 2016 <www.unmillenniumproject.org>.

[2] "ICT for Development: Contributing to the Millennium Development Goals." infoDev, World Bank Group. Nov. 2003. Accessed Mar. 2016. <www.infodev.org>.

[3] Duff, Alistair S. "The Rawls-Tawney Theorem and The Digital Divide In Postindustrial Society." *Journal of the Association for Information Science and Technology.* 13 Dec. 2010.

[4] "History of the Institute - IIT Delhi." Indian Institute of Technology - Delhi. N.D. Accessed Mar. 2016. <www.iitd.ac.in>.

[5] *Code of Ethics For The Information Society Proposed By The Intergovernmental Council of The Information For All Programme (IFAP).* United Nations Educational, Scientific and Cultural Organization. 10 Oct. 2011. Accessed Mar. 2016 <www.unesdoc.unesco.org>.

[6] *Ibid.*

---

[7] Sumit Roy, UW Professor of Electrical Engineering. Personal Communication. Mar. 2016.

[8] Allyson W. Haynes. "Online Privacy Policies: Contracting Away Control Over Personal Information?" *Penn State Law Review*. Mar. 2007. Accessed Mar. 2016 <www.works.bepress.com>.

[9] Jeffrey Rosen. " The Deciders: The Future Of Privacy And Free Speech In The Age Of Facebook And Google." *Fordham Law Review*. Feb. 2011. Accessed Mar. 2016 <www.ir.lawnet.fordham.edu>.

Understanding the Risks in the Indian Automobile Manufacturing

Jyotsna Saxena
Publication Month: June 2017

Abstract: This paper discusses the history and current environment of the automobile-manufacturing sector in India. The analysis begins by providing the historical and cultural context necessary for identifying and understanding the key risks to the sector in both the public and private sectors. Building upon this knowledge, the author explores some of the potential solutions aimed at improving both domestic and international confidence in this key sector, which is a dominant contributor to the country's economic output.

Introduction

The "Make in India" campaign, the brainchild of India's Prime Minister Narendra Modi, was launched in September 2015 to bolster the contribution of the manufacturing sector towards the country's Gross Domestic Product (GDP).[1] The campaign's goal is to put India at the forefront of global manufacturing by encouraging investments, motivating innovation, and supporting skill development. In 2016, the week of February 13 to 18 was India's first ever "Make in India Week."[2] Prime Minister Modi kicked off the weeklong showcase of India's capabilities in the field of manufacturing. In his speech, he highlighted the four 'Ds' that work in favor of the Indian market – democracy, demography, demand, and deregulation.[3] He supported this claim with the statistic that the Foreign Direct Investment (FDI) inflows have increased by 48 percent since May 2014, at a time when the global GDP was not that strong. This is indeed an exciting time for the Indian manufacturing sector with new processes (de-licensing and deregulation), new infrastructure (development of industrial corridors and smart cities, fortified Intellectual Property Rights regime), new sectors (FDI availability in defense production, construction, and railways infrastructure), and a new mindset (a pro-business, pro-industrialization government).[4] It is important to note that the risks faced by the Indian manufacturing sector overall are equally applicable to the automobile- specific segment of manufacturing – so too are the government regulations and policies undertaken to mitigate these risks.

In order to be well oriented with the topic of this paper, it is essential to understand why this government initiative has gained so much traction in all quarters, leading to it being touted as *the* development factor for the country's growth. From 1947 (year of independence) until 1990, the Indian economy was closed and controlled by the state, where business development was in the hands of the government. This period has been specifically labeled as the "Permit/License Raj" (rāj, meaning "rule" in Hindi), which was initiated by the first prime minister of the country, Jawaharlal Nehru.[5] In this period, if any private company aspired to manufacture a commodity, it had to acquire a license from the government to be able to do so. This process was tied up with red tape, thereby making it rather cumbersome for private sector companies to flourish. As if this were not enough, the State also had a say in what was being produced, how much quantity was being produced, the selling price of the commodity, and even the sources of capital for production.[6] This practice continued for more than four decades and the then governments were in support of import substitution industrialization.[7] Consequently, business leaders and marketers shied away from getting their systems and people involved in an unconducive business environment. By 1980, the consequences of this planned economy were highly noticeable – low growth rates, pessimism among businessmen, macroeconomic instability, and marginalization of India in the world market.[8]

In 1991, the Indian government began the shift from a planned economy to a market economy, restructuring its role in the economic administration, opening the market to the private sector - including foreign investment. Man economic and trade policies were modified in a systematic manner to make the market more favorable for investors. Deregulation was undertaken across the manufacturing sector to attract competent business entities and enhance productivity. Industrial licensing was eliminated in almost all industries except defense production, atomic energy generation, and railway transport.[9] Gradually import licensing was abandoned in 1993 for capital goods and raw materials. Processes that limited the quantity and quality of manufactured consumer goods and agricultural products were done away with in 2001. Financial policies had to be eased to accommodate the demand that rose out of opening up the economy. Interest rates and reserve requirements were liberalized.[10] According to the World Bank Indicators, the annual GDP growth in 1990 was 5.5 percent, slowed to 3.8 percent in 2000, and is currently hovering at 7.3 percent in 2015.[11] It has remained steady in the first half of fiscal year 2015-16, making India the world's fastest growing economy, according to KPMG India.[12] Also, to align with the manufacturing sector's contribution to the GDP, a point can be made that in 2000, manufacturing contributed to the GDP by approximately $71 billion (USD) and this figure soared to about $348 billion in 2014, a fivefold increase. The Indian government is expecting manufacturing to contribute 25 percent of India's approximate current GDP of $2 trillion.

Public Sector Major Players

The first step is to identify the government entities involved in the Indian automobile manufacturing sector and their respective roles in the decision-making process. Multiple governmental and non-governmental entities influence the growth and policies in the manufacturing sector and subsequently the automobile industry. Initial research shows that the Ministry of Commerce and Industry (MCI) and the Ministry of Heavy Industries and Public Enterprises (MHIPE) are the leading government ministries that govern the policies and reforms in this sector. The Department of Industrial Policy and Promotion (DIPP) under the MCI[13] is in charge of strategizing for industrial development, facilitating Foreign Direct Investment (FDI) policy, and policies related to Intellectual Property Rights (IPR) among other functions.[14] As part of the Make in India initiative, an agency named 'Invest India', a joint effort of DIPP and Federation of Indian Chambers of Commerce & Industry (FICCI) (a non-government trade association), was set up to provide expansive investment opportunities.[15] MHIPE and Society of Indian Automotive Manufacturers (SIAM) have together come up with an Automotive Mission Plan 2006-2026 in order ensure that India emerges as the destination of choice for the design and manufacture of automobiles.

The long-term goal is to eventually have India rank in the top three automotive industries in the world by 2026.[16]

Public Sector Risks

The following section outlines the risks and potential mitigation prospects concerning the related government agencies face in handling global investors, the country's corporate entities, and progressive reforms.

1. Lack of innovation - Most of the Indian Original Equipment Manufacturing units (OEMs) launch several new models of vehicles, but no pioneering ideas have gained any momentum in the automobile-manufacturing sector.[17] Even with the Global OEMs, only the globally successful models are launched in the Indian markets.[18] This largely affects competition negatively among the companies within the industry as it limits the options available in the market. Competition is directly proportional to productivity which impacts the country's per capita income. High productivity and flexible policies that stimulate innovation are key factors in retaining the market advantage that the global OEMs are looking for.[19] To handle this risk, the Automotive Mission Plan 2006-26 has brought about a 200 percent weighted tax reduction in the Research and Development expenditure to in-house and outsourced R&D facilities.[20] This has attracted a lot of attention of the foreign companies, who are now expanding their R&D operations. Some examples include Mercedes-Benz, Mahindra and Mahindra, Tata Motors, and Hero MotoCorp.[21]

2. Environmental Regulations and Emission Norms - The automobile industry is directly impacted by the verdict of the judiciary in cases against the companies of this sector who are often blamed for rise in the atmospheric pollution.[22] These decisions are often taken in favor of the prosecution, which has encouraged the perception that the automobiles industry is the reason for polluting the environment. There are no clearly demarcated emission standards that would facilitate

235

transparent and fair court proceedings. This makes global automobile companies more hesitant in expanding their operations in India. The Automotive Mission Plan (AMP) 2026 mandates that a scientific and transparently conducted study be done of the cities where automobile-manufacturing plants are based, to outline the causes of air pollution. In addition, emission standards are set to be specified structurally to help stakeholders take informed decisions.

3.   Political Obstructionism[23] - A very native feature of the Indian political system, political obstructionism is a major risk that impedes the speed of development and consequently growth of the country overall. The law of majority in the parliament houses affects the execution of the various laws or reforms that are pitched in the upper house.[24] In order to mitigate the consequences of political obstructionism, Competitive Federalism has been charted. Under this framework, all 29 states will be ranked along a 98-point action plan.[25] If an investor seeks to invest in a particular region, they would be required contact the state authorities. Each state has their own policy competing to enhance the ease of doing business and attract investors.

4.   Complex Tax and Customs Formalities - Automobiles are the most heavily taxed manufactured products in India and pose a lot of burden on the sellers and buyers alike.[26] The Curtain Raiser document for the AMP 2016-2026 plan mentions a 53 percent to 73 percent tax incidence for cars, which poses a major risk for the companies in this sector. To top this, the domestic tax system is a cobweb of multiple taxes applicable at different points in the automobile manufacturing lifecycle, as well as the existing heavy excise duties. Propositions like Goods and Services Tax (GST), excise duty concessions, and a fiscally supportive government have been included in the AMP 2026 as an attempt to mitigate this risks.

5.   Poor Return Of Invested Capital (ROIC) Values - McKinsey & Company - a global management consulting firm – reports

that only 46 percent of manufacturing companies (and 41 percent of automobile companies) have an return on invested capital (ROIC) greater than the average cost of capital in 2006.[27] This makes investment in India a less lucrative proposition for foreign companies. Again, this is a significant risk if India aims to increase the automobile manufacturing sector's contribution to the country's GDP to $300 billion by 2026. Therefore, the government ministries and agencies need to work on ensuring that these percentages increase and the foreign companies keep India at the top of their list of countries when they think of expansion.

6. <u>Lack of a Robust Online Legal Infrastructure</u> – There are various online portals established to sell the manufacturing sector to the world (Make in India, Invest India, DIPP), but there are very few efforts made to digitize the judicial system. During the Make in India week, the Prime Minister himself stated that the "formation of the Company Law Tribunal is at the final stage."[28] The fact that it is not already in place and functioning demonstrates that the provision to deliver justice in a streamlined manner has not been top priority so far. While it is true that these facilities are available on-ground, one would expect them to be available online in the face of technological advancements and the government's own directive of "Digital India."[29] This could be taken as a learning lesson for future policy implementation in the hope that the proposed tribunal would be in place soon. However, efforts should be made to streamline other tribunals of the judiciary (Income Tax, Securities and Excise) before the need for their digitization springs up and eventually lead to delay in the delivery of justice.

Private Sector

When reviewing the private automobile manufacturing companies, it is possible to see how far they have come since the License Raj period. Until 1982, the automobile manufacturing market was dominated by three manufacturers - Hindustan Motors, Premier Automobiles, and

Standard Motors Products. Then Maruti Udyog (now Maruti Suzuki) was founded in 1982 as a government initiative in collaboration with Japan's Suzuki.[30] In the liberalization era, the market opened to both joint venture and foreign-owned brands. The automobile industry consists of four sub sectors: two-wheelers (2W), three-wheelers (3W), passenger vehicles (PV), and commercial vehicles (CV).

Private Sector Risks

This section covers the risks faced by the companies of this sector and their mitigation with examples.

1.Fuel Economy - For the growing middle class in India, the decision of buying a car is solely based on oil prices. The 2W segment has an 81 percent market share[31] (also the largest) because of fuel-efficient products being rolled out by manufacturers. The same is applicable for four-wheelers. Manufacturers need to create models catering to such buyers if they wish to make an impact in the sector. Not every manufacturer understands this feature of an Indian car buyer. Maruti Suzuki has been the market leader with largest car manufacturing in India. A quick search on the Internet shows that in the five most fuel-efficient cars in India, four have been manufactured by Suzuki.[32]

2.Labor productivity and training- McKinsey & Company reports that production planning, supply chain management, quality, and maintenance are the four key operational areas that affect Indian manufacturers' productivity.[33] This influences a worker's productivity directly and it has been found that Indian workers are four and five times less productive than Chinese and Thais, respectively.[34] Similar sentiments were echoed in an analysis by Cisco of the manufacturing sector.[35] Companies expanding their operations in India would need to incorporate these facts into their labor training and strategy. If they fail to do so, the cost of capital would increase because of project delays arising out of poor productivity. Maruti Suzuki, for example, arranged for training its workers in six technical institutes. They utilize these training sessions not only to enhance a worker's productivity but also to inculcate a sense of the company's culture.[36]

When Tata Nano initiated such training programs for their workers, they were able to deduce that the company's decision to construct a factory at a site would lead to displacement of residents living at that site. Here, the company faced the risk of facing backlash from the residents of that site against a factory construction, potential political intervention, and an indefinite halt in the construction. However, when they promised to get the residents on board with the project and train them to enhance their productivity, they were able to stick to their business plan.

3.Lack of Infrastructure - Even with flexible policies and pro-investment market regulations, manufacturers like Tesla are shying away from setting up shop in India.[37] This is primarily because of three reasons - inadequate infrastructure, less demand and high import duties. At present, India does not have the have the infrastructure in place to set up charging stations for Tesla's customers and build an Electric Vehicle (EV) network.[38] Secondly, it is not as though the demand for Tesla's models is so high that the manufacturer would think twice before saying no to this business proposition. Thirdly, pricing will be a challenge to sustain a market in India for Tesla. With high import duties, it will be difficult to control the prices of even its third-generation car, which is aimed for sale in emerging markets like India.[39] While the current policies and market seem favorable for 2Ws, 3Ws, 4Ws, PVs and CVs, India has a long way to go before it can create a robust environment for the deep penetration of next-generation automobile technology.

Next Steps

The automotive manufacturing sector in every country is dependent on other sectors like transport, physical infrastructure (road, rail, port and power), digital infrastructure (streamlined online portals for carrying out business operations remotely) and social infrastructure (automotive hubs), labor, and land acquisition. All these factors play an important role in ensuring the business continuity in the automotive manufacturing sector. For example, trucks carrying cargo in developed countries can cover up to 500 kilometers a day whereas this figure is around 250-300 kilometers in India due to bad road conditions. In Hong Kong, it takes up to 12 hours for ship loading and unloading, whereas in India it takes up to 4 days to complete the work. In order to boost the transportation speeds, the Dedicated Freight Corridor project is scheduled to be completed by 2019.[40]

The current policy and reforms is bound to reap profits adding to the growth of the Indian automotive manufacturing industry. However, there are certain things that can still be incorporated by the manufacturing companies to accelerate the process of meeting set targets. Productivity can be boosted by making controls across the supply chain more sophisticated. Cisco has identified some useful solutions that could reinforce the potential of this sector.

1.Intelligent Network Manufacturing - This vision entails an integrated solution that collects data right from the manufacturing plant floor and transmits it to the business systems. [41] This is referred to as the 'Ethernet to the Factory' solution that empowers the employees with information on-demand abilities, thereby enabling the visibility to the factory floor without disrupting the production line.[42]

2.Collaborated Product Development - This solution is worth implementing to increase the participation of stakeholders in the decision-making processes and enforce high standards of transparency in the functioning of the company. [43] When all the stakeholders are subjected to the same information, collaboration becomes easier, decisions are taken faster, and ultimately productivity is enhanced.

Conclusion

The government on the other hand should focus on creating a conductive business environment by boosting the infrastructure and digitizing the judicial systems. When investors are confident of these factors, the potential for successful business increases manifold, and investors become more willing to test the market. So in essence, if all the dependent sectors are strengthened, then manufacturing can reach greater heights in fulfilling the demands of the people and the government. In addition, more efforts can be made to ensure that the government's online portals - the gateway to the manufacturing sector - add value to the investors' decisions in addition to just being updated. For example, creating a section that contains the 'success stories', opinions, and other relevant information on the companies who are currently running their operations from India would go a long way in helping investors make an informed decision.

---

[1] "Major Initiatives." Prime Minister of India. N.D. Accessed Mar. 2016 <www.pmindia.gov.in>.

[2] "Make in India Week." Make in India Week. Feb. 2016. Accessed Mar. 2016 <www.makeinindia.com>.

[3] "PM's Speech at Inauguration of Make in India Week, Mumbai." Prime Minister of India. 13 Feb. 2016. Accessed Mar. 2016 <www.pmindia.gov.in>.

[4] "Make in India." Prime Minister of India. N.D. Accessed Mar. 2016 <www.pmindia.gov.in>.

[5] "License Raj." *Wikipedia*. Wikimedia Foundation. Web. 07 Mar. 2016.

[6] Ibid.

[7] "Import Substitution Industrialization." *Wikipedia*. Wikimedia Foundation. Web. 07 Mar. 2016.

[8] Bhagwati, Jagdish. "What Went Wrong: Derailing after the 1950s, Phase II." *www.anu.edu.au*. Web. 07 Mar. 2016.

[9] Ahluwalia, Montek S. "India's Economic Reforms." Planning Commission, Government of India. Mar. 1994. Accessed Mar. 2016 <www.planningcommission.nic.in>.

[10] Bhagwati, Jagdish.

[11] "World Development Indicators." The World Bank. May 2015. Accessed Mar. 2016 <www.data.worldbank.org>.

[12] "India Soars High." KPMG in India. Feb. 2016. Accessed Mar. 2016 <www.assets.kpmg.com>.

[13] "Ministry of Commerce and Industry." National Portal of India, Government of India. N.D. Accessed Mar. 2016 <www.india.gov.in>.

[14] "Roles & Responsibilities." Department of Industrial Policy & Promotion. Accessed Mar. 2016 <www.dipp.nic.in>.

[15] "India Soars High."

[16] Ibid.

[17] BMR Advisors. "Indian Automotive Industry: The Road Ahead." *Forbes India*. 20 Oct. 2015. Accessed Mar. 2016 <www.forbesindia.com>.

[18] "About Digital India - Introduction." Digital India. N.D. Accessed Mar. 2016 <www.digitalindia.gov.in>.

[19] India. Department of Heavy Industries. *Automotive Mission Plan, 2006-2016: A Mission for Development of Indian Automotive Industry*. New Delhi: Ministry of Heavy Industries & Public Enterprises, Govt. of India, 2006. Print.

[20] Philip, Lijee. "Why Global Carmakers Are Moving R&D Work to India." *The Economic Times*. 11 Sept. 2014. Accessed Mar. 2016 <www.economictimes.indiatimes.com>.

[21] Ibid.

[22] "Automotive Mission Plan: 2016-26 (A Curtain Raiser)." Society of Indian Automobile Manufacturers. Aug. 2015 Accessed Mar. 2016 <www.siamindia.com>.

[23] "India's Automotive Industry - The Road Ahead." *Control Risks India, Oxford Economics*. 15 Sep. 2015. Accessed Mar. 2016 <www.controlrisks.com>.

[24] Ibid.

[25] "India Soars High."

[26] Philip, Lijee.

[27] Dhawan, Rajat, Gautam Swaroop and Adil Zainulbhai. "Fulfilling the Promise of India's Manufacturing Sector." *McKinsey & Company*. Mar. 2012. Accessed Mar. 2016 <www.mckinsey.com>.

[28] "PM's Speech at Inauguration of Make in India Week, Mumbai."

[29] "About Digital India - Introduction."

[30] "Company at a Glance." Maruti Suzuki. N.D. Accessed Mar. 2016 <www.marutisuzuki.com>.

[31] "Automobile Industry in India." India Brand Equity Foundation. N.D. Accessed Mar. 2016 <www.ibef.org>.

[32] "Top 5 Most Fuel-Efficient Cars in India." *The Economic Times*. 30 Jan. 2015 Accessed Mar. 2016 <www.economictimes.indiatimes.com>.

[33] Dhawan, Rajat, Gautam Swaroop and Adil Zainulbhai.

[34] "India's Automotive Industry - The Road Ahead."

[35] Bhasin, Anil. "Manufacturing: The Next Triumph Card for India." Cisco India. N.D. Accessed Mar. 2016 <www.cisco.com>.

[36] "India's Automotive Industry - The Road Ahead."

[37] Rajghatta, Chidanand. "Tesla Drives past India, into China." *The Times of India*. 25 Oct. 2015. Accessed Mar. 2016 <www.timesofindia.indiatimes.com>.

[38] "Tesla Motors Inc: Why Was China Chosen Over India For Future Production Unit?" *Business Finance News*. 26 Oct. 2015. Accessed Mar. 2016 <www.businessfinancenews.com>.

[39] Bidyanta, Soumyadeep. "India Is Not Ready for Tesla Motors." *Yaabot*. 22 Oct. 2015. Accessed Mar. 2016 <www.yaabot.com>.

[40] "Progress in Dedicated Freight Corridor." Press Information Bureau, Government of India. Aug. 2015. Accessed Mar. 2016 <www.pib.nic.in>.

[41] "Top 5 Most Fuel-Efficient Cars in India."

[42] Ibid.

[43] Ibid.

Chapter V
Organizational Risks

Organizational Risks of Bring Your Own Device (BYOD)

Evan Cottingham
Publication Month: June 2017

Abstract: This paper discusses the rapidly evolving, business-critical issue of "Bring Your Own Device" (BYOD) programs, and the considerations and risks applicable across organizations in all sectors. While the benefits of BYOD programs are clear, the associated risks are clearly documented as well, and must be taken into consideration by any organization considering implementing or with an existing BYOD program.

The enterprise Information Technology (IT) sector is amidst a revolution as individuals within the workforce have moved the sector in the direction by utilizing personally owned and valued technologies. This effort of the workforce population - in terms of IT – to essentially blur the lines between their home lives and work has been labeled the "consumerization of IT." The phrase "consumerization of IT" can be defined as the dissemination of information technologies that originate and emerge within the consumer market into the IT sector of business or government organizations. The driving force behind this consumerization are the workforce employees who are purchasing devices, downloading applications, and utilizing personal online services while integrating such technologies into the workplace environment and job duties.[1] Employees are increasingly recognizing the opportunities for greater individual productivity allowed by these consumer electronic products, and the market has followed, further accelerating this pattern.

The concept of "Bring Your Own Devices" (BYOD) offers a concrete illustration of the consumerization of IT movement. The core idea behind BYOD stems from consumerization, however refers specifically to the movement of consumer IT devices into organizational IT. Specifically BYOD can be defined as bringing their personally owned devices into the workplace and using these devices to connect to a company's network and access company data in order to complete their work related tasks.[2] Within the context of the consumerization of IT,

BYOD has served as an initiative for organizations that wish to embrace the consumerization movement.

The growth of this movement within organizations is evidenced by the recent trend in BYOD adoption. To get a sense of the current state of BYOD adoption, Cass Information Systems Inc. conducted a study to assess the BYOD landscape within organizational IT going into 2016. In the "Cass BYOD and Mobility Study 2016," more than 200 telecommunications and IT professionals and managers were surveyed in the U.S. and Canada regarding BYOD adoption within their respective companies. Exemplifying the growing trend of BYOD use, 60 percent of those surveyed stated that the number of BYOD users within their organizations had increased from the previous year. The emergence of personal device use within the workplace is also evidenced by the 85 percent of respondents claiming that their organization contains at least some BYOD users, and the 36 percent stating that there are at least 1,000 BYOD users within their company.[3] Additionally, Gartner Inc. - an IT research and advising firm - offers insights into the future of BYOD incorporation within organizations through their own analysis of the consumerization trend. Most notably, Gartner estimates that by 2017, half of employers will require workers to utilize their personal devices for work purposes. Furthermore, Gartner predicts that by 2018, "70 percent of mobile professionals will conduct their work on personal smart devices."[4] This drastic growth trend is largely due to organizations buying into the promised benefits of permitting personal device use within the workplace. One such perceived benefit is increased employee productivity. This viewpoint asserts that allowing work to be conducted on a personal device promotes an employee's mobility during the workday. So long as a mobile device is able to connect to the company's network and access the necessary information, work related tasks can be completed away from the workplace. According to the Cisco Internet Business Solutions Group's "Financial Impact of BYOD" study, the average BYOD user in the U.S. saves 81 minutes per week at work.[5] In terms of employee efficiency, with consideration for the number of employees within an enterprise, this figure suggests a significant amount of saved time company-wide that can be focused towards other tasks or projects.

Employees have also indicated that BYOD use improves overall satisfaction. BYOD gives employees the flexibility to work on devices with which they are comfortable and familiar. It effectively eliminates the burden of being forced to learn to work with company-issued IT devices. Additionally, Samsung reports that 78 percent of employees believe that because BYOD promotes the use of a single mobile device for data access, it effectively enables an improved balance between their work and personal lives.[6] Furthermore, by eliminating the need for company-issued devices, BYOD offers costs savings and reduces IT spending on hardware purchasing, as the responsibility shifts to the employee. Similarly, repair or replacement costs become employee responsibilities as well.

Establishing a program to allow personal device use within the workplace promises an overall improvement to productivity and profitability to organizations. However, there are major security tradeoffs that must be considered. The push towards tapping into the consumer IT market through BYOD adoption is a departure from the traditional centralized IT department - personally owned consumer devices are replacing the use of company sanctioned and distributed devices. This places BYOD devices into the category of "Shadow IT" - a term used to encompass "hardware or software within an enterprise that is not supported by the organization's central IT department."[7] This lack of centralized IT support implies the overall lack of control, management, or visibility of organizations over such technologies. Re-contextualizing BYOD devices as a form of Shadow IT, such devices should not only be viewed as opportunities for profit or a competitive advantage, but also as enterprise security risks as well.

As of October 2014, according to a survey of IT executives conducted by cyber security software provider Check Point, costs of incidents attributed to personal mobile devices at work have cost organizations over $250,0000.[8] Considering this potential for significant financial loss due to insecure BYOD devices, it is imperative that organizations are aware of the risks of personal device use within the workplace. With this awareness, companies could then make informed decisions with consideration for these risks when developing their own BYOD program or policy.

The security risks associated with BYOD devices, in general, stem from the absence of organizational IT support and the lack of control that this implies. This is evident in the difficulty to track BYOD devices within an organization. Because such devices are owned by the employee and not the company, they are not included in an organization wide inventory or asset management system. In terms of security, utilizing an asset management system is a necessity simply because "you cannot secure what you do not know exists."[9] With this exclusion from an asset management system, BYOD devices may operate, handle data, or communicate over the enterprise network unbeknownst to the organization.

According to the "2014 Information Security Guide" developed by Confluence, the collaboration software branch of software company Atlassian, an asset management system provides a company with insight into what they have, where it is, who owns it, who maintains it, and its importance to the institution.[10] However, for BYOD devices such insights are often unavailable. Establishing ownership and location of a device within the company allows for the attribution of a role or responsibility to the device. This in turn allows the company to determine the criticality of the tasks it is used to complete, the data or information it handles, and therefore, the device itself. This may include information such as which operating system the device is running. If such system information is not collected, it is impossible for an enterprise to assess a BYOD device's alignment with their IT standards and consequently hinders the organization's ability to accurately assess its overall security posture.

Another security risk lies in the lack of BYOD device monitoring that exists within companies. A BYOD device brought within a workplace to access its data and do work, because it is a consumer product not owned by the company, is not initially configured by policy to report to a centralized IT monitoring system. This leaves a company's systems administrator blind to information such as the resources being used on the device, processes that are being run, programs or commands that are being executed, or who may be logged onto the device.[11] Lack of visibility for such information poses a significant security risk. This is because examining processes or executed applications/commands is an effective method of determining the presences of malicious software (malware) on the device. Due to this lack of reporting and monitoring, activity on a BYOD device within an enterprise is obscured. Therefore, it is possible that potential malicious processes or programs could execute and run on a device continuously without detection.

With the lack of visibility into BYOD devices, this leads to the risk of non-compliance. Without centralized IT support and monitoring, it is difficult to ensure that an employee's personally owned device that is brought into the workplace is compliant to the company's established IT standards or policies. This includes regulations imposed upon the security measures implemented on a device. This also includes ensuring that the operating system is up to date, any vulnerabilities are patched, and that the device has a company approved antivirus software installed on it. Furthermore, because these are personal devices, the employees themselves are solely responsible for taking these steps and doing their due diligence in these areas. The actions that employees take regarding the security of their own devices are not necessarily regulated by the company. Without the proper security measures in place, BYOD devices can become vulnerabilities in the enterprise environment.

Security is especially of concern as BYOD devices have access to a company's network and process or store business data in order for the completion of tasks. A vulnerable device with outdated security controls in the work environment puts this data at risk for exfiltration in a variety of ways. Through web browsing or downloading malicious applications, a user may install malware that may plant a backdoor - "a technique in which a system security mechanism is bypassed undetectably to access a computer or its data"[12] - onto the device, giving a malicious actor access to the business data that may be stored on the device. Similarly, a compromised device could be brought into the work environment and serve as a point of access into the company's network. Scenarios such as this give rise to breaches known as Advanced Persistent Threats (APTs) which "strive to remain undetected in the network in order to gain access to the company's...valuable data"[13] which includes "intellectual property, trade secrets, and customer data... threat actors may also seek other sensitive data such as top-secret documents from government or military institutions."[14] An inverse scenario poses similar risk. Consider, for instance, a mobile employee who wishes to work at a coffee shop. To accomplish their tasks, they might connect their device to the shop's public Wi-Fi. This certainly promotes productivity, however, network traffic in such public spaces is generally unencrypted, meaning anyone in range can view network activity (through a method known as "snooping").[15] Should the employee engage in transactions involving company data stored on their phone, there are few barriers to a malicious actor intercepting the traffic and stealing that data.

The organization's focus on addressing issues and mitigating the risks associated with personal device use should be on management and gaining improved control over such devices; and to do so begins with implementing a BYOD policy. A BYOD policy must be formulated with consideration for the risks inherent in BYOD devices and the company data or resources with which these devices would be interacting. To do so effectively, the organization should conduct an independent comprehensive risk assessment emphasizing the personal devices that would be brought into their environment. Given the numerous security risks, a risk assessment process for BYOD devices should be conducted separate from, but in addition to, the organization's overall risk assessment. With that said however, it is important to gain an understanding for the relationship of BYOD risk with the other aspects of the business. According to the Deloitte & Touche LLP publication, "Risk Assessment in Practice," assessing risk interactions is an essential component of the risk assessment process. Determining BYOD risks and how they may interact with other conditions contributes to gaining a holistic understanding of BYOD risk within the company. Deloitte offers techniques to consider when assessing risk interactions such as risk interaction matrices, bow-tie diagrams, or aggregated probability distributions.[16]

With a deep understanding of the risks and opportunities, the BYOD policy should impose regulations on such devices, especially regarding security. Compliance should be described and enforced within the policy, outlining the necessary security measures that must be in place on an employee's personal device in order to access the company network. Compliance can be enforced through the use of "quarantine networks" for non-compliant devices. If a non-compliant device attempts to connect to the organization network, an automated process could be put in place to run scripts on the device to check for insecure processes such as an outdated operating system, unpatched vulnerabilities, or the absence of antivirus software. If the device is determined to be non-compliant, it may access a quarantined network, separate from the company's internal employee network, that only permits the device to connect to resources needed for the device to become compliant - such as updating or installing antivirus software.

The integration of a mobile device management (MDM) system helps to support BYOD compliance. Such systems assist businesses in monitoring, managing, and securing employee "mobile devices that are deployed across multiple mobile service providers across multiple mobile operating systems being used in the organization."[17] MDM solutions also serve to allow the management of the applications, network, and data used by a mobile device by the organization's IT department.[18] There are MDM software options available such as those provided by AirWatch, a subsidiary of VMware. AirWatch is an industry leader and highly reputed provider of enterprise-wide mobility management software. AirWatch MDM software features options such as mobile device configuration to allow for centralized management, wrapping to allow the application of policy to mobile applications, and a device enrollment program to establish an inventory of personal mobile devices within the organization.[19]

The policy should also include an employee education and awareness program that details device compliance and proper BYOD use within the workplace. Additionally, it is equally important that the risks and ramifications of non-compliance and improper personal device use are also communicated. Heightened risk awareness should instill in employees better practices regarding the security of their device, in not only the workplace, but elsewhere as well. However, an education program alone is not effective. A culture of understanding for secure device practices must be established within the company. This makes policy implementation a matter of setting the tone at the top. To create a culture of secure and effective BYOD use, the policy must be implemented from the top level of management down in order to ensure its adoption and enforcement.

Through the risk assessment process, it may be determined that the conveniences and benefits of a BYOD program do not justify the risks. If this is the case, the organization may want to enact a policy disallowing personal devices in the workplace. Such a policy could be enforced organization-wide or within specific business units. The latter pertains to situations in which certain departments handle more sensitive company data than others. For example, a company's finance department may impose a no-BYOD policy as it handles the company accounts and relevant information. Whereas a company's development team has a BYOD program enacted as it handles data that is deemed less business critical. An organizational scenario such as this creates the need for the segregation of business units and their data. The idea behind unit segregation is that employees within one unit are unable to access the data of another. This can be accomplished through the integration of multiple separate intranets for each division. There are commercial options available for this purpose such as the Bitrix24 Company Structure tool's "Multiple Divisions" intranet feature, which allows each branch to have their own structure while departmental integration is maintained.[20] The use of separate departmental intranets is recommended when one business unit permits BYOD and another does not. Although the device would be within the same company, they do not support the same functions and therefore should not have the ability access irrelevant, highly sensitive business data.

The integration of personal devices in the workplace is projected to grow at a staggering rate in the coming years. More and more businesses are adopting BYOD programs in hopes of realizing the promised benefits to productivity and morale and gaining a competitive advantage over other organizations. However, an organization must consider the security risks involved with allowing personal devices within the workplace. With consideration for these risks, the proper mitigation measures must be put into place. In doing so, the enterprise can be well equipped to embrace the consumerization movement.

[1] Beal, Vangie. "Consumerization of IT." *QuinStreet Inc.* N.D. Accessed Dec. 2016 <www.webopedia.com>.

[2] Evans, Dean. "What Is BYOD and Why Is It Important?" *Future plc.* 07 Oct. 2015. Accessed Dec. 2016 <www.techradar.com>.

[3] "Cass BYOD & Mobility Study 2016." Cass Information Systems. 2016. Accessed Dec. 2016 <www.cassinfo.com>.

[4] Gilbert, Jake. "BYOD Security: It's Here to Stay. What Can You Do?" SailPoint Technologies. 24 May 2016. Accessed Dec. 2016 <www.sailpoint.com>.

[5] "The Financial Impact of BYOD: A Model of BYOD's Benefits to Global Companies." CISCO Internet Business Solutions Group. May 2013. Accessed Dec. 2016 <www.cisco.com>.

[6] "SAMSUNG Mobile Index Reveals BYOD Trend at a Tipping Point with Mobile Devices, Becoming Central Hub For Personal, Professional Lives." Samsung Electronics America. 8 Jan. 2013. Accessed Dec. 2016 <www.samsung.com>.

[7] Rouse, Margaret and White, Caitlin. "What Is Shadow IT (Shadow Information Technology)?" *TechTarget.* Oct. 2012. Accessed Dec. 2016 <www.searchcloudcomputing.techtarget.com>.

[8] "BYOD Security Incidents Skyrocket with Growing Adoption." *Computer Business Review.* 29 Oct. 2014. Accessed Dec. 2016 <www.bcronline.com>.

[9] "Asset Management." *2014 Information Security Guide.* Atlassian Confluence. 31 Jul. 2015. Accessed Dec. 2016 <www.spaces.internet2.edu>.

[10] Ibid.

[11] Weeks, Alex, et al. "The Linux System Administrator's Guide" The Linux Documentation Project, Free Software Foundation. 2003. Accessed Dec. 2016 <www.tldp.org>.

[12] "What Is a Backdoor?" *Technopedia Inc.* N.D. Accessed Dec. 2016 <www.technopedia.com>.

[13] "Data Exfiltration: How Do Threat Actors Steal Your Data?" Trend Micro Incorporated. 2013. Accessed Dec. 2016 <www.trendmicro.com>.

[14] Ibid.

[15] Hoffman, Chris. "Why Using a Public Wi-Fi Network Can Be Dangerous, Even When Accessing Encrypted Websites." *How-To Geek.* 02 Jan. 2014. Accessed Dec 2016 <www.howtogeek.com>.

[16] Dr. Curtis, Patchin and Carey, Mark. "Risk Assessment in Practice." Deloitte & Touche LLP. Oct. 2012. Accessed Dec. 2016 <www.deloitte.com>.

[17] Beal, Vangie. "MDM - Mobile Device Management" *Webopedia.* N.D. Accessed Dec. 2016. <www.webopedia.com>.

[18] Ibid.

[19] "AirWatch by VMware." VMware. N.D. Accessed Dec. 2016 <www.air-watch.com>.

---

[20] " Company Structure and Organizational Chart in Bitrix24." Bitrix Inc. N.D. Accessed Dec. 2016. <www.bitrix24.com>.

Uber Recovery

Joe Pollack
Publication Month: July 2017

Abstract: Originally written in May 2017 and updated in June 2017, this paper discusses how Uber's success in disrupting the transportation industry has not prevented the decay of the company's internal culture and resulting risks to its future success. Uber's toxic culture has clearly stemmed from senior leadership and a lack of accountability; it has had far-reaching consequences and has allowed for illegitimate business practices that the public is beginning to discover. The author examines how an enterprise risk management plan could be developed by utilizing the COSO framework. Uber will need to implement immediate, drastic, and widespread changes to shift the direction of the company's future.

In the past decade, technology has disrupted numerous traditional industries, presenting tremendous opportunity for growth as well as a significant array of risks. The rise of social acceptance of the sharing economy, or social sharing of goods and services, has enabled technology companies the ability to disrupt once stable industries. One such industry is the transportation industry being disrupted by ride-sharing services such as Uber Technologies, herein Uber. Uber applies the sharing economy to the transportation industry, and it is beginning to research and develop autonomous vehicle technology to further revolutionize the transportation industry as well as shipping and logistics. Disruption is the result of unprecedented innovation, meaning few existing governmental regulations often apply. The implication of this lack of regulation is that Uber is essentially operating in the "Wild West," without many rules or regulations, expanding aggressively and with the sole goal of industry disruption. One consequence of Uber's success is its internal culture. While some may credit Uber's success to its culture, most would characterize it as unhealthy, detrimental, and toxic. Uber's unmitigated cultural risk has already caused tremendous cultural, reputational, and financial losses, and will continue to do so without proper treatment. To truly address the issues they are facing, they will have to make dramatic and widespread changes both internally and externally. An enterprise risk management plan can be developed by utilizing the COSO framework, enabling Uber to mitigate its risk exposure and to practice proactive risk management moving forward.

To characterize Uber's risk profile, it is important to first understand its current state. Uber has already suffered tremendous reputational, cultural, and financial harm due to inadequate risk management. These risks can be generally credited to a lack of accountability, present throughout the business.

A defining characteristic of Uber's culture is a lack of accountability. Susan Fowler, a former Uber engineer, published a report detailing an account of sexual harassment and the inadequate response by Uber's human resources department. Upon reporting the sexual harassment, "[upper] management told [her] that he 'was a high performer' (i.e. had stellar performance reviews from his superiors) and they wouldn't feel comfortable punishing him for what was probably just an innocent mistake on his part."[1] While Uber's internal sexual harassment policies are unknown, Uber enforces strict policies for its customers, detailing that "[any] behavior involving violence, sexual misconduct, harassment, discrimination, or illegal activity while using Uber can result in the immediate loss of [one's] account."[2] If their policies for their employees are aligned with their policies for their customers, then this inaction is a control failure in Uber's human resources department. Regardless of Uber's policies, this blatant disregard for serious sexual harassment allegations is a direct reflection of Uber's toxic culture. Fowler continues, saying this was not the first time in her career she had been sexually harassed. Previously, she had just reported the incident to human resources and continued working while the incident was resolved. The fact that Uber did not investigate and resolve her claims further exhibits Uber's lack of accountability for its employees. The result of mismanaging this risk has caused Uber tremendous reputational harm, both internally and externally.

In large part, this sexist and misogynistic culture is shaped by the "tone at the top," from Uber CEO Travis Kalanick and other upper management. Gabi Holzwarth, Kalanick's ex-girlfriend, describes an account of events occurring at a South Korean escort-karaoke bar. She describes that, "miniskirt-clad women 'sat in a circle, identified by numbered tags.'" She then tells that '[four] male Uber managers picked women out of the group, calling out their numbers, and sat with them.'" According to the report, visitors "get acquainted with the women and sing karaoke before going home with them."[3] This account illustrates Uber's misogynistic culture and describes its manifestation and perpetuation by upper management. This incident was reported to Uber human resources by a female marketing manager who was present that evening. Not only was the matter left unresolved, but following Susan Fowler's public account of sexual harassment, Emil Michael, Uber's senior vice president of business, contacted Holzwarth, requesting her to conceal the truth and tell media, if asked, that they just went for karaoke and "had a good time." This seemed to be a feeble attempt at reactive crisis management more than proactive risk management. Holzwarth later released the story, saying, "she wouldn't have considered speaking publicly had Mr. Michael not attempted to 'silence' her." In addition, Kalanick and other upper management shaped the misogynistic and aggressive culture in more subtle ways. For instance, Kalanick "once referred to Uber as "Boob-er" because it improved his dating prospects" and "[in] 2014, [Emil] Michael made headlines after he suggested that the company should target reporters who write about the company negatively."[4] It is apparent that upper management is directing the negative tone and culture of the company, meaning that for the culture to improve, upper management will need to change their behavior or be replaced.

In addition, Uber's high appetite for risk, resulting from their hypercompetitive nature, is shaped from the "tone at the top." An Uber driver released video depicting Kalanick, "perched in the middle seat, flanked by two female friends," arguing with the driver "over falling fares." One of the women comments that she heard Uber is having a hard year, to which Kalanick responds, "I make sure every year is a hard year. That's kind of how I roll. I make sure every year is a hard year. If it's easy I'm not pushing hard enough." It is clear that the hypercompetitive culture of the company is the result of Kalanick. This behavior is so ingrained in the company that "'[toe]-stepping' is one of Uber's cultural values."[5] Uber's culture has degraded into an environment in which, "[everyone uses] those values to excuse their bad behavior." This fiercely competitive workforce has been described by employees such that, "[one] can never get ahead unless someone else dies."[6] While Uber's success can be credited to Kalanick, so can the dysfunctional culture. Following this February 2017 incident, Kalanick released an internal statement apologizing to the driver and saying he needed to "fundamentally change as a leader and grow up."[7]

Moving forward, Uber will need to implement immediate, drastic, and widespread changes to minimize risk impact and mitigate future risk. It is abundantly clear that the toxic culture and cultural risk stems from senior leadership and a lack of accountability. To address the tremendous reputational damage resulting from Fowler's description of company policy, Kalanick held an "honest, raw, and emotional" company wide meeting.[8] Kalanick announced they were going to launch an internal audit concerning the issues raised by Fowler. The audit is headed by U.S. Attorney General Eric Holder, who formerly lobbied on Uber's behalf and whose law firm, Covington & Burling, is retained by Uber to consult on safety issues[9], Arianna Huffington, an Uber board member, Angela Padilla, a member of Uber's in-house counsel, and Liane Hornsey, chief of Uber's human resources department.[10] While launching an internal audit could be effective, the individuals Uber chose to lead its audit have serious conflicts of interest in reporting real problems within Uber. It seems as though Uber is, again, trying to avoid being held accountable. This enforcement of accountability will need to come from senior leadership, which, now, seems unlikely. Increased transparency at the senior leadership level is a minimum, but if inappropriate behavior continues, a change in senior leadership may be necessary.

Uber's toxic culture has had far-reaching consequences, and has allowed for illegitimate business practices that the public is beginning to discover. The majority of their illicit activity involves inappropriate use of data for surveillance of customers, competition, and law enforcement. In the past several months, numerous examples of Uber's illegitimate practices have surfaced, causing tremendous reputational damage.

First, evidence of Uber's illicit business practices was present back in 2014, when news outlets discovered Uber's "God View" program, in which it openly tracked customers using the platform. Almost unrestricted access to data combined with a toxic culture resulted in gross misuse of customer data. The program allowed Uber employees to "spy on the movements of 'high-profile politicians, celebrities, and even personal acquaintances of Uber employees, including ex-boyfriends/girlfriends, and ex-spouses.'" Peter Sims, a venture capitalist, said he was tracked "by a visitor to Uber's Chicago offices, where the God View data was shown on a large public screen." Samuel Ward Spangenberg, Uber's former forensic investigator, "told Uber executives including the company's head of information security, John Flynn, and its HR chief Andrew Wegley, of his concerns around the lack of security, and was fired 11 months later." He reported that Uber "stored driver and employee information in an insecure manner" and intentionally "operated a vulnerability management policy which allowed data to be stored that way if the company deemed there to be a 'legitimate business purpose' for doing so." Spangenberg's responsibilities included enforcing security controls surrounding Uber's data. Spangenberg describes his job "[as] part of Uber's incident response team" in which he would "be called when governmental agencies raided Uber's offices due to concerns regarding noncompliance with governmental regulations." Uber's procedure was to "lock down the office and immediately cut all connectivity so that law enforcement could not access Uber's information."[11] It is clear that Uber had formal, well-defined, and enforced information security controls in place, meaning Uber intentionally disregarded implementing security protocols regarding its users' data. These practices also illustrate Uber's adversarial perspective on law enforcement. It is important to note that Uber actively worked to keep its data secure from law enforcement while completely neglecting data privacy internally. Moving forward, Uber can mitigate risk of data abuse by restricting access to application data, implementing mechanisms to protect users' privacy. In addition, Uber can alleviate customer concerns and reputational damage by openly developing and enforcing a strict privacy policy regarding user data.

In addition, Uber's "Hell" program was a surveillance program designed to harm their competition and gain an unfair competitive edge. With this program in place, Uber was able to monitor its own drivers by showing "Uber employees which drivers worked for both Uber and Lyft — information that it could then use to entice drivers away from Lyft."[12] Uber also leveraged other channels for surveillance. A popular email add-on, Unroll.me, scraped users' inboxes for receipts from Uber's competition. Unroll.me would then sell this information to Uber so Uber could target advertisements at these users.[13] While this program is another example of Uber's abuse of data, it only emphasizes the information technology industry's need for increased transparency and customer advocacy. In an age when many companies' source of revenue is selling user data, it is incredibly important that users are aware of how their data is being used and what opportunities for abuse exist. Moving forward, Uber needs to develop a transparent privacy policy describing how it manages its users' data. To mitigate some of the reputational harm, it could become an outspoken advocate for consumer information privacy.

Finally, Uber's Greyball program abused customer data to target law enforcement. Originally intended to evade law enforcement when Uber illegally expanded into new cities, the Greyball program leveraged data "collected from the Uber app and other techniques to identify and circumvent officials who were trying to clamp down on the ride-hailing service." Uber's culture is so tolerant of illegal activity that "Greyball was approved by Uber's legal team."[14] Uber has a history of targeting individual users. In 2015, Kalanick had to meet Tim Cook because of "secretly identifying and tagging iPhones even after its app had been deleted and the devices erased — a fraud detection maneuver that violated Apple's privacy guidelines."[15] In this meeting, Tim Cook threatened to remove Uber's application from Apple's application store, which would eliminate access to millions of users, an action that would effectively incapacitate Uber.

With an understanding of Uber's current state, the COSO framework can now be used to develop a proper enterprise risk management plan. The first three steps of the COSO framework consist of identifying the risks, developing assessment criteria, and assessing the risks to which Uber is currently exposed. Identifying an organization's risks is the first step in "[understanding] the universe of risks making up the enterprise's risk profile." When developing assessment criteria, it is important to analyze the likelihood, impact, type of impact, vulnerability, speed of onset, as well as the inherent and residual risk. In order to assess the risks to which Uber is exposed, the previously established assessment criteria are used. In addition, risk interactions will be considered.[16]

Uber is exposed to reputational risk due to the damaging accounts of its internal behavior. While it has launched an internal audit, if Uber fails to implement meaningful changes or permits its culture to remain unchanged, it will suffer further reputational risk. Uber is extremely vulnerable to this risk, especially without direction and support from upper management. However, risk presents the opportunity for positive and negative outcomes, meaning if Uber implements significant changes it could improve its reputation, resulting in both financial and cultural benefits. The internal audit is supposed to be concluded end of May 2017, meaning this risk is soon to come to fruition.

In addition, Uber is also exposed to tremendous financial risk on several fronts. First, Uber is at risk of losing customers due to its damaged reputation. Backlash to Kalanick's membership in Trump's advisory council alone resulted in a trending hashtag "#deleteUber" as well as an estimated 200,000 accounts being deleted. Uber is also losing customers because of open and careless abuse of data for surveillance. However, again, if they do not take proper action and protect their user's privacy, they risk losing additional customers. Unfortunately, it seems that even if they do improve, their reputation will remain damaged meaning customers will be reticent to return to the service. It may take years for Uber's reputation to recover following the discovery of its surveillance programs. Second, it faces financial loss due to increased competition in the race to autonomous vehicles. Waymo, Google's self-driving car program, has recently partnered with Uber's main competitor, Lyft. In addition, Uber faces increased competition from Tesla, as well as the partnership made up of Apple and Didi Chuxing. To compound increasing competition, Uber has recently clashed with technology giant, Google, over Google's self-driving car technology in its Waymo program. A former Waymo employee started his own company that Uber later acquired.[17] While Uber claims it did not exploit Google's autonomous car technology, the due diligence during acquisition should have dissuaded Uber from acquiring the company. Google Waymo has launched a lawsuit against Uber, which could not only directly cause Uber financial harm in the form of punitive damages, but could also slow its progress towards commercializing self-driving car technology. Google has requested the courts halt Uber's use of self-driving car technology. The implications of this outcome would mean its competitors would be able to capitalize on the autonomous vehicle market before Uber. In both cases, the timeline for risk impact is years due to the lengthy legal process and due to the fact that autonomous driving technology is not yet ready for widespread consumer availability. Not only is the likelihood and impact from increased competition high, but also Uber, in its current state, is extremely vulnerable to this risk. Finally, there is immediate financial risk exposure in Uber's leadership because Kalanick's parents were just in a tragic boating accident, resulting in the death of his mother and leaving his father in critical condition.[18] This could result in increased uncertainty within Uber's leadership, potentially slowing meaningful cultural changes or other business initiatives within the company.

Uber is facing serious cultural risk in its current state. One high-impact risk to which Uber is especially vulnerable is low employee morale due to its negative reputation and poor working environment. To stay competitive, Uber will need to continue attracting and retaining top talent. This risk is extremely likely to manifest due to the company's current public image and is arguably the most dangerous because, as the company loses key employees, remaining employees will feel further discouraged, increasing their motivation to leave. Uber is most likely already facing this risk, meaning it will need to take immediate action to mitigate it. Although Uber is extremely vulnerable to this risk, it is also the risk over which Uber has the most control.

More generally, risk interactions expand to the larger industry landscape. First, Uber's situation is incredibly significant because Uber is within both the transportation industry and the information technology industry. It is one of the major players in both spaces and it likely sets the expectation of rapid growth and disruption. Facebook's motto "move fast and break things" resembled Uber's "toe stepping," however Facebook realized the inherent cultural and financial risks, and proactively changed it in 2014.[19] If Uber does not begin practicing proactive risk management and enforcing accountability, it could create a precedent and cause a ripple effect throughout its industries that growth, innovation, and disruption are valued more highly than ethics and transparency.

The fifth step in the COSO framework is to prioritize risks. The highest priority risk, and the area in which Uber should initially focus its efforts, is its dysfunctional culture. Uber should focus on its culture both because it is the area over which Uber has the most control and because it is this toxic culture that is the source of its numerous risks including its sexual harassment lawsuits and surveillance programs. Improving culture could serve as a first step in mitigating the reputational and financial risk to which Uber is exposed. It is important to note that residual risk will still exist from its negative publicity and other previously unmitigated risks. As Uber is improving its culture, it is important that it begins fostering transparency and accountability throughout its business. Next, Uber should focus on minimizing its financial risk by focusing on developing a sustainable revenue model. Some of its financial risk, such as that derived from low employee morale, will be treated as an externality from its improving culture. To mitigate risk associated with its slow progression in autonomous vehicle technology, Uber will need to internally develop and champion a shared vision for the future of the company. In addition, they could explore collaborating or leasing self-driving car technology from another company, such as Tesla. Last, Uber should repair its reputation with its customers, employees, and the public. While this risk is critical, Uber has the least control over this risk.

The final step in the COSO framework is to respond to risks. Moving forward, Uber will need to implement drastic and widespread changes. First, it needs to lead a proper internal audit with an independent third party. The internal audit Kalanick launched is fraught with conflicts of interest, effectively barring meaningful discovery. Second, Uber needs to improve upper management whether that means mandated leadership training or replacements. Third, Uber needs to develop and enforce a new code of ethics, including improving their privacy policy. In addition, Uber will need to begin following governmental rules and regulations. It is already beginning to accede to city and state laws. For example, though Uber formerly would not buy a $150 permit from the California Department of Motor Vehicles to test autonomous vehicles, they finally acquiesced and obtained a permit.[20] This is not only a testament to their stubborn nature but also an initial indication of improvement. Ultimately, Uber needs to promote accountability, which will naturally follow meaningful outcomes from the internal audit, changed tone at the top, and internal whistleblower protection.

Despite rising to a $70 billion valuation and revolutionizing an industry, Uber is at risk of collapse if it does not begin to implement proper risk management and mitigation practices. Uber's gross misuse of data in its surveillance programs is the direct result of its hypercompetitive and "toe-stepping" culture. In order to survive, the ride sharing giant will first need to dramatically change its culture, starting at the top. Accountability and enforced control procedures need to be present throughout the organization. Finally, to repair relations with the public, Uber will need to become more transparent in its initiatives and corporate behavior. As more and more technology companies disrupt traditional industries, issues will arise regarding the lack of regulation for these innovative business models. This also means the government will need to adapt, creating and enforcing regulation to support the rising popularity of the sharing economy. While Uber has the potential to change the world, it must first change itself.

Addendum

Since writing, Uber has undergone major developments. Starting on June 13, 2017, Kalanick "took a leave of absence."[21] On the same day, the results of the internal audit launched earlier in the year were released. The audit, led by Eric Holder, produced "The Holder Report," which outlines numerous suggested changes for Uber to implement. Notable changes include diminishing Kalanick's role in the organization, and increasing accountability and training throughout the organization.[22]

Eight days after the release of "The Holder Report," prominent Uber investors forced Travis Kalanick's resignation.[23] Kalanick's exit presents a unique opportunity for Uber to course-correct, while presenting numerous underlying risks associated with hiring a new CEO. The type of CEO Uber needs could face tension leading the organization. Almost "10% of Uber's estimated non-driver workforce" have spoken out on Kalanick's behalf, "appealing for former-CEO Travis Kalanick to be brought back 'in an operational role.'"[24] To be clear, this does not mean Uber should hire another leader with Kalanick's traits. Instead, the company should be cognizant of the cultural tension during this transition. Uber should strive to find a CEO that embodies integrity and equality. Some individuals within Uber, including board member Arianna Huffington, believe a "woman [CEO] would be ideally suited to fix Uber's mess."[25] Uber is already considering several possible candidates for CEO, including Sheryl Sandberg. Sandberg's incredible professional experience and history of empowering women could replace the toxic and misogynistic cultural tone Kalanick created. However, according to an anonymous source, "Sandberg doesn't have any plans to leave her job at [Facebook]."[26] Part of the reason is Uber's reputation, which is a clear deterrent to prospective employees at all levels.

Uber is at a pivotal moment in its life. With Kalanick's resignation, Uber has the opportunity to rebuild itself and put itself on an improved path. Implementing the suggestions of "The Holder Report" and creating a strong, corrective tone at the top will increase Uber's chances of recovery. Uber is currently in a weakened position and it will need to focus on improving its internal culture while also staying competitive externally.

[1]Isaac, Mike. "Uber Investigating Sexual Harassment Claims by Ex-Employee." *The New York Times*. 19 Feb. 2017. Accessed Jun. 2017 <www.nytimes.com>.

[2]"Uber Community Guidelines." Uber. N.D. Accessed Jun. 2017. <www.uber.com>.

[3]"Uber CEO Kalanick Took Workers to an 'Escort-Karaoke' Bar." *New York Post*. 27 Mar. 2017. Accessed Jun. 2017 <www.nypost.com>.

[4] Liptak, Andrew. "A Female Uber Employee Spoke out after a Company Trip to a South Korean Escort Bar." *The Verge*. 25 Mar. 2017. Accessed June 2017 <www.theverge.com>.

[5] Newcomer, Eric. "In Video, Uber CEO Argues with Driver Over Falling Fares." *Bloomberg*. 28 Feb. 2017. Accessed Jun. 2017 <www.bloomberg.com>.

[6] Wong, Julia Carrie. "Uber's 'hustle-oriented' Culture Becomes a Black Mark on Employees' Résumés." *The Guardian.* 07 Mar. 2017. Accessed Jun. 2017 <www.theguardian.com>.

[7] Newcomer, Eric.

[8] Hawkins, Andrew J. "Uber Employees Say All-hands Meeting about Sexism Allegations Was 'honest, Raw, and Emotional'." *The Verge.* 21 Feb. 2017. Accessed Jun. 2017 <www.theverge.com>.

[9] Overly, Steven. "Why Uber Is Turning to Eric Holder in a Moment of Crisis." *The Washington Post.* 21 Feb. 2017. Accessed Jun. 2017 <www.washingtonpost.com>.

[10] Statt, Nick. "Uber's Review of Sexism Allegations Will Be Run by Eric Holder and Some Uber Employees." The Verge. The Verge, 20 Feb. 2017. Accessed Jun. 2017 <www.theverge.com/2017/2/20/14677862/uber-sexism-allegations-eric-holder-travis-kalanick>.

[11] Hern, Alex. "Uber Employees 'spied on Ex-partners, Politicians and Beyoncé." *The Guardian.* 13 Dec. 2016. Accessed Jun. 2017 <www.theguardian.com>.

[12] Farber, Madeline. "Uber Reportedly Had a Secret 'Hell' Program to Track Lyft Drivers." *Fortune.* 13 Apr. 2017. Accessed Jun. 2017 <www.fortune.com>.

[13] Isaac, Mike, and Steve Lohr. "Unroll.me Service Faces Backlash Over a Widespread Practice: Selling User Data." *The New York Times.* 24 Apr. 2017. Accessed Jun. 2017 <www.nytimes.com

[14] Isaac, Mike. "How Uber Deceives the Authorities Worldwide." *The New York Times.* 03 Mar. 2017. Accessed Jun. 2017 <www.nytimes.com>.

[15] Isaac, Mike. "Uber's C.E.O. Plays with Fire." *The New York Times.* 23 Apr. 2017. Accessed Jun. 2017 <www.nytimes.com>.

[16] *Risk Assessment in Practice: Governance Risk Compliance.* Deloitte. Accessed Jun. 2017 <www2.deloitte.com>.

[17] Mac, Ryan. "Meet the Former Google Engineer Who Allegedly Stole Secrets For Uber." *Forbes.* 24 Feb. 2017. Accessed Jun. 2017 <www.forbes.com>.

[18] Nusca, Andrew. "Lessons in Uber CEO Travis Kalanick's Tragedy." *Fortune.* 30 May 2017. Accessed Jun. 2017 <www.fortune.com>.

[19] Murphy, Samantha. "Facebook Changes Its 'Move Fast and Break Things' Motto." *Mashable.* 30 Apr. 2014. Accessed Jun. 2017 <www.mashable.com>.

[20] Etherington, Darrell. "Uber Get Its Self-driving Vehicle Test Permit In California." *TechCrunch.* 09 Mar. 2017. Accessed Jun. 2017 <www.techcrunch.com>.

[21] Chappell, Bill, and Merrit Kennedy. "Uber's Travis Kalanick Announces Leave Of Absence; Company Adopts Harassment Policies." *NPR.* 13 June 2017. Accessed Jun. 2017 <www.npr.org>.

[22] "Holder Recommendations on Uber." *The New York Times.* 13 June 2017. Accessed Jun. 2017 <www.nytimes.com>.

[23] Isaac, Mike. "Uber Founder Travis Kalanick Resigns as C.E.O." *The New York Times*. 21 June 2017. Accessed Jun. 2017 <www.nytimes.com>.

[24] Burns, Janet. "Over 1000 Uber Employees Have 'Demanded' Travis Kalanick's Return In Letter To Board." *Forbes*. 22 June 2017. Accessed Jun. 2017 <www.forbes.com>.

[25] Atkinson, Claire. "Uber wants Sheryl Sandberg to be its next CEO." *New York Post*. 21 June 2017. Accessed Jun. 2017 <www.nypost.com>.

[26] "Sources say Sheryl Sandberg is Uber's top choice for CEO." *The New York Times*. 22 June 2017. Accessed Jun. 2017 <www.nytimes.com>.

Privacy and Security

The Largest Data Breach in the History of the Internet

Dominik Żmuda

Publication Month: July 2017

Abstract: This paper discusses the risks and fallout associated with Yahoo announcing in September 2016 that in late 2014, data associated with more than 500 million user accounts had been stolen. Virtually all possible events associated with risk exposure arose from the biggest data breach in the history of the Internet.

Privacy and security are always the top-most concerns when dealing with and handling sensitive personal information, including personally identifiable information (PII) and personal user data. All organizations, enterprises, and companies establish their own methods of data security and protection within a certain context and most often, different types of data are handled differently - purely based on the risk associated if that data should be lost or mishandled. As defined by the International Organization for Standardization (ISO), risk is "the effect of uncertainty on objectives,"[1] whereby it is possible to gain or lose something of value based on wagering something else (i.e. risking your life to save your drowning dog).

We have witnessed many events throughout the lifetime of the Internet whereby data had been accidentally lost, leaked, or hacked as a result of potential internal control failures within the governing organization or enterprise of that specific data. While many different types of risk exist within each organization (strategic, compliance, financial, reputational, etc.), operational risk is the highest at stake when dealing with the nature of privacy and security. Internal failures are a direct cause of operational risk within the company's people, process, systems, or even external events (a third-party breaching data, for example).[2]

The year of 2016 will arguably be remembered as the year of discovery within the technological sector. New technologies have emerged, obsolete systems were rediscovered, and privacy and security has tremendously increased because of surrounding events (the most famous being the Federal Bureau of Investigation vs. Apple, Inc. dispute whereby the FBI put pressure on Apple to hack a terrorist's iPhone).[3] While privacy and security have tremendously increased, we cannot apply this principle to all contexts - this year alone we have discovered many enterprises' services and products we all use, know, and love have been breached with the potential of our personal information being at risk.[4] In 2016, we witnessed the announcements of some of the largest data breaches in history, including the U.S. Department of Justice, the Internal Revenue Service, LinkedIn, MySpace, Dropbox, and the biggest of them all, Yahoo.

In September 2016, Yahoo, one of the biggest online search engines, announced that in late 2014, data associated with more than 500 million user accounts had been stolen (over half of all active accounts).[5] This breach amounts to be the biggest in the history of the Internet, bigger than the LinkedIn and MySpace breaches combined. The company claims the breach was not previously discovered and is "state-sponsored," though has not disclosed which country is responsible. Stolen data includes names, email addresses, telephone numbers, security questions and answers, dates of birth, and encrypted passwords.[6] Living and working in a safe and secure online environment in this day and age is necessary - and many believe total security and privacy exist online and all of our personal information and data is protected. It is not - it is vulnerable to anyone and everyone, and if they desperately need the information, they will find a way - they always have.

Yahoo's data breach is the most significant in the history of the Internet as it is the biggest breach having taken place during the lifespan of the entire Internet with 500 million user-related accounts stolen; 200 million of that information has been posted on the dark web for sale.[7] While the company claims the attack was carried out by a "state-sponsored actor," it has not mentioned what state might be involved; speculations rose around Russia or China. After the announcement of the breach, nearly two years later, most (if not all) Yahoo users and customers were furious the breach hadn't been announced earlier, though Yahoo claims it had no insight before August of 2016, when it acknowledged a potential hack.

Yahoo's breach presents exposure of several different types of risk stemming from the event, not only to the users and company itself, but also to the entire technological world. Due to negligence, Yahoo has essentially placed millions of users at risk of personal information loss or theft as a direct result of the hack. The risk exposure associated with this event is massive, and possesses potential losses to various aspects of the enterprise including user loyalty, operational losses, financial losses, and liability exposure.[8] Fallout included customers who stopped using Yahoo services and products, users filing lawsuits (23 so far) against the company, and Yahoo's brand image being depleted and no longer trusted.

Virtually all possible events associated with risk exposure arose from the biggest data breach in the history of the Internet - Yahoo has now become a brand in which people cannot trust. The sole fact that Yahoo delayed the announcement of the data breach for over two years is a major issue as users and customers need to be notified immediately in the case of data breach, that way they are able to update their personal information on other accounts or services that may have been linked to their Yahoo account. Although Yahoo claims it had not known of the breach until a few weeks before the public announcement in September of 2016, Fortune, a leading news source, claims "some employees at Yahoo were aware of a recently disclosed major hacking incident when it occurred in 2014."[9] The same article further mentions the company paid more than $1 million to set up an internal investigation committee to research and possibly mitigate the breach before the public could be notified. Yahoo's Chief Executive Officer, Marissa Mayer, was fully aware of the event but "withheld the information from investors, regulators and acquirer Verizon until September."[10] Several sources including the *BBC*, *CNET*, and *The New York Times* claim that Yahoo had knowledge about the event after it occurred and did not announce it to the public until two years later - betraying all users of their services and the general public.

Yahoo knew the breach was major: millions of names, passwords, phone numbers, email addresses, etc. - data pertaining to 500 million user accounts. Investigators and the public began to speculate and try to understand why Yahoo took more than two years to announce the breach. The most plausible reason may be the fact that Verizon was in the process of acquiring Yahoo and their respective services for $4.83 billion[11] - a deal which just closed in 2016. Furthermore, Verizon states that not only did they find out two days before the public, they also have no more information about the breach than what is available to everyone.[12] Marissa Mayer was clearly trying to hide the fact that her enterprise was breached, as the news could have diminished Yahoo's relationship and ended the deal with Verizon. Furthermore, various sources have reported that during the past two years there were "frequent changes in leadership of [the] security team [at Yahoo]."[13] It is a possibility the security team could not handle the large breach or was simply unprepared with no disaster recovery planning in place, and therefore before the public announcement, Yahoo needed to internally "cleanup" and restructure. We can come to a conclusion that Yahoo was clearly trying to hide the breach to those outside of the organization as they were not only unprepared to handle such an event, but also because Verizon might have 'pulled the plug' on the acquisition.

This is not the first time a large data breach has been announced years later. In 2016 alone, it was announced that LinkedIn was hacked (165 million credentials stolen) back in 2012 and MySpace (360 million credentials stolen) in 2013.[13] So why does it frequently take years to announce data breaches by enterprises? A few major reasons include internal investigations, verifications of breach, rapid improvement of current breached systems, and of course, potential pending acquisition of the enterprise by another organization. It is, however, very unethical to wait two years to publicly come forward and admit a system was hacked. *The Conversation* has thoroughly analyzed the Yahoo breach and reports, "as a major internet company with an extremely large user base, it's reasonable to expect Yahoo might detect – and disclose – breaches much sooner than other firms."[14] Yahoo's delayed announcement not only cost them millions of user's trust, but also their public image of being a faithful and reliable enterprise. As Benjamin Franklin once said, "It takes many good deeds to build a good reputation, and only one bad one to lose it."[15]

Yahoo has definitely set a historical moment in the lifetime of the Internet by acknowledging to withstanding the largest hack in the history of the World Wide Web. It is, of course, perfectly reasonable to believe Yahoo maintained the necessary security protocols and procedures and the breach was 'not their fault'. Hazards and vulnerabilities do not only exist in this event or in Yahoo as an enterprise, but rather in the entire technology sector. Data breaches and potential hacking is always possible, even if you have the most secure system in the world; this breach is no exception and therefore the only blame placed on Yahoo should be for them not issuing a timely announcement.

The vulnerability of data theft and of a potential breach is inevitable, no matter how secure a system is. According to Forbes, the top five data breach vulnerabilities include employees, unsecure mobile devices, cloud storage applications, third-party service providers, and malicious attacks.[16] Often times hackers find loopholes in existing systems and exploit those tiny vulnerabilities to breach a system and once they're in, they have access to virtually everything; while a pathway to a system might be tiny, once it is exploited there is potential for total, unauthorized access. The main reason why we see enterprises improve products and release updates is exactly because of this, and it is crucial to understand nothing is one-hundred percent secure and new vulnerabilities are discovered daily – that is why systems need to be updated and issues need to be reported - even if they do not seem like a major deal.

While we do not know exactly how Yahoo's data was breached, we can only assume the hacker was able to break-in through a vulnerability, exploit it, and gain access to the bigger overall system to steal millions of credentials. Yahoo is continuously working with law enforcement to investigate the breach[5] and identify possible loopholes in their system, it could be possible the vulnerabilities have been discovered, but not yet publicly disclosed. In the case of technology and the online, connected network of computers, servers, and other devices, constant risks, hazards, and vulnerabilities will always exist. There will never be a fully hack-proof system and once a device is connected to the Internet, it is vulnerable.[17] Hackers will always find a way, even if it will take months or years to breach a device. Yahoo's data breach event does not possess any new significance, it is yet another event whereby an organization was hacked and data has been stolen; the scale of the breach, however, is significant. Hazards and vulnerabilities will continue to exist as long as devices are connected together, through the Internet, and no one person or organization will ever be foolproof or immune to data breaches.

Yahoo is a global organization, providing services to users worldwide - the most commonly used ones being the search engine and email services. Yahoo being a non-governmental company based in the U.S. means that while it must follow all of the rules and regulations set forth, the government has no more control over the enterprise than they do of other organizations. There are general business practices and standards each organization must follow, however if the organization is not necessarily providing services directly to the U.S. government, the government then does not have much say over how the enterprise conducts business and what the internal procedures and policies are.

After the largest data breach in the history of the internet, Yahoo has filed a report with the U.S. Securities and Exchange Commission (SEC) stating it did not know about "any incidents of, or third party claims alleging ... unauthorized access."[18] While Yahoo is working with law enforcement to investigate the breach, the government is not able to necessarily force Yahoo to conduct an internal investigation in a certain manner. As best stated by Reuters, Yahoo's breach "has highlighted shortcomings in U.S. rules on when cyber attacks must be revealed and their enforcement."[18] There are currently no government reporting and/or government regulations that could have prevented this event from occurring. The government has limited control about how companies and enterprises secure their data internally and what each enterprise's security standards are. Furthermore, there is only limited regulation regarding data breach disclosure. There, however, is a possibility that just because of the sheer size of the breach, the government will be able to show more power over Yahoo and their investigation. The breach could push the SEC's guidelines to the limits due to a number of factors - including Yahoo's announcement of the breach taking two years, intense public scrutiny, and the sole fact that the breach is the biggest in the history of the Internet.

There are currently no governmental actions or policies that could have changed the outcome of the breach. In addition, the SEC's 2011 rules on disclosure of breaches for public companies are vague and have not called Yahoo to disclose when the company learned about the 2014 breach.[19] Lawyers and politicians are hoping this breach will open the government's eyes and force it to modify the current SEC rules regarding data breach disclosures as "less than 100 of 9,000 public companies have reported a data breach since 2010."[16] The SEC did impose new regulations in 2014 regarding disclosure of cybersecurity events, however they do not apply to public companies, but rather for broker dealers and investment advisers.

The SEC has never taken action against any company for delays or failures of data breach disclosures, it did however initiate two actions regarding insufficient data protection, both of which are still in progress. According to lawyers, the main reason for no strengthened regulations as far as the government is concerned is because data breaches are "difficult to assess" and the gravity of their effect is not always known at the beginning. A proposed legislation by President Obama and the Democratic Party would legally require companies to disclose breaches within thirty days of internal company acknowledgement. The President states "If we don't act, we'll leave our nation and our economy vulnerable,"[20] however there is a problem - there are currently 47 different data breach statutes across the U.S., each of which apply to different states, and it has been a nightmare in the past to find common ground and policy. The "thirty-days notification provision" would require enterprises to quickly disclose breaches, in addition to reporting to the government about a said breach. Beyond the reporting process, the Federal Trade Commission (FTC) would then be empowered to set and enforce "federal data notification and security standards." While this proposed regulation has not yet been successfully approved, hope is shown for the future of bringing together one common law for data breach disclosures.

While there are currently no government reporting or government regulations that could have prevented the Yahoo data breach from occurring, there is hope for the future regarding data breach notifications to the public and the government. Currently, there are no specific laws regarding how a company should maintain their safety, security, and data protection - at least there is hope for a "disclosure of data breaches" law that would force companies to quickly report breaches. Data breaches affect users the most, as their personal information is then vulnerable to anyone and is at risk of a variety of factors including identity theft. It is of key importance that a law be regulated to force enterprises to disclose breaches in a timely manner for the safety and security of the company itself, the government, and most importantly of all, the loyal users.

The Yahoo data breach is arguably the most significant event taking place in the entire lifespan of the Internet and World Wide Web. At 500 million pieces of user information being breached, just the astounding size of the event makes it significant alone. It is important to note that Yahoo may not necessarily be at fault of anything (apart from the late announcement of the breach), but could rather be a random victim of a malicious attack. The enterprise still has not acknowledged as to why the announcement of the hack took two years, but it has been proven that internally many employees were well aware of the breach after it happened in 2014. The one, single greatest cause for the delayed announcement was Verizon's pending purchase and acquisition of Yahoo for $4.83 billion, a deal which just closed months ago.

The various risks surrounding the event are astounding: millions of users could be victims of data and identity theft simply because Yahoo took an astonishing amount of time to come forward with the message; had Yahoo disclosed information earlier, users would have been able to update their personal information on all related websites and services to be less vulnerable to the breach. The operational risks arising from this event include failures in the company's people, process, systems, and external events. The breach was an external event, however the operation of the process of disclosing and identifying the breach were internal procedures and policies of Yahoo. Many enterprises and companies should use Yahoo's data breach event as a way to improve their own policies, procedures, and security standards. The single, most recommended, item of key importance is to disclose a breach or hack as soon as the event takes place - this will enable all users to take the necessary precautions and measures to ensure their data and identity is safe. Announcing the breach years later betrays the user's trust and faith in a company because by then, the personal information and data from all of the user's services and websites might be floating around in the hands of malicious hackers. Early disclosure of breaches is better and shows the company has ethics and high standards when it comes to safeguarding their customers and users.

Another key recommendation that should be placed into action to reduce the risk around such an event from reoccurring is to have enterprises implement data breach detection systems. These systems would simply run in the background and if a breach or hack was detected, the said system would be able to preserve all company data and take it offline by disconnecting it from the Internet or hacker, and access would be disabled. In the case of a data breach detection system, all of the servers would essentially go offline - neither the users or hackers would have access, but data would be preserved and would not be vulnerable. Taking an entire company offline would cost millions of dollars, but would be a more effective way than to have millions of personally identifiable user information breached. This system would essentially preserve an enterprise's public image while ensuring user information is safe.

Yahoo's 2014 data breach will always be remembered in the history of the Internet as one of the most significant events due to the sheer size of data being breached. Many users and customers have lost faith and trust in Yahoo due to the data breach announcement taking more than two years - perhaps not just the enterprise is at fault here, but also the government as no strong laws and regulations currently exist dealing with data breaches. The events surrounding the breach have not only drawn a pathway for the government to create new laws and policies regarding cybersecurity issues, but also for the technology sector to keep innovating through risk[21] and improving the current systems to ensure reliability, safety, security, and data protection measures exist and are constantly improved upon. As set forth by the National Institute of Standards and Technology (NIST), enterprises need to ensure the five Framework Core Functions of Cybersecurity risk mitigation (Identify, Protect, Detect, Respond, and Recover)[22] are continuously and concurrently carried out to ensure maximum safety and protection.

Had Yahoo followed these key steps, the entire organization would be better regarded as having taken thorough action in the case of the largest data breach of the Internet. While we will never be one hundred percent safe when dealing with the world wide web and internet, there is hope to become safer and smarter as new vulnerabilities and weaknesses become discovered and new technologies emerge, changing the way we interact with the world.

---

[1] "ISO 31000 - Risk Management." ISO 31000. International Organization for Standardization, n.d. Web. 30 Nov. 2016 <http://www.iso.org/iso/home/standards/iso31000.htm>.

[2] Griffin, Dana. "Types of Business Risk." Types of Business Risk | Chron.com. Chron, n.d. Web. 30 Nov. 2016 <http://smallbusiness.chron.com/types-business-risk-99.html>.

[3] "Breaking Down Apple's IPhone Fight With the U.S. Government." The New York Times, 21 Mar. 2016. Web. 30 Nov. 2016 <http://www.nytimes.com/interactive/2016/03/03/technology/apple-iphone-fbi-fight-explained.html>.

[4] Leary, Judy. "2016 Data Breaches." IdentityForce, n.d. Web. 30 Nov. 2016 <https://www.identityforce.com/blog/2016-data-breaches>.

[5] Fiegerman, Seth. "Yahoo Says 500 Million Accounts Stolen." *CNNMoney.* Cable News Network, 23 Sept. 2016. Web. 01 Dec. 2016 <http://money.cnn.com/2016/09/22/technology/yahoo-data-breach/>.

[6] Gallucci, Nicole. "Yahoo Confirms Massive Leak of 500 Million User Accounts." Mashable, 22 Sept. 2016. Web. 30 Nov. 2016 <http://mashable.com/2016/09/22/yahoo-confirms-data-breach>.

[7] Burr, Edmondo. "200 Million Yahoo Accounts Show Up For Sale On Dark Web." *Your News Wire.* N.p., 02 Aug. 2016. Web. 01 Dec. 2016 <http://yournewswire.com/200-million-yahoo-accounts-show-up-for-sale-on-dark-web/>.

[8] Baranoff, Etti, Patrick L. Brockett, and Yehuda Kahane. "Risk Management for Enterprises and Individuals 1." Scribd. Scribd, n.d. Web. 01 Dec. 2016 <http://catalog.flatworldknowledge.com/bookhub/1?e=baranoff-ch01_s04#baranoff-ch01_s04_s01_t01>.

[9] Hackett, Robert. "Yahoo Knew About the Breach in 2014." *Fortune.* N.p., 09 Nov. 2016. Web. 01 Dec. 2016 <http://fortune.com/2016/11/09/yahoo-hack-data-breach-sec/>.

[10] Murgia, Madhumita, Tim Bradshaw, and David J. Lynch. "Marissa Mayer Knew of Yahoo Breach Probe in July - FT.com." *Financial Times.* N.p., 23 Sept. 2016. Web. 06 Dec. 2016 <http://www.ft.com/cms/s/0%2Fd0d07444-

81aa-11e6-bc52-
0c7211ef3198.html?ft_site=falcon&desktop=true#axzz4S5JMLWip>.

[11] Alesci, Cristina, Seth Fiegerman, and Charles Riley. "Verizon Is Buying Yahoo for $4.8 Billion." *CNNMoney*. Cable News Network, 25 July 2016. Web. 03 Dec. 2016 <http://money.cnn.com/2016/07/25/technology/yahoo-verizon-deal-sale/>.

[12] Szoldra, Paul. "Yahoo Gave Verizon Only Two Days Notice of the Massive Breach of 500 Million Users." *Business Insider*. Business Insider, 22 Sept. 2016. Web. 04 Dec. 2016 <http://www.businessinsider.com/yahoo-verizon-breach-2016-9>.

[13] Kirk, Jeremy. "MySpace, LinkedIn Data Just a Click Away." *BankInfoSecurity*. N.p., 30 June 2016. Web. 05 Dec. 2016 <http://www.bankinfosecurity.com/myspace-linkedin-data-just-click-away-a-9233>.

[14] Ye, Yanfang. "Why Did Yahoo Take so Long to Disclose Its Massive Security Breach?" *The Conversation*. N.p., 30 Sept. 2016. Web. 05 Dec. 2016 <http://theconversation.com/why-did-yahoo-take-so-long-to-disclose-its-massive-security-breach-66014>.

[15] Eccles, Robert G., Scott C. Newquist, and Roland Schatz. "Reputation and Its Risks." *Harvard Business Review*. N.p., Feb. 2007. Web. 06 Dec. 2016 <https://hbr.org/2007/02/reputation-and-its-risks>.

[16] Basu, Eric. "The Top 5 Data Breach Vulnerabilities." *Forbes*. Forbes Magazine, 05 Nov. 2015. Web. 03 Dec. 2016 <http://www.forbes.com/sites/ericbasu/2015/11/05/the-top-5-data-breach-vulnerabilities>.

[17] Mann, Jason. *The Internet of Things: Opportunities and Applications across Industries*. N.p.: Enterprise Research Service, 2015. PDF.

[18] Volz, Dustin. "Yahoo Hack May Become Test Case for SEC Data Breach Disclosure Rules." *Reuters*. Thomson Reuters, 30 Sept. 2016. Web. 04 Dec. 2016 <http://www.reuters.com/article/us-yahoo-cyber-disclosure-idUSKCN1202MG>.

[19] Pymnts. "Yahoo's Breach Epitaph - SEC To Change Breach Disclosure Rules | PYMNTS.com." *PYMNTS.com*. N.p., 03 Oct. 2016. Web. 04 Dec. 2016 <http://www.pymnts.com/news/security-and-risk/2016/yahoos-breach/>.

[20] Amorosi, Drew. "Obama Wants Federal Data Breach Notification Law." *DatacenterDynamics*. N.p., 03 Feb. 2015. Web. 05 Dec. 2016 <http://www.datacenterdynamics.com/content-tracks/security-risk/obama-wants-federal-data-breach-notification-law/93420.fullarticle>.

[21] "The Art of Managing Innovation Risk | Accenture Outlook." *Accenture Outlook*. N.p., n.d. Web. 06 Dec. 2016 <https://www.accenture.com/us-en/insight-outlook-art-of-managing-innovation-risk>.

[22] *Framework for Improving - Critical Infrastructure Cybersecurity.* N.p.: National Institute of Standards and Technology, 12 Feb. 2014. PDF.

Delta Airline's Power Outage Risk Analysis

Sukhman Tiwana
Publication Month: July 2017

Abstract: This paper discusses the power outage that sent shockwaves through Delta Airline's operations in August 2016 for multiple days, resulting in significant financial and reputational losses. The crisis revealed some underlying system and operational weaknesses. The author examines some of the potential steps Delta can take to reduce risks and improve future operations.

Introduction

A switchgear failure resulted in a crisis for Delta Airlines Corporation, causing multiple negative impacts to its business. On August 8th 2016, Delta lost access to Georgia Powers and its reserve generator, due to a power outage. This resulted in a "shutdown of Delta's data center, which controls bookings, flight operations and other critical systems."[1] Even when the power was restored, Delta's "critical systems and network equipment didn't switch over to backups. Other systems did."[2] Because of this power outage, Delta recognized vulnerabilities in its current systems. Due to this occurring in its Atlanta headquarters, it cancelled 2,300 flights over three days and its revenue for August 2016 declined approximately $100 million.[3] It faced operational risk failures in external vendors, dependencies on systems, and vendor risk that resulted in the risk of reputation damage, financial loses, and processes flaws. Delta could have prevented some of the revenue lost by better maintaining its systems, but the power outage was a black swan event. Delta is not the only airline company that has struggled with its Information Technology (IT) management; this has been a common issue across the airline industry. There are regulations in place that should assist these companies in their management, but even the auditors ignore or do not identify flaws.

Risk Environment

Delta's initial risk came from its high dependencies on an external vendor for power - Georgia Powers. The IT systems and networks cannot be supported without the external vendor maintaining its operational and IT systems.[4] Delta needs to ensure that any vendor they use is updating and maintaining its technology systems and software. The vendor could have used a damaged switchgear or failed to replace the switchgear in a timely manner. Potentially, the power company also needs to improve its processes. However, the power outage may have been unpreventable, much like a natural disaster, because it did not have any warning signs. There is a chance that switchgear went out without any warning.

However, the power outage revealed Delta's systems risk. The risk came from Delta not merging its technology properly during new company additions. Perhaps Delta did not want system merges to affect its existing business processes and customers. Therefore, the company could have focused on finding the fastest way to merge its IT infrastructure without evaluating the impact and stability of the overall system. The *Wall Street Journal* reports that "the vulnerabilities in Delta's computer system ... raises questions about whether a recent wave of four U.S. airline mergers that created four large carriers controlling 85% of domestic capacity has built companies too large and too reliant on IT systems that date from the 1990s. Delta merged with Northwest Airlines eight years ago."[5] Potentially, Delta may not have merged the IT systems of these four companies efficiently, resulting in Delta having issues with its computers not restoring to backup mode when the power did come back.[6] Regardless of the cause, the airline's systems were not able to handle the downtime and recover its state.

Because of these mergers, Delta's software systems may have been running on outdated technology, which goes back to 1990s, and if this is the case then its system runs the risk of breach and stolen data. When Delta merged with Northwest Airlines, it hired IT specialists from other companies to "upgrade their technology infrastructure to make it more durable, adding redundant power supplies to their computing centers and other facilities, [and] increasing the number of backup telecom providers."[7] It seems they added onto the existing IT infrastructure for both of these corporations, thought this approach did not solve the underlying technology problem. Adding technology is the quickest way to merge technology, but creating a new infrastructure is challenging and time consuming.

Business Impact

Delta's miscalculations of the IT systems influenced its business processes across the board. Any damage to its technology infrastructure could result in impacting "customer service ... business disruption and its adverse financial and reputational consequences."[8] They are aware of the potential damage from the systems being down for long periods; however, they did not treat or terminate this risk and instead, tolerated the risk, which resulted in increasing its overall risk. According to IT experts, "these systems — which run everything from flight dispatching to crew scheduling, passenger check-in, airport-departure information displays, ticket sales and frequent-flier programs — gradually have been updated but are still vulnerable."[9] Its systems failure disturbed its business processes and customer experience because the passengers were unable to fly to their destinations in a timely manner. In addition, their airport staff was unable to do their work efficiently because the company's systems were down. *The Washington Post* reports that some agents' "fallback seemed to be returning to pen and paper: Some airport agents started writing out boarding passes by hand."[10] The agents did not have pre-printed forms that they could use to make this process efficient. They were writing the entire boarding pass by hand and trying their best to provide services to their customers. Many airports' staff worked around the clock because per the CEO of Delta, Ed Bastian, "there aren't a lot of crews to bring in to replace them. That's not how the system is designed."[11] Even though Delta mentioned in its 10-K Form from the fiscal year ending in December 2015 that it had "prevent disruptions and disaster recovery plans," its plan was not effective because it lacked a rotational employee program.[12] Their staff experienced fatigue and stress, which resulted in bad customer service and increased the risk of losing their customers.

The airline's business process increases its financial risk, because their customers and staff were unhappy with their process, by reimbursing its customers and paying its employees for overtime. Its current business process is paying its staff overtime, which results in financial damage for

Delta. According to Delta Professionals, "Delta extended its offer of compensation to customers significantly affected by delays or cancellations to cover Tuesday. The airline also provided hotel vouchers to several thousand customers, including more than 2,000 on Monday night in Atlanta."[13] Delta struggled to arrange flights that met its customers' needs at no additional cost, which also affected their "passenger revenue per available seat mile (PRASM)" because now they were providing business to their competitors.[14] According to *Fortune*, Delta's PRASM "declined 9.5 percent in August from a year earlier" because the airline paid for overtime and reimbursed its customers.[15] Delta had no other choice but to absorb the financial loss because it was forced to choose between reputation and financial loss. It valued its customers and employees because it had spent years trying to gain trust and maintain a long-term relationship with most of them. Additionally, there was a higher financial risk in the coming months because it had to repair and improve its IT infrastructure, which took a toll on its budget.[16] The company may have been able avoided financial losses by having a crisis management plan or by troubleshooting its systems to check if they were outdated.

The Delta Airlines' reputation was at risk due to this power outage because it was not living up to its promises of flying a customer to their destination. In the *Harvard Business Review*, Robert G. Eccles, Scott C. Newquist, and Roland Schatz say that "Three things determine the extent to which a company is exposed to reputational risk." These are reputation reality gaps, changes in beliefs and expectations, and weak internal coordination.[17] Delta had a weak internal coordination because it did not have a strong method in place for crisis management. Its employees were unable to do their work for at least four days because that is how long it took to get a partially working system back up and running, which reveals that its internal coordination was not efficient.[18] According to its 10-K Form from fiscal year ending in December 2015, Delta mentioned how its business depends heavily on IT and that any downtime could result in reputational damage and poor customer service.[19] Delta's reputation was certainly damaged in August, because even after allowing changes to booking at no cost, customers continued to vent their frustration on social media platforms.[20] The *Wall Street Journal* reports that "on a typical day, there are about 3,600 social conversations involving Delta on Twitter, according to social media analytics firm Networked Insights. On Monday morning, there were 43,000."[21] Even the people who were not physically experiencing the bad customer service were aware of the service through social media. Customers spent hours at the airport while Delta agents figured out flight status, booked hotels, and booked new flights. There were passengers who complained about wasting their time and being frustrated with the management process, even though the airline agents passed out blankets, water, pizza, and gave updates on the status of flights while their customers were waiting.[22]

Airline Industry IT Risks

Delta is not the only airline that has vulnerabilities and hazards in its systems, disaster recovery plans, and process management - there are others in the airline sector that face similar crisis due to its technology. Southwest Airlines cancelled 2,300 flights due to a router failure at their data center in July 2016.[23] It took Southwest 13 hours to reboot the carrier's computer systems, which is similar to Delta's experience where the system recovery was the major pain-point. *The New York Times* said:

"In Southwest's case, a backup system was in place, but the airline said that system was not triggered as it should have been when the router failed. And Delta said on Monday that it was investigating why some of its own critical operations had not switched over to backup systems."[24]

Both companies were struggling with its backup systems in place. United Airlines also faced issues with its computer systems last year and American Airlines had a bug in its iPad software, which resulted in cancelations of flights.[25] Therefore, some of the airline sector does not have updated and powerful technology to manage its company's infrastructure during a crisis, event, or incident. They do not have IT systems and the plan in place to recover quickly without affecting their business, which results in influencing their financial revenue due to the cancellations of flights. *NPR* reports "experts say the airlines are struggling to merge and upgrade their IT infrastructure to keep pace with rapid growth."[26] The airline industry struggles to keep up with the rapid growth and change in technology, which were the reasons behind the lack of mitigating the risk of processes and systems. Therefore, since they did not have processes and systems in place that met their needs, they were unable to come up with sufficient disaster recovery plans. In order for the airline sector to lower their risk, they need to change their technology management style before they damage their reputation or finances to a degree where they cannot recover.

To mitigate risk in the airline industry, there are both U.S. governmental and international regulations in place. One of the regulations is called Sarbanes-Oxley (SOX) Compliance, which requires the signing officer to be responsible for checking the business's internal controls and only sign the paperwork if they meet the guidelines.[27] In addition, SOX Compliance requires that the company's "entire IT infrastructure—from server and network security to IT practices and operations—must be reinforced and configured to maintain and demonstrate compliance in the event of an audit."[28] Delta Airline did not have IT practices and operations in place that meet its IT infrastructure needs. Therefore, the auditors should have caught this system flaw, which means they not only have vendor risk in terms of their power suppler, but also with their auditors. In addition, the auditor should have highlighted how Delta Airlines does not have a disaster recovery plan in place, which might have prevent the need for staff to create paper-based boarding passes, which increased their risk of fraud occurrence during those three days because anyone could have created them.[29] Therefore, during this crisis, Delta Airlines highlighted its weak internal controls, which means it is likely non-compliant with the SOX Compliance regulation. The auditors should have spotted the gaps in the disaster recovery plan or their proposed plan.

Recommendations

To improve its management system and avoid a black swan event leading to a greater crisis, Delta needs to change their business management style. Therefore, to reduce its vendor risk, it needs to meet with its vendors to ensure its internal control management meets its needs, since power supply is essential to IT systems and its business. It can take this opportunity to cross check its policies and guidelines with each vendor. It also needs to change its systems because of the new regulation, which is General Data Protection Regulation (GDPR) Compliance that goes in effect in 2018. The GDPR Compliance was enforced by the European Parliament & Council to manage European citizens' personal data. This law gives the citizens of Europe the right to control and regulate their personal data.[30] Therefore, when this law goes in effect, Delta Airlines IT infrastructure should be able to secure and manage data without any problem. Per their 10-K Form for ending fiscal year of December 2015, it "regularly review and update procedures and processes to prevent and protect against unauthorized access to our systems and information and inadvertent misuse of data."[31] However, even after regularly reviewing its systems, it was unable to get its system in backup mode, which might have been due to its merging scheme and lack of management of IT systems. It should create an effective plan for merging with other companies and its IT infrastructure. In addition, it should plan on how it is going to manage and update its IT systems regularly.

Another recommendation is to improve its disaster recovery plan and its overall IT systems. To do this, Delta should hire an auditor to conduct analysis and suggest changes to its system, which would reduce its system risk and improve its processes. Alongside this, Delta should create an improved disaster recovery plan that works alongside its IT, and it should train its employees on what they should do during an event, incident, or crisis. In order to come up with a stable plan, it should ask its employees of what they discovered as an issue during the power outage. The company does not have to agree with the suggestions, but this will help them understand what the crisis management was like, and what it needs to improve. The Delta Airlines could create forms that agents' fill out in replace of printing boarding passes when they are facing IT problems. In addition, it should have a printed copy of the schedule for the flights and should communicate with employees at the gate using a phone. Delta should have a disaster plan accommodating its IT systems when they are down. When Delta has established a process for disaster and technology recovery, it should check it with various scenarios. Because of this, it will reduce its financial risk through an employee rotational plan incorporated into the recovery plan resulting in employees not working around the clock. This way, employees could provide services to customers with energy, which would reduce the company's reputational risk. In order to ensure that its reputation is not at risk, Delta should create a "strategic alignment, cultural alignment, quality commitment, operational focus, and organizational resiliency."[32] These five frameworks of managing reputational risk will ensure that the board is overseeing the company, the company's values are followed, its customers are satisfied, and it has a controlled environment.[33] Ultimately these management frameworks will improve Delta Airlines' customer and employee interactions and the organization will have a unified understanding of guidelines and principles. Because of these changes in its overall business, it could be the ideal airline for its IT systems, processes, and disaster recovery mechanisms.

---

[1] Carey, Susan. "Delta Equipment Malfunction Triggered Loss of Power." *The Wall Street Journal*. 09 Aug. 2016. Accessed Dec. 2016 <www.wsj.com>.

[2] "Delta Operations Update for Tuesday, August 9." Delta Air Lines. 9 Aug. 2016. Accessed Dec. 2016 <www.pro.delta.com>.

[3] "Here's How Much Delta Lost On Its Massive Flight Outage." *Fortune*. 2 Sept. 2016. Accessed Dec. 2016 <www.fortune.com>.

[4] Carey

[5] Ibid.

[6] "Delta Operations Update for Tuesday, August 9."

[7] Carey

[8] *Delta Air Lines Form 10-K For the Fiscal Year Ended December 31, 2015*. U.S. Securities and Exchange Commission. *Form 10-K For the Fiscal Year Ended December 31, 2015*. Accessed Dec. 2016 <www.sec.gov>.

[9] Carey

[10] Peterson, Andrea. "Delta's Massive Computer Outage Is Part of a Much Bigger Problem." *The Washington Post*. 8 Aug. 2016. Accessed Dec. 2016 <www.washingtonpost.com>.

[11] Isidore, Chris, Jethro Mullen, and Joe Sutton. "Delta Flights Resume but Cancellations and Delays Continue." *CNNMoney*. 8 Aug. 2016. Accessed Dec. 2016 <www.money.cnn.com>.

[12] *Delta Air Lines Form 10-K*.

[13] "Delta Operations Update for Tuesday, August 9."

[14] Here's How Much Delta Lost On Its Massive Flight Outage."

[15] Ibid.

[16] Carey

[17] Eccles, Robert G., Scott C. Newquist, and Roland Schatz. "Reputation and Its Risks." *Harvard Business Review.* Feb. 2007. Accessed Dec. 2016 <www.hbr.org>.

[18] Carey

[19] *Delta Air Lines Form 10-K For the Fiscal Year Ended December 31, 2015.*

[20] Carey

[21] Carey

[22] Isidore

[23] Kurtz, Annalyn. "Delta Malfunction on Land Keeps a Fleet of Planes From the Sky." *The New York Times.* The New York Times, 8 Aug. 2016. Web. 05 Dec. 2016.

[24] Kurtz

[25] Kurtz

[26] Booker, Brakkton. "Delta Air Lines Cancels Nearly 700 Additional Flights." *NPR.* 9 Aug. 2016. Accessed Dec. 2016 <www.npr.org>.

[27] "Sarbanes-Oxley Act Section 302. Sarbanes Oxley 302 Made Easier." SOX Law. N.D. Accessed Dec. 2016. <www.soxlaw.com>.

[28] "Sarbanes-Oxley (SOX) Compliance: Comprehensive, Cost-effective and Risk-based." *Tripwire.* N.D. Accessed Dec. 2016. <www.tripwire.com>.

[29] Peterson

[30] "Regulation (EU) 2016/679 of the European Parliament and of the Council of 27 April 2016." *Official Journal of the European Union,* EUR-Lex. 27 Apr. 2016. Accessed Dec. 2016 <www.eur-lex.europa.eu>.

[31] *Delta Air Lines Form 10-K For the Fiscal Year Ended December 31, 2015.*

[32] "Board Oversight of Reputation Risk." *Board Perspectives: Risk Oversight 83 (2016): 1-4.* Protiviti, Sept. 2016. Accessed Dec. 2016 <www.protiviti.com>.

[33] "Board Oversight of Reputation Risk."